-------- # THE KNITTER'S --------

BOOK OF YARN

This book belongs to

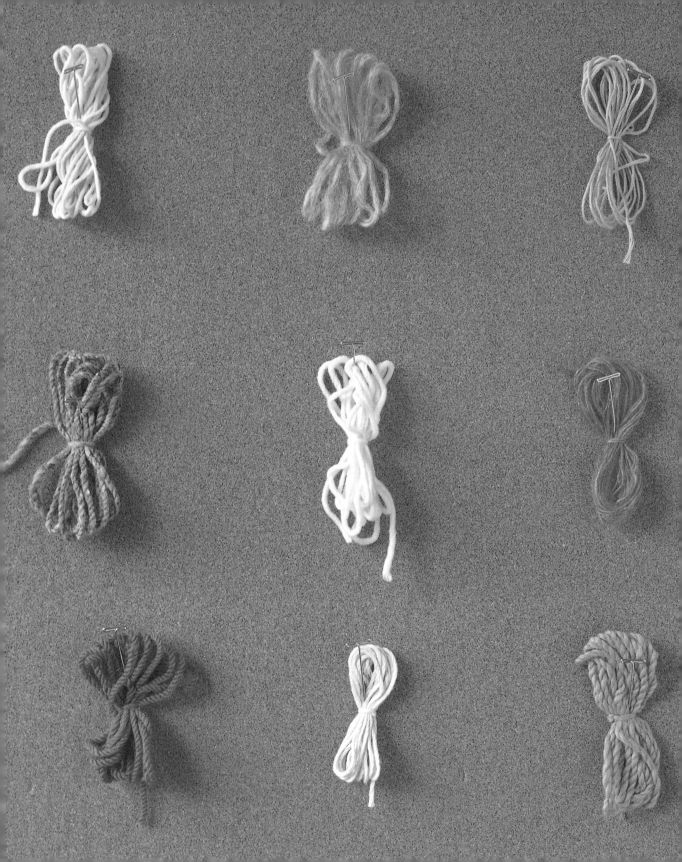

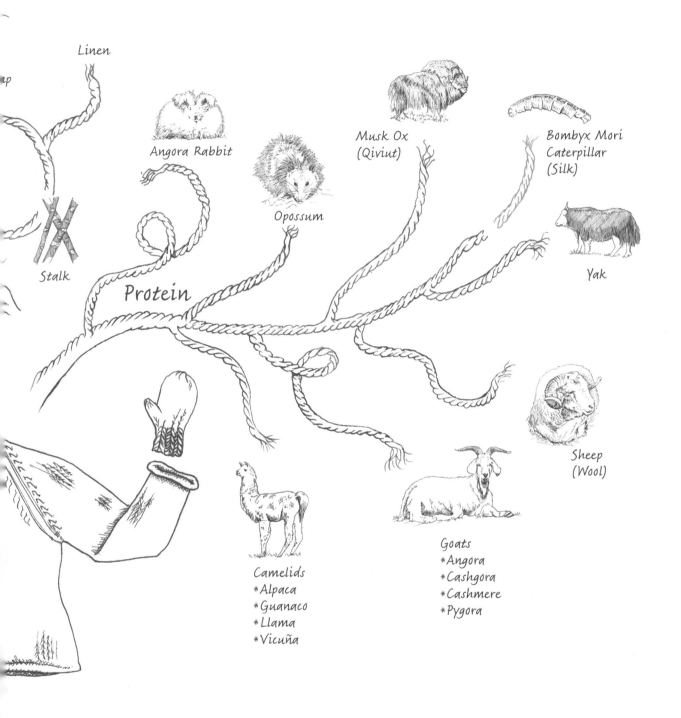

Linen

up

Angora Rabbit

Opossum

Musk Ox
(Qiviut)

Bombyx Mori
Caterpillar
(Silk)

Stalk

Protein

Yak

Sheep
(Wool)

Camelids
*Alpaca
*Guanaco
*Llama
*Vicuña

Goats
*Angora
*Cashgora
*Cashmere
*Pygora

THE KNITTER'S
BOOK OF YARN

THE ULTIMATE GUIDE
to Choosing, Using, and Enjoying Yarn

by Clara Parkes

POTTER
CRAFT

Published in the United States by Potter Craft,
an imprint of the Crown Publishing Group,
a division of Random House, Inc., New York.
www.crownpublishing.com
www.pottercraft.com

POTTER CRAFT and colophon, and POTTER
and colophon are registered trademarks of Random
House, Inc.

Library of Congress Cataloging-in-Publication Data
Parkes, Clara.
    The knitter's book of yarn : the ultimate guide to
choosing, using, and enjoying yarn / by Clara
Parkes. — 1st ed.
    p.   cm.
Includes index.
ISBN 978-0-307-35216-3
1. Knitting. 2. Yarn.   I. Title.
TT820.P28   2007
677'.028245—dc22   2007009363

Printed in China

Graphic design by Goodesign
Photography by Alexandra Grablewski
Illustrations by Kate McKeon

Thanks to the Craft Yarn Council of America
(www.yarnstandards.com) for their Standard Yarn
Weight System Chart, which appears on page 236

10 9 8 7 6 5 4 3 2 1

First Edition

Table of
CONTENTS

THE KNITTER'S BOOK OF YARN

Introduction

ALL KNITTERLY CREATION STEMS FROM ONE SIMPLE ELEMENT: YARN. IT IS THE BAKER'S FLOUR, THE JEWELER'S GOLD, THE GARDENER'S SOIL. YARN IS CREATION, CONSOLATION, AND CHAOS ALL SPUN TOGETHER INTO ONE PERFECT BALL. IT'S A SIMPLE CONCEPT, TWISTING FIBERS TOGETHER INTO A CONTINUOUS THREAD OF YARN. BUT THE VARIETY OF FIBERS, BLENDS, AND SPINS IS TRULY INFINITE. SO IS OUR RELATIONSHIP WITH YARN. WE LOVE IT, WE COVET IT, WE ARE KNOCKED SENSELESS BY IT, YET SOMETIMES WE ARE BAFFLED, THWARTED, AND BETRAYED BY IT.

Few materials undergo so many transformations during their lifetime. From the plant or animal where it originates, it gets clipped and fluffed and dipped and blended and twisted and dyed, displayed as a skein in your local yarn shop (LYS), wound into a ball and worked into just the right garment, washed and blocked, and finally worn.

With so many steps and choices along the way, it's inevitable that one or two things will go wrong. I'm not talking about the dropped stitches and funky decreases. I'm talking about the bigger mistakes we usually don't discover until it's too late: The socks that grow twice as long in the first wash, the cardigan that droops and sways like a church bell when you wear it, the gorgeous scarf that feels like sandpaper against your delicate neck.

These are what I call *yarn-related errors*. Sometimes they're caused by eager yarn manufacturers who need to sell more of a yarn, even if it isn't entirely right for the pattern. But more often they stem from a deeper knitterly dilemma we all face at one point or another: matching the right yarn to the right project.

In an ideal world, we'd fall in love with a yarn, find the perfect pattern that calls for this yarn, and knit our way into the sunset. Or we'd fall in love with a pattern *and* the yarn it calls for, both of which would be easily available, and we'd all live happily ever after.

Sadly, this is rarely how it works. We fall in love with a yarn and simply must have it, giving little thought to what it will become. We collect patterns, books, and magazines for projects we may never complete. And we struggle to bring the two together.

Some yarns have little if any pattern support from their manufacturer—especially the smaller-scale farms and hand-dyers. But even when the company does provide patterns for its yarns, sometimes we just don't like them. Perhaps we like the aesthetics of a designer who works with one yarn company but we love the yarns of another. Maybe we need to find lower-cost yarn alternatives. Or we're seeking patterns for a yarn in our stash that has long since been discontinued, or trying to find yarn for a pattern written ages ago for a yarn long gone.

Discontinued yarns are one of the biggest headaches for knitters. By the time this book reaches you, chances are that several of the yarns mentioned in these pages will no longer be available. No matter how hard we try, we'll never be able to escape this reality. We must learn to work around it.

And that's why this book exists. I believe each of us has the potential to be a *yarn whisperer*, to hold a skein in our hands, look at it, touch it, listen to it, even smell it, and instinctively know what the yarn wants to become. With this innate understanding, we'd never need to rely on a specific pattern again.

Some of us are relatively new to knitting and approach impromptu pairings with anxiety and uncertainty. Others, having gone it alone for years, have developed their own instinct—yet they still may have occasional doubts.

I want to give a formal vocabulary to that instinct and help you refine it further.

While I've assembled a vast selection of yarns in these pages, it is by no means intended as a compendium of every yarn available. Considering the frequency with which yarns enter and leave the market today, such an effort would be futile.

Instead, the yarns in this book serve as examples of the most common fiber types, preparations, spins, and ply combinations that you'll likely find in your local yarn shop and unearth in your stash. They come from large-scale manufacturers and importers, medium-sized companies, boutique dye shops, community spinneries, and old-fashioned sheep farms. Some are ironclad standards, while others are smaller, magical blends from noteworthy people whose story I felt needed to be told.

Because the best way to learn is by *doing*, within each chapter in Section 3: Ply Me a River you'll find several patterns designed expressly for that yarn's specific spin, ply, and/or fiber type. You're not only reading about yarn, but you get to pull out a skein, cast on, and feel its precise design potential for yourself.

The patterns come to us from some of the most inquisitive design minds in the knitting world—people I admire not only for their work but for their instinctive love and understanding of yarn. They also share insight about what, in those yarns, led them to design what they did.

By the time we reach the end of our journey, you will have a much better understanding of yarn, how it's made, who makes it, how it gets to you, and what it longs to become in your hands. The next time you pick up a skein and someone asks, "What are you going to do with it?," you'll be able to respond with inspired confidence.

SECTION 1

Fiber Foundations }————

BEFORE WE CAN GRAB THAT BALL OF YARN AND START KNITTING, WE FIRST NEED TO UNDERSTAND WHAT IS ACTUALLY *IN* THAT BALL. JUST AS OUR PLANET IS DIVIDED INTO ANIMAL, VEGETABLE, AND MINERAL MATTER, SO THE FIBER WORLD IS DIVIDED INTO PROTEIN, CELLULOSE, CELLULOSIC, AND SYNTHETIC FIBERS. EACH FIBER GROUP HAS MULTIPLE VARIETIES, EACH OF WHICH CAN BEHAVE DRAMATI-CALLY DIFFERENTLY FROM ONE TO THE NEXT, BOTH ON THE SKEIN AND IN THE GARMENT. UNDERSTANDING HOW THESE FIBERS WORK IS YOUR FIRST STEP TOWARD YARN FREEDOM.

A QUICK TIP

Terms in boldface are defined in the Glossary at the end of the book.

PROTEIN FIBERS

page 12

Protein fibers are essentially the hairs that grow on animals. They all contain carbon, hydrogen, oxygen, nitrogen, and sulfur. The one exception is silk, which falls somewhere between protein and cellulose because it is extruded from the silkworm after it feasts on plants—but, for the sake of order, we'll place it in the protein category.

CELLULOSE FIBERS

Cellulose fibers are derived from the cellulose that occurs naturally in plants. Cotton has the highest cellulose content (normally 95% cellulose, 5% water) and is somewhat unusual in that it is derived from the seed pod of the cotton plant. The other popular cellulose fibers, such as linen and hemp, are called bast fibers because they're derived from the stalks of plants.

page 34

CELLULOSIC FIBERS

Cellulosic fibers are also made from the cellulose of plant material (most often cotton and trees) that has been chemically processed down to a base liquid form before being extruded and regenerated into a spinnable fiber form. The most common cellulosic fibers are rayon and Tencel.

page 38

SYNTHETIC FIBERS

page 42

Synthetic fibers—including polyester, nylon, and acrylic—are manmade using entirely artificial materials.

Protein Fibers

The oldest and most prevalent protein fiber is wool, which is the hair grown on a sheep. But goats, camels, rabbits, and other animals—including household pets and even humans—also produce protein fibers.

Just as our own hair differs from person to person, protein fibers vary dramatically depending on the animal and the specific *breed* of animal that grew them. They can be long or short; thick or fine; hollow or filled with tiny air pockets; curly, wavy, or completely straight. But they all have a few things in common.

If you look at fibers under a powerful microscope, you'll see that they are covered with tiny **scales**—rather like the scales of a fish. You can experience them for yourself by running your fingers up and down your hair. Slide your fingers away from your scalp and they'll move smoothly; in the other direction, they encounter a faint amount of drag and resistance. You're feeling the scales moving with and against the direction of your fingers.

SCALES

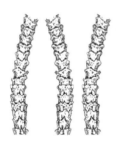 Scales deserve a section of their own because they play such an important role in how protein fibers look, feel, and behave. First, they act as miniature fingers that help hold fibers together to form a strong, durable yarn. They give fibers something to hold on to during the spinning process. At the same time, they also provide a microscopic buffer between fibers, making them at once enmeshed and distinctly separate. And scales are also the reason why a wool sweater, when machine-washed in hot soapy water, will emerge a shrunken felted mass—but we'll get to felting later.

A simple rule of thumb to remember is that the finer the fiber, the finer and more numerous the scales; the rougher the fiber, the larger and fewer the scales. A superfine **Merino** fiber, for example, may have as many as three thousand scales along each *inch* (2.5cm)

of fiber. The scales are so microscopic that even the most sensitive person won't be able to feel them—which is why Merino is highly regarded as a scratch-free wool. When the light hits this finely fragmented surface, it reflects back with a matte, almost pearlescent light, which is what gives Merino its lustrous sheen.

On the other end of the spectrum we have **longwools** and rougher fibers, which tend to be larger in diameter with fewer scales covering the fiber surface—sometimes as few as six hundred scales per inch (2.5cm). Although these larger scales still won't be immediately perceptible to the touch, they can have a rougher feel against your skin. But with fewer scales to break the fiber surface, these wools can have a far more reflective, almost luminous quality when light hits them.

Larger scales don't always indicate roughness, however. Angora has chevron-shaped scales that contribute to a powdery appearance and slippery surface, as do the larger but smoother scales on the surface of cashmere and qiviut fibers. Mohair also has large scales that contribute to a gorgeous, reflective quality—and the first shearing can be as soft as cashmere.

Part of what makes a fiber warm is its ability to trap still air, and scales play a role here, too. Their endless nooks and crannies along the fiber shaft give ample room for air to hide. Spun woolen style, with the fibers jumbled every which way, even a thin strand of yarn can be remarkably warm. Meanwhile, the smoother protein fibers that have been aligned and combed and spun worsted-style tend to compact into a dense, fluid material that's strong but not nearly as warm. This is why an airy Shetland shawl can actually be warmer than a firmly spun pair of mittens.

The only animal-produced fiber that doesn't have scales is silk—a fiber that's a category unto itself. Although it's produced by a living creature, silk isn't a *grown* hair—it's a liquid that the silkworm extrudes after feasting on mulberry leaves, and this liquid hardens when it comes into contact with air. The smooth, scale-free surface of silk helps account for its notoriously brilliant, reflective qualities—but it also helps explain why it's so slippery to spin. Cellulose fibers, such as cotton and linen, have no scales; nor do cellulosic fibers, such as rayon and Tencel, or pure synthetic fibers.

SHEEP: WOOL

 **Wool** in yarn is like restaurants in San Francisco. You could knit a different blend every day for a year without using the same yarn twice. It's as varied as the sheep on which it grows, running the gamut from rugged and ropelike to delicate and ethereal, with just about everything in between. Even within the same sheep breed, you'll find subtle differences from animal to animal, farm to farm. If you'd like to learn more about specific sheep breeds and the fibers they produce, I strongly recommend Nola Fournier and Jane Fournier's *In Sheep's Clothing: A Handspinner's Guide to Wool*. Here we'll focus on wool as it pertains to commercial yarns.

The first thing to know about wool is that it is hygroscopic—a great trait for clothing and an equally great word for your next crossword puzzle or cocktail party. *Hygroscopic* means that the fiber is able to absorb up to 30 percent of its weight in moisture while still feeling warm and dry against your skin. This helps the fabric breathe, readily absorbing and releasing moisture to maintain a steady ecosystem of comfort against your skin, no matter how cold or damp the external weather may be.

Wool is naturally flame-retardant and has long been a favorite material for firemen's blankets and industrial fabrics in public buildings. When exposed to flame, wool simply extinguishes itself without a peep. The constant level of moisture in the fiber keeps wool from conducting static electricity, which not only causes those annoying shocks but also acts as a magnet to pull fine dirt and dust particles deep into your garment.

Wool is also extremely resilient and highly extensible, which essentially means you can stretch it a third of its length, or two-thirds when wet, and it'll recover to its original shape. Despite over a century of effort, not a single manmade fiber yet possesses all these amazing qualities.

How We Get It

Sheep are generally shorn twice a year—once in the spring and once in the fall. Depending on the animal and the frequency of the shearing, the fiber length (often called **staple length**) averages anywhere from 2 inches (5cm) in the fine wools to 12 inches (30.5cm) in the longwools.

The mass of fiber shorn from a sheep is called a **fleece**, and it contains everything that was on the sheep at the moment it was shorn—including vegetable matter, dirt, and **lanolin**, a greasy substance that is secreted from the sheep's sebaceous glands. Lanolin helps repel water from the sheep's coat (which can be especially handy for sheep that live in wet climates) and may also help protect the sheep's skin from infection.

Finer fiber fleeces tend to have far more lanolin (sometimes 35 percent of the overall fleece weight), while some Shetlands and Icelandics are so clean that they can be spun "in the grease," that is, without any washing whatsoever.

Depending on the stringency of the processing, wool can be either squeaky clean, like a fine, triple-sifted cake flour, or left a little *au naturel* with more vegetable matter and lanolin in the fiber—rather like a hearty whole grain. Many of the traditional fishermen's sweaters were made from lanolin-rich yarn to help keep fishermen warm and dry in stormy seas.

In Yarn

With just a few exceptions, most commercial wool yarns are made from a blend of fibers that the manufacturer has chosen for their specific crimp, **loft**, fineness, staple length, strength, warmth, resiliency, and perhaps most important, cost and availability. Rarely do you get a skein that's labeled 100 percent of one specific sheep breed—the exception being wool whose breed name enhances its price and marketability, such as Merino, Icelandic, Shetland, Rambouillet, or Blue-faced Leicester. Yarn manufacturers normally purchase their wool from brokers using fiber diameter (or **micron** count), staple length, and cleanliness as their selection criteria.

Labels will, however, sometimes hint as to the grade of wool fibers being used—especially if they're more expensive. As with most protein fibers, the younger the animal, the finer and more highly valued the fibers. Look for expressions like *superfine, fine,* and *lamb's wool* on the label, but always use your fingers as the ultimate gauge of fineness.

Interestingly enough, Federal Trade Commission regulations allow for the term *wool* to be used not only for fiber made from the fleece of the sheep or lamb, but also for the hair of the angora and cashmere goat, camel, alpaca, llama, or even vicuña. Rarely will a yarn company allow those more expensive fibers to go unmentioned on the label, but do note that—at least as of this writing—they are legally allowed to do so.

Evaluating Yarn

While handspinners have the luxury of being able to walk into a field, point to a specific sheep, and say, "I'll take that one," we must content ourselves with skeins of yarn simply marked *wool*. Fear not, however; there are ways to analyze the yarn and figure out what it is and what it wants to be. I'll talk more about the specific spinning preparation, twist, and ply of yarns later—for now we'll focus on analyzing the general qualities of the wool.

The three factors to consider when evaluating wool and almost all other protein fibers are fiber diameter (a fineness measured in microns), staple length, and crimp structure. So the first thing to do is pull some individual strands of fiber out of your yarn. Try to avoid pulling strands from the cut end of the yarn because those may not represent the true fiber lengths.

What do these fibers look like? How long are they? Are they smooth, evenly wavy, or wildly kinked and crimped? Compare a few fibers. Are their lengths similar or do they vary dramatically? Do they feel the same, or do they have different thicknesses and appearances? Is the dye evenly saturated, or are the strands in the very center somewhat lighter? How does the light reflect off them—does it shine, or is it chalky and matte? Here's why you want to ask those questions.

Fineness

Fineness is often measured in terms of fiber diameter, with a common measurement being the micron, or unit of micrometer. One micron equals one thousandth of a millimeter, or .00004 inch. If numbers aren't your forté, just remember that the smaller the micron "count," as it's often called, the finer the fiber. The more rugged longwools can range from the high 30s to the mid-20s, while finer wools, such as Merino, can range from 24 to 18 microns. The finer the diameter of a fiber, the softer it feels against your skin. (To give you a point

VIRGIN WOOL
FUN FACT

Occasionally you'll come across a skein of yarn labeled *100 percent Pure Virgin Wool*. No, this is *not* referring to the sheep's modesty. It's a reference to the days when people would sell their old knits and woven goods to shoddy mills, where they'd be unraveled or shredded and remanufactured into blankets or yarn. By putting *Virgin Wool* on garment or yarn labels, the manufacturer is indicating that this is the fiber's first foray into the world of textiles. If you were to knit a wool garment, unravel the yarn, and reknit it into something else, technically it would no longer be virgin wool.

of comparison, human hair can vary anywhere from 50 to more than 100 microns.)

Length

The natural length of a fiber (or staple length) varies, depending on the sheep breed and the frequency of shearing—here we're assuming the standard cycle of twice a year. A general rule of thumb is this: The shorter the fibers, the softer they will be against the skin. But as with all good things, there's a drawback in terms of wearability. Since abrasion attracts the ends of fiber, working them loose from the fabric until they form pills, the more fiber ends you have per inch (2.5cm) of yarn, the greater the number of pills you may get. This is why even the best Merino yarn may eventually pill.

Staple length can also be influenced by improper shearing, rough processing, or even a poor fleece with breaks in the fiber—which is why it helps to examine the actual fibers and see if they look damaged.

Conversely, longer fibers may not feel as soft, but they will wear far better than the short ones because they have longer spans of pure, uninterrupted fiber held tightly together with twist. For any knitted project where abrasion is an issue, such as socks, you may want to stick with longer fibers.

Crimp

Just as some people have wavy hair and others have straight hair, wool fibers have endless variations in crimp. **Crimp** helps fibers absorb and balance twist, and it also helps them trap still air, which—in turn—makes your fabric warmer. The finer fibers, such as Merino and Rambouillet, will have extremely tiny wavelets running down the length of the fiber. On the other hand, longwools, such as Bluefaced Leicester, have large, almost ringletlike curls.

The result, when spun, is a little different than you'd think: Those fibers with the tinier crimp end up with more bounce, loft, and warmth—perfect for cozy sweaters, hats, blankets, and anything where softness, stretch, and warmth are prized.

The fibers with the bigger ringlets, on the other hand, tend to flatten out into denser, stronger, more lustrous yarns. You'll want to use these for projects where drape and shimmer are needed, such as elegant sweaters, shawls, and throws.

While not all wool breeds get prominent label attention from the big yarn companies, you can still find them by seeking out smaller-scale yarn companies and farms. For example, Elsa Sheep and Wool Company offers an exquisite pure Cormo straight from her Colorado farm (on page 107 you can see a pair of Amy King's Guernsey Socks knit from this yarn). And Rovings, based in Canada, imports delicate Polwarth fiber and spins it up into a dreamy lace yarn for shawls. The next time you go to a fiber festival, seek out the farm yarns made with unusual breeds and have fun experiencing these different fiber behaviors for yourself.

Guernsey Socks (page 106) knit in Cormo and Icelandic wools

Sensitivities

Debate rages not only among knitters but among doctors and dermatologists as well about whether there truly is such a thing as a *wool allergy*. A couple of theories are making the rounds. If you experience any sensitivity to wool, try one of the solutions on the next page before giving up on the fiber completely.

First, be sure to test the finest of the superfine fibers, such as Merino. The theory here is that part of what causes irritation is the ends of fiber that protrude from the yarn and rub against your skin. The thinner the fiber and the tinier the scales, the lighter the rubbing against your skin and the less irritation you'll feel.

Another theory is that some people may be sensitive to the lanolin in wool. If you suspect this may be the case, try a superfine wool like Merino that has been completely processed and has very little trace of lanolin left. These yarns will be smooth and completely devoid of any lanolin scent, vegetable matter, or any other traces of the farmyard. (Karabella Aurora 8 is a perennial favorite in this category.)

Finally, if you suddenly find yourself sensitive to wool, consider the garment you're currently working on. I've seen a few cases where something foreign in a specific yarn was causing irritation—perhaps a strange kind of vegetable matter, unexhausted dyestuff, spinning oil, or even the type of soap used to wash the yarn before skeining. In one case, simply washing the skein in mild soapy water did the trick.

But if your senses can handle it, I urge you to experience the sensation of minimally processed wool straight from the farm at least once in your knitterly life. These fresh materials have a vibrancy and life all their own, and the lanolin scent can be as rich and grounding as the smell of fresh-baked bread.

Special Treatments

The advent of the washing machine almost rendered wool extinct, because, in its natural state, wool is not machine-washable. To keep the world from being taken over completely by manmade, machine-washable fibers, the wool industry started working on a way to create a machine-washable wool.

Instead of trying to breed a sheep that produces scale-free fibers, textile scientists tried to eliminate the scales from existing fibers. Soon **superwash wool** was born. Early efforts involved carbonizing the scales

by rapidly burning them off at a high temperature, but this proved too harsh on the fibers. (If you find a skein of superwash wool from the '50s or '60s and it feels scratchy and unpleasant, this may be why.) Later developments involved applying a fine resin to the fibers, which essentially glued the scales onto the fiber shaft. Today's superwash wools may also contain *biopolished* wool that's been bleached to remove the fiber's protective outer lipid barrier and then treated with enzymes that literally eat away the scales.

Because the scales have been eliminated in one way or another, superwash wools tend to have a denser **hand** and a more lustrous appearance. The altered surface can sometimes impact the fiber's ability to take dye, so you may want to check yarns for colorfastness. The only exception here seems to be the superwash Merino sock yarn that's so prevalent with hand-dyers these days. I don't know why, but that particular kind of yarn eagerly sucks up every drop of dye, holds it forever, and reflects it back brilliantly.

Perhaps the most important drawback of the superwash process, however, has to do with stretching. Since the fibers lack the scales that normally help hold everything together, some superwash wools can stretch dramatically with washing. (And because it's superwash, you can't just toss it in the washing machine to shrink it.) Your best course of action is to buy a single skein of yarn and knit a sizable swatch with it. Wash the swatch and let it hang dry. Hanging handknits is normally a no-no, but in this case we want to induce stretching to see just how far it goes.

If you find a superwash wool you like, you'll only need to swatch it once to be sure. Then you can return to it again and again.

ANGORA GOATS: MOHAIR

Often hastily dismissed as "that fluffy, scratchy stuff," **mohair** is actually one of the most versatile fibers in the world. It's certainly one of my favorites, but that may be just because I find the inquisitive, friendly goat such a charmer.

A bit of confusion exists about where mohair comes from. Is it a kind of sheep? Or perhaps the hair of an elusive mountain Mo? No. Mohair comes from the angora goat. (Which debunks the second myth that angora is produced by angora *rabbits*, not angora goats.)

The notion of goats with silken hair can be traced back to the fourteenth century BC, but the angora goat as we know it most likely evolved from a thirteenth-century AD breed in the Ankara region of Turkey—hence the term *angora* goat. The name *mohair*, on the other hand, is supposedly a variation on the Arabic word *mukhayar*, which roughly means "choose." European traders may have associated that term with mohair cloth (perhaps because they were always "choosing" it?).

When Elsie Davenport originally wrote *Your Handspinning* in 1953, mohair fibers were a rarity in England. "Fine, strong, very lustrous yarn can be spun by the worsted method, especially from the hair of young animals," she wrote. "But one's only chance of doing so in this country is through the good offices of the curator of a zoo." Fortunately, this is no longer the case. Today, more than 60 percent of the world's mohair is grown in South Africa, with the United States in second place. The majority of U.S. mohair comes from Texas. In other countries, however, mohair for handknitters and spinners hasn't always been so prevalent.

Mohair has all the wonderful qualities of wool: It is flame-retardant, soil-resistant, and can absorb moisture without feeling damp or cold. It is also warmer and stronger than wool, with larger, flatter scales that contribute to an overall silky-smooth appearance. The fiber absorbs dye readily and, thanks to that smooth surface, reflects it back brilliantly.

While mohair has a reputation for being scratchy, its softness varies dramatically depending on the age of the animal. The younger the goat, the softer the fiber. Superfine kid mohair, which is the very first shearing when the kid is only six months old, can rival cashmere for softness. (Rowan Kidsilk Haze is made from this grade.) Next comes kid mohair (such as Anny Blatt Fine Kid),

then yearling, then fine adult, and then adult mohair. If you see a brushed mohair yarn with just *mohair* on the label, chances are the grade is either fine adult or adult. Since the finer grades cost more, yarn companies will almost always indicate them on the label. Sometimes you'll see hybrid listings, like *super kid* or *baby*, which usually fall somewhere between superfine kid and kid—but let your fingers be your ultimate guide.

In Yarn

When we say mohair, most people think of the brushed, fluffy stuff—and indeed that's probably the most common way you'll find mohair in yarn. To accomplish this fuzzy look, mohair fibers are plied with a fine nylon binder thread (or a nylon/wool blend) at such a rate that the mohair loops back on itself, creating a bouclé loop effect. The yarn is then re-plied with a second binder to secure the loops.

Sometimes yarn companies stop there and sell the yarn as a bouclé yarn, or they'll run it through another machine to brush out the loops and create the fuzzy brushed mohair we know and love. Most major yarn manufacturers have at least one brushed mohair in their product line, with weights varying from heavy worsted to laceweight.

Few yarn companies sell mohair in pure, nonbrushed form for handknitting. (You can find far stronger, firmer yarns for industrial weaving, but your hands will not enjoy trying to knit with them.) One longtime exception is Lancaster, Texas–based Brooks Farm Yarn, a perennial favorite at all the major U.S. fiber festivals. (You can see the yarn in action in Shelia January's Optic Waves Shawl on page 94.) Most likely, yarn companies avoid pure unbrushed mohair yarns because mohair is such a dense, slippery fiber, with very little elasticity or memory. Knit up alone, it produces a heavy fabric with tremendous luster and drape, but the smooth scales and lack of crimp can cause the yarn to release fuzz more quickly. In the case of Brooks Farm Yarn, which does tend to leave fuzz behind, the sacrifice is well worth it. Just wear clothes the same color as your handknit and nobody will be the wiser.

Most yarn companies prefer to use mohair in blends. Wool is a perennial favorite because it lends body, loft, and stability to the mix. Silk is also a perfect mate for mohair, since it has a similarly brilliant sheen and relaxed drape. While both silk and mohair have great reflective qualities, the silk tends to absorb color more readily. Once spun and brushed, the silk shimmers brilliantly from beneath a lighter halo of mohair fuzz. Knit One, Crochet Too Douceur et Soie and Rowan Kidsilk Haze are two longtime favorites that combine mohair and silk. (You can see Kidsilk Haze in action in the Scaruffle on page 214.) Artyarns Silk Rhapsody (shown in the Diamonds and Pearls Shawl on page 202) takes the notion one step further by pairing a strand of single-ply silk with a strand of laceweight brushed mohair. They're simply stranded together, rather than plied, so that each remains more distinct in the fabric.

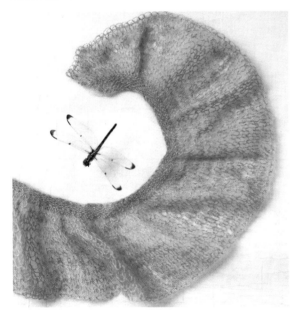

The Scaruffle (page 214) knit in a mohair blend

A few yarn companies skip the nylon completely and use a pure wool binder in their brushed mohair to make a softer, warmer, 100 percent natural yarn. Often the halo isn't as intense at first, but the wool has a gentler, "woolier" feel. The only potential drawback is that the nylon tends to be stronger and wear longer than wool—but unless you're knitting jerseys for a football team you probably won't notice much difference. Anny Blatt Fine Kid brushed mohair is a perfect example and one of my very favorites.

Sometimes yarn companies will add a small amount of mohair to a wool yarn to give it a delicate sheen. One of the best examples is Brown Sheep Lamb's Pride, which has 85 percent wool and 15 percent mohair. The presence of mohair in a predominantly wool yarn can be especially appealing in felted items. See Amy King's Retro Cloche, page 228, for an example of Lamb's Pride after it's been felted. The wool provides a thick foundation while the mohair skiffs the surface like mist on a pond.

CASHMERE GOAT: CASHMERE

Were I marooned on a desert island and only allowed one fiber for the rest of my life, it'd have to be **cashmere**. Not because the fiber is comfortable in hot tropical climates, because it isn't. My reason is more spiritual than practical. When I work with this airy, soft, luxurious fiber, I have a blissful sense of the divine.

Cashmere is the downy undercoat of the Capra hircus Laniger, otherwise known as the cashmere goat. Originally from the Himalayas and named after the Kashmir region of India (although very little cashmere is produced there now), these rugged animals grow a dual coat of fibers that protect and insulate them from freezing winds and subzero temperatures.

The dual coat consists mostly of long, coarse, pointy **guard hairs**. Entirely unsuitable for handknitting, these rugged 3½- to 4½-inch (9–11.5cm) long fibers are often used for brushes or other household items. But beneath the guard hair grows a fantastically soft and extremely insulating downy undercoat that's the cherished fiber we call *cashmere*. It's a short, delicate fiber averaging 1¼–3½ inches (3–9cm) in length and 16 microns—that's about one-third the diameter of the finest human hair. The fiber's light weight (over 30 percent lighter than wool) and insulating capacity (eight times warmer than wool) help it provide warmth without overwhelming bulk. The fiber has crimp, but not as much elasticity as wool.

Cashmere is a notoriously expensive fiber, but there's a reason. While a cashmere goat may produce up to a pound (454g) of fiber each year, the actual cashmere content averages only 6–8 ounces (170–227g)—that's about 400–475 yards (366–434m) of worsted-weight yarn, enough for a scarf. You'd need at least three times that amount for a medium-sized woman's sweater.

How We Get It

Cashmere is harvested in one of three ways. When the cashmere goat molts in the spring, it releases its fibers in large clumps. Although the clumps can be pulled off by hand, in China and Mongolia most commonly they are combed off by hand using a coarse comb. The combing process yields a high percentage of pure cashmere with less guard hair. In other countries, however, the entire fleece may be shorn. Since all the fibers are being cut at once, you'll have a higher amount of guard hairs that will need to be removed.

Guard hairs are an issue with cashmere. Regardless of how the fiber was procured or how many guard hairs are in the fleece, those guard hairs need to be removed. The process is called **dehairing**, and it involves running the scoured fleece through a series of extremely fine metal combs that separate the down from the guard hair. Care, skill, and proper equipment are required to do it properly. Otherwise, the length of the fine fibers may be damaged (causing the fabric to pill and wear faster).

Where It Comes From

As the biggest cashmere producer in the world, China now supplies two-thirds of all cashmere products to the international market. To create these products, China is the biggest single importer of Mongolian cashmere, snatching up some 50 percent of the raw fibers for its own textile industry. Traditionally, China sold these raw fibers to Western mills, but—having recently abandoned a 13 percent tax-rebate policy for dehaired-cashmere exports—Chinese firms have discovered that exporting raw materials to foreign mills is less profitable than exporting *processed* cashmere products, such as yarn.

Historically, Italy, Scotland, England, and Japan led the world in luxury cashmere processing, but China has made major inroads in the last ten years to upgrade its manufacturing machinery and techniques and improve the overall quality of its production. For knitters, this means we can expect to see an even greater influx of cashmere yarns coming to stores directly from Chinese mills. And as China's processing techniques improve, it will become increasingly difficult to feel any difference between high-end Italian-spun and new Chinese-spun cashmere.

Buyer Beware

Because cashmere is considered a premium fiber, manufacturers will often add just a small percentage of it to their yarns. They try to balance the luxury branding of cashmere with the affordability of adding just a small amount. Unfortunately, as of this writing, at least one major yarn company has come under scrutiny after several independent lab reports showed that its popular cashmere blend had no cashmere in it whatsoever.

CASHMERE STANDARDS

QUICK NOTE

Cashmere produced from small-scale processing mills (where most cashmere from smaller U.S. cashmere farms is processed) is not held to the industry standard, and the equipment used by small mills does not have the same degree of precision as the larger mills. This doesn't necessarily mean the yarn will be of lesser quality. In fact, the most exquisite cashmere yarn I've touched to date came from a now-defunct cashmere farm in the United States. But do be aware that the standards will be a little different.

The Wool Products Labeling Act of 1939 requires that the yarn label clearly indicate the exact fiber content—in percentage or *all,* if 100 percent—as well as the country of origin. In January 2007, Congress enacted an amendment to the 1939 act that restricts manufacturers from labeling a product as "cashmere" if the average fiber diameter exceeds 19 microns. Also, anything containing more than 3 percent (by weight) fiber with an average diameter exceeding 30 microns cannot be labeled cashmere either. Beware of yarn labels that simply say *cashmere* or *cashmere blend* without any indication of *how much.* And always trust your own fiber instinct. If something feels wrong, move on to another yarn.

In Yarn

To make best use of the short, delicate cashmere fibers, and to enhance their naturally fluffy state, yarn manufacturers will often prepare cashmere in the lofty woolen style. This is where the fibers are left in a jumbled state before spinning. The fiber is equally adaptable to all weights, from lace to bulky. Yarn companies have recently played around with using cashmere in multiple-ply cabled yarns, where the cable structure lends extra strength and elasticity. Because the fiber is short and delicate, it requires a little more **twist** to hold it in place. For this reason most manufacturers have shied away from using cashmere in a single-ply yarn.

A two-ply laceweight cashmere from Habu Textiles

Determining Quality

Cashmere quality can vary dramatically from yarn to yarn—even more so than other protein fibers. Fortunately, there are some simple ways to evaluate the quality of the fiber before you buy.

First, hold a skein in your hand. Run your fingers along the surface. Does the yarn melt into your fingers? Do you immediately feel compelled to rub it against your face? Or do you turn it over to reread the label because the yarn feels too stiff and lifeless to be cashmere? Really good cashmere will make you stop dead in your tracks and emit at least one "ooooooh" as you touch it. This isn't a scientific gauge of quality, but it's one I've grown to trust over time.

Now, try to pinch a section of the fluff and pull it away. Does it all come off easily in your fingers, or do just a few fibers come loose? This will tell you if the fiber has been spun tightly enough to hold together under duress.

Next, check to see if the fiber was properly dehaired. This is important because some manufacturers try to skimp on the dehairing so they can bring the yarn to market faster and for less money. Fortunately, guard hairs are easy to spot. Unlike the powdery down fibers, guard hairs are hollow, with no crimp or core. When dyed, they tend to have a shiny, almost translucent appearance. And when they are spun into yarn, they immediately try to work their way out. So the first thing to look for is slightly firmer, shiny—perhaps even silver—fibers poking out of the yarn.

Some guard hairs are inevitable, but remember that the more guard hairs you have in the mix, the less cashmere you have. The resulting fabric will be scratchier, it won't wear as well, and it won't keep you as warm. The high-end luxury cashmere market standard is no more than two-tenths of 1 percent of guard hair, while more mainstream yarn manufacturers will accept as much as one-half of 1 percent guard hair. I don't recommend trying to pull out the guard hairs as you knit—I've done this and (a) it doesn't work and (b) it'll drive you nuts!

Finally, be aware that many mills treat cashmere fibers with a lightweight oil to reduce buildup of static electricity during spinning. The faster they try to run the equipment (because time is money), the more oil they'll need to apply to keep static at bay. Ideally, you want a cashmere that's been slowly, lovingly spun with minimal oils added. But it's also fine to knit with the oil-laden yarns. In fact, some people find that the oil helps them maintain tension and control of their stitches, especially when working in laceweight yarns.

The fun part is when you're done and you wash your garment for the first time. Cashmere already has a natural tendency to bloom with wash, but when the fibers have been held down with oil, the bloom can be even more stunning. If you don't like surprises—even good ones—knit and wash a test swatch first.

Classic Elite Princess

In Blends

As I've already mentioned, cashmere is often used in blends because it's so expensive. Cashmere adds two qualities to any blend: warmth without bulk, and a fine, almost powdery, softness. Two of the most common blends are cashmere with Merino (the Merino adds elasticity, loft, and durability) and cashmere with silk (the silk adds tensile strength and a brilliant shimmery luster). But you'll also find cashmere blended with baby alpaca, which gives a marvelous hint of weight and drape to the finished fabric. Regardless of the mix, cashmere is so lightweight that a little bit will go a long way.

You can also go one step further and try what I call *kitchen sink yarns* that mix cashmere with all sorts of fibers—such as Knit Picks Panache, which has 40 percent baby alpaca, 20 percent cashmere, 20 percent silk, and 20 percent extrafine Merino. Here you'd have a foundation of weighty, relaxed alpaca loosened up by the lightweight softness of the cashmere, a hint of sheen from the silk, and elasticity and crimp from the Merino.

You could also add synthetic fibers to the mix, as in Classic Elite Princess, which we used for Jennifer Hagan's Princess Mitts on page 172. This five-ply yarn blends 40 percent Merino, 28 percent viscose, 15 percent nylon, 10 percent cashmere, and 7 percent angora, making it warm and plush but also long-wearing. As more yarn companies experiment with broader fiber blends, we'll have even more yarns available from which to choose.

On the Needles

What should you knit with cashmere? While "everything" immediately comes to mind, I do have some general guidelines. If you're going to splurge on this notoriously soft fiber, it makes sense to use it for items that will stay in direct contact with your skin. Scarves, shawls, throws, sweaters, hats, mittens, gloves, pillows—all are fair game. The soft-as-a-baby's-bottom feel makes cashmere perfect for, well, babies (though not necessarily their bottoms). Just remember that the fiber requires extra care in the wash. If you're knitting an item for a new mother who is handwash-challenged, be sure to stick with a machine-washable blend, such as Rowan Cashsoft—but be aware that it only contains 10 percent cashmere, set against 57 percent extra-fine Merino and 33 percent microfiber.

There's a debate raging about whether cashmere is appropriate for socks. Some people insist that it isn't. These are probably the same people who file their taxes on time, eat the crust on their bread, and change their car's oil every three thousand miles. I am not one of those people. Therefore, I am a strong proponent of cashmere socks. You just have to follow some guidelines.

Cashmere is a delicate fiber. When spun woolen-style, even the finest cashmere blends will pill and grow thin over time. So yes, this makes it a silly choice for socks. But how often do your feet get a chance to be bathed in the pure bliss of cashmere? That's what cashmere socks provide. Unless your last name happens to be Rockefeller, you probably won't wear these

Butterfly Moebius (page 188) knit in a cashmere/silk blend

The cashgora breed is technically defined as three-quarters cashmere and one-quarter angora goat. As you'd imagine from such a mix, the fleece tends to include both longer, lustrous fibers (with the dense drape of mohair) and finer down hairs, with a few rough guard hairs as well. The downy fiber isn't quite as fine as cashmere, averaging 22 microns compared to the 16-micron average for finer cashmere. Because the breed is still evolving, you may find some quality variation from breeder to breeder. Keep this in mind if you ever order cashgora, sight unseen, from a new vendor.

PYGORA

The **pygora** goat is also a relatively new breed, resulting from efforts to cross-breed the pygmy and angora goat. While the ultimate goal of the breeding may have been to increase the angora goat flock, these not-quite-angora-but-no-longer-pygmy goats have been assigned a name all their own.

The fiber is not yet available in the mainstream yarn market, but you may find it at fiber festivals and farms. As with cashgora goat, the fleece is a mix of longer, lustrous fibers and fine, short down fibers, along with some guard hairs that vary in roughness but should generally be removed.

socks every day. But they'd be perfect for those special occasions when true pampering is in order. Perhaps you're nursing a broken heart, or a bad cold, or just bundled up on the couch watching your favorite movie—a pair of handknit cashmere socks is like chicken soup, only better.

CASHGORA

Although no large commercial yarn company yet offers a **cashgora** yarn, interest in this new breed is on the rise. The cashgora goat is the result of efforts to cross-breed the cashmere and angora goats, the goal being to create an animal that produces cashmerelike fibers but with greater length and luster. Most of the breeding efforts have taken place in Australia and New Zealand, but some cashgora breeders are in the United States as well.

PASHMINA

The rise in popularity of **pashmina** shawls has led to some confusion about what pashmina actually is. Older reference books identify pashmina (and pashim/pashm/pushmina) as a breed of goats raised in Kashmir and other northern Indian provinces, whose finest downy undercoats are called *turfani pashim* or *phum*, and from whose fibers the famous pashmina shawls are made.

More recently, however, the term has included everything from fine cashmere to a blend of cashmere and silk, cashmere and wool, and even 100 percent acrylic. Similar blends are sometimes also marketed as *cashmina* or *pashmere*. The confusion has led to the word *pashmina* no longer being a legally recognized labeling term in the United States.

If you come across a yarn labeled *pashmina,* look for the fine print that indicates actual fiber content—something that is required in the United States by the Wool Products Labeling Act of 1939. If there's no hint (100% cashmere or all cashmere, 70% cashmere and 30% silk, 100% acrylic, etc.), let the buyer beware.

ANGORA

The least expensive and most easily available luxury fiber, **angora** has a warmth that rivals cashmere and softness that rivals qiviut. Best of all, it comes from cute little bunnies that look for all the world like furry footstools with ears.

According to Erica Lynne (author of the excellent reference book *Angora: A Handbook for Spinners*), angora is so prized in Germany that they have a special name for it: *menschenheilkaninchen.* Loosely translated, it means "mystical, magical, human healing rabbit." Think about it: Angora weighs next to nothing and yet keeps you eight times warmer than wool. Even when saturated with twice as much moisture as wool can handle, angora still feels warm. Slip a knitted angora tube over any arthritic joint or aching muscle and you may quickly find relief.

Where It Comes From

Angora comes from the angora rabbit (not to be confused with the angora goat, which produces mohair). These animals can weigh anywhere from 5 to 11 pounds (2.3–5kg), and they produce an average of 8 ounces (227g) of fiber a year (about enough for a woman's sweater).

Because angora rabbits have few sebaceous and sweat glands, angora fiber is extremely clean—in fact, you'll get about 99 percent pure angora right off the animal. Some manufacturers will spin the fibers without any processing at all. If you travel to any of the major fiber festivals in the United States, you may find an angora breeder holding a rabbit in her lap and spinning yarn directly off its coat.

There are three general classes of angora rabbits: French, English, and German. French is a full-bodied fleece, English is far softer and more delicate, and German is somewhere in between. Commercial yarns rarely indicate the specific breed of animal from which the fibers came.

Regardless of breed, all angora rabbits grow three distinct types of fiber: the strong, straight erector hair; the slightly finer protector hair, or **awn**; and the short, extremely soft crimped hair, or **down**, that's closest to the skin. Both erector and protector hairs are considered guard hairs from a yarn standpoint.

A common misconception is that good angora yarns are made entirely of down hairs. Some may prefer this, if they can find it, but the truth is that all three fibers *can* be used in angora yarn. The firmer guard and awn hairs actually serve as structural supports to keep the finer down fibers open and lofty and to protect the mix from accidental feltings.

Characteristics in Yarn

Spinning equipment costs money to run and maintain. If you're spinning thousands of yards (or meters) of yarn, decreasing the number of twists per inch (2.5cm) of yarn by even one rotation may result in significant energy cost savings. And, naturally, since yarn manufacturers want to keep operations economical, they often work to find the minimum amount of twist needed to keep the fibers together and still produce a reasonable yarn.

This approach works for crimpy wools that naturally want to hold together, but the short and smooth angora fibers need twist in order to hold together in yarn. Scrimp on twist and you'll face copious amounts of fuzz on yourself and everything around you. This is part of why angora has suffered from a bad reputation over the years as nothing more than a source of fuzzy frustration. But the truth is that if the fibers have been blended and prepared properly, and the yarn has been given enough twist, your resulting garment will both feel fantastic and wear beautifully.

Besides twist, the other thing that directly impacts the fuzz factor is how the fiber was harvested from the animal. The first thing to note is that angora rabbits are *not* killed for their fur. The fiber is plucked, combed, or shorn.

Plucking and combing yield the finest grade of fiber, because the fibers are left completely intact, from tip to base, just as they grew on the rabbit. The fiber is harvested when the animal is naturally shedding, so it is not a cruel or painful process. But because both plucking and combing are very time-consuming, the resulting fibers can be extremely expensive. Shearing, on the other hand, is a speedy process that results in shorter jumbled fibers that don't benefit from the same order and structure. The fibers may be shorter, which leads to more fuzz and faster wear, but the cost is lower.

Only a few luxury angora breeders in France, Hungary, and the former Czechoslovakia still produce prime plucked or combed fibers for the major handknitting yarn market. You may also find small amounts of prime plucked angora in England, Spain, Switzerland, Belgium, and Poland, and you can also find gorgeous "boutique" angoras from smaller breeders here in the United States—I recommend fiber festivals for this.

But on the global scale, China dominates the angora market. Chinese angora fibers tend to be much softer but also shorter, resulting in the need to blend them with small amounts of longer-staple, higher-grade angora or other fibers in order to hold the yarn (and resulting fabric) together. Chile and Argentina follow closely in production volume. Korea is also a competing force in the angora market, and all angora from Korea is shorn. As with Chinese angora, Korean fibers tend to be shorter and benefit from blending with longer fibers for durability.

Testing for Quality

Handspinners may get to choose a prime plucked angora for their projects, but handknitters have no such luxury. We're given yarn labels that simply say "angora" without any indication of its grade or the age of the animal from which it came or whether it was plucked, combed, or cut. We must use our instinct, our senses, and check the reputation of the vendor.

For starters, know that France has been the world's leading producer of prime plucked and combed angora fibers since the late 1800s. The French still have the breeding infrastructure and the highly tuned equipment and skill to process the fibers properly.

Anny Blatt Angora Super

Second, study the mix to see if it contains an even blend of fibers, or if there's an overabundance of slightly firmer, pointier protector fibers. I mentioned that some of those hairs can be a good thing, but too many will result in a scratchy fabric you won't want anywhere near your sensitive skin.

Finally, try pinching a small amount of the fluff and see how much comes off in your fingers. Remember that you'll be knitting this yarn into a tighter fabric, and that your small knitted stitches will help hold those fibers together. So some fluff in your fingers is okay. But if you pull and every strand of fluff comes off in your fingers, consider it a warning of fluffier days to come.

If you ever get a chance to use handspun angora, accept it without hesitation. Handspinners can control the quality of the fiber and the degree of twist to such a degree that you'll encounter nary a stray strand of fluff as you work. These yarns tend to wear far better than their industrially spun counterparts.

In Blends

Angora has a strong presence. It's extremely warm, extremely lightweight, and extremely fluffy. Because of this, yarn companies often use angora sparingly to add elements of warmth and fluff to other fiber blends.

But the issue of blending is especially tricky with angora. Manufacturers must list fiber blends by percentage *weight,* not percentage *volume.* Angora is an extremely lightweight fiber. If you were to compare 6 ounces (170g) of angora with, say, 6 ounces (170g) of a much denser alpaca, you'd see just how much more angora fiber it takes to achieve the same weight. If you see a yarn with 20 percent angora, that's actually quite a lot of fiber. By the time you get to 70 percent or 75 percent angora, that fiber will pretty much dominate the mix. I like the fluff, so I tend to choose yarns that have a high percentage of angora but are anchored by a more full-bodied fiber, such as Merino.

Knitting with Angora

Angora has very little body or elasticity, which means that garments with excessive ribbing or form-fitting shaping will be pretty much lost on it. I once made a pair of pure angora socks that work perfectly as long as I don't move my feet. When I do, they slide right off.

Angora benefits from stitches that are proportionate to its bulk. That's what helps hold the fluff and fiber together. For this reason I don't recommend using angora for large, airy stitch patterns or patterns calling for needles significantly larger than the ones specified on the label.

I've heard people say angora is too hot for a sweater, but it really depends on the sweater. For the Vines Cardigan (shown at right; pattern on page 102), we chose a cropped raglan shape and slightly open stitch motif along the shoulders to allow for maximum air circulation. We also kept the sleeves at three-quarter length, which helps control heat and keeps fuzz away from your hands. But if the notion of a full-sized sweater is too daunting, you can also have great fun using angora

Vines Cardigan (page 102) knit in an angora/wool blend

in hats and anything that's worn around the neck (scarf, moebius, shawl, you name it).

Knitting Tips

Angora has very little crimp to hold your needles snug. That's why I recommend using wood or bamboo needles that have a little extra surface drag to help maintain control over your stitches. Smooth metal needles just beg for a chance to slide out of your work at the slightest provocation. And that's not good, since the fuzz of the angora makes it difficult to see (and rescue) your stitches.

Because of this lack of body and elasticity, angora fabric may stretch out of shape over time. If stretch is a serious concern, try finding a yarn that blends angora with a fiber with more memory, such as wool. If you want to indulge in angora socks, I'd recommend a wool blend with no more than 50 percent angora.

CAMELIDS

Almost as prolific and varied in fiber production as the goat family, the **Camelid** family includes five fiber-producing animals: the camel itself (the one "true" camel species) and four South American descendants, the alpaca, the llama, the guanaco, and the vicuña.

From a yarn perspective, the most prevalent Camelids are alpaca and llama, with camel running a close third. Although guanaco and vicuña produce some of the finest fibers on earth, the guanaco is an endangered species. The United States recently downgraded vicuña to a protected species, which means small amounts of vicuña fiber can be legally imported into this country. But don't expect to find commercial yarns with either fiber in your local yarn store any time soon.

There is also a small subalpaca breed, called *paco-vicuña,* which exhibits vicuña traits and has been specially bred to enhance these traits. No paco-vicuña fibers are in large-scale commercially available yarns, but, as the breed continues to grow and be refined, this is sure to change.

CAMEL

The only "true" camel in this category is the **camel** itself. There are actually two camel types: the single-humped Dromedary, which thrives in arid desert regions and grows only a short coat of fiber; and the two-humped Bactrian, which lives in far colder climates and grows a thick protective coat in winter. The one knitters care about is the Bactrian camel, whose dual coat includes not only scratchy guard hairs but surprisingly soft and warm down hair.

The majority of camel hair in commercial yarns comes from China, Mongolia, Iran, Afghanistan, and Russia, with additional amounts now coming from New Zealand, Australia, and Tibet.

Bouton d'Or Ksar

Characteristics

Like the cashmere goat, the camel goes through a natural **molting** season every spring, releasing its thick winter coat (averaging about 5 pounds [2.3kg]) in large clumps. The fibers are hand-gathered, sorted, and scoured, and the guard hairs are removed.

The remaining down fibers average 1–3 inches (2.5–7.5cm) in length, with a micron range of 19–24. Generally speaking, camel down has a softness similar to Merino, but it behaves like cashmere. It has crimp but very little elasticity, and it does not felt easily. The fiber also doesn't bleach easily, so you'll normally find it used in yarns whose color either masks or enhances the natural tan shade of the camel fiber.

On its own, camel fiber spins into a soft, lightweight yarn. But most yarn companies tend to use camel in wool blends. Wool balances out the airy lightweight camel down and gives body and bounce to the resulting fabric. One of my favorite camel blends is Ksar from Bouton d'Or.

It's a worsted-spun, machine-washable, 50/50 blend of wool and baby camel. At first glance you'd think it was just wool. But if you really work it with your hands, you'll start to feel something a little different. Keep paying attention and you'll be able to detect a different kind of fiber that lightens and insulates without nearly the weight of wool.

ALPACA

While many fiber-bearing animals originated in the Middle East and Asia, the alpaca is a distinctively South American animal that—along with its cousin, the llama—descended originally from the Camelid family. Carefully bred and prized for its fiber since 4000 BC, the alpaca was almost rendered extinct by Spanish conquistadors. But today, the world alpaca population has been restored to nearly 3 million animals worldwide.

The bulk of the world alpaca trade is centered in Arequipa, Peru. Almost 99 percent of the world's alpaca population is still found in the highlands of Peru, Chile, and Bolivia. Millions of alpacas may roam freely there, but the export of alpacas to other countries has been tightly controlled. Before the mid-1980s, just a few alpacas were imported to the United States for use as novelty animals. As such, many of these docile, quiet animals ended up in places like petting zoos, where the onslaught of eager, outgoing children sometimes prompted the animals to defend themselves by spitting. This earned alpacas a bad and unjustified reputation as ill-tempered beasts. But spend a quiet day with the animals on their own turf, and you'll quickly fall in love.

Alpaca import and breeding programs in the United States began in earnest in the mid-1980s. Today, the U.S. alpaca industry maintains a somewhat exclusive (and expensive) reputation, with nearly every alpaca registered and tracked, and prized animals fetching upwards of $50,000 apiece. The market for U.S.-produced alpaca *fiber,* however, is nowhere near as vigorous or profitable as the market for the animals themselves. Pretty much all commercial yarn—with the exception of a few farms and boutique spinneries—uses alpaca from South America. And a great portion of those yarns are spun in Peru.

The Fiber

There are actually two different types of alpacas: **Suri**, which produces long, silky locks; and **Huacaya**, which produces a denser fiber with a little more crimp. Huacaya make up roughly 90 percent of the current alpaca population, but you can occasionally find Suri or Suri/Huacaya blends at fiber festivals and farms. Both animals grow both coarse "beard" hairs, which must be removed, and the soft wool-like hair used in yarns and fabrics.

Alpaca fibers are longer than fine sheep wools, ranging in length from 4½ to 11 inches (11.5–28cm) or longer, depending on how frequently they've been shorn. The finer grades run in the 4½- to 8-inch (11.5 to 20.5cm) range. They have a high tensile strength that translates into durable, long-wearing garments. Alpaca fiber has similar moisture properties to wool, being able to absorb a good deal of moisture while maintaining a warm and dry feel against the skin. Alpaca differs from wool, however, in that it has far fewer scales, which helps contribute to its lustrous appearance. Also, the alpaca does not secrete lanolin, so the fleece is far cleaner and more hypoallergenic for those with lanolin sensitivities.

The alpaca fleece comes in more than twenty-two different colors, ranging from bright white to many shades of brown to a deep jet black. This makes alpaca an ideal choice for people who crave colorwork but prefer to use all-natural, undyed materials. Unlike sheep's wool, which tends to be bleached to a pure white and then dyed to suit the manufacturer, alpaca fiber does not bleach readily. This means more care must be taken in matching the natural fiber color with the finished color goals.

Those large scales mean that alpaca won't felt as readily as its fine sheep's wool counterparts, but it does produce beautiful results, given extra time and care. Because the fibers haven't been bleached, even bright white alpaca yarn will felt—which makes it a suitable felting substitute for bright-white wools. Those wools often won't felt because of damage to the fibers from the bleach. (For more on felting, see page 222.)

On the Needles

When choosing a project for an alpaca yarn, you should keep three things in mind: touch, drape, and warmth.

The fiber averages 18–26 microns, which puts it in the same league as cashmere and baby kid mohair. Alpaca has a smooth, dense, and lustrous hand, absorbing dye readily and reflecting it back with brilliance and luster.

When knit, alpaca produces a dense, relaxed fabric that drapes beautifully on the body. Alpaca is well-suited for garments that will rest directly against the skin—even that of babies. Actual softness can vary somewhat, depending on the grade of alpaca used in your yarn. Handknitters should stick with superfine alpaca. For more delicate, tender (and expensive) fibers, look for yarns labeled *baby alpaca*. The softest fibers of all—royal alpaca—are normally reserved for the fashion mills, but you can occasionally find them in handknitting yarns.

In plain stockinette, the smooth alpaca fibers can reveal even the slightest irregularities in your stitches. For this reason, alpaca can benefit from patterns that incorporate some stitchwork such as moss or seed stitch. But keep in mind that cables and heavier stitchwork should be added prudently because they increase the overall weight of the garment. Some weight is good for drape, but alpaca is already a dense fiber—so too much drape can be uncomfortable to wear and quickly pull things out of shape.

For this same reason, any kind of ribbing in pure alpaca will be decorative only—the yarn won't reliably keep your fabric snug. If cables and ribbing are your thing, that's OK, too. Just stick with a yarn that blends alpaca with a loftier, more elastic fiber, such as wool. (This is what Norah Gaughan does with her Cabled Swing Cardi on page 134.)

And finally, remember the warmth factor. Although not as warm as cashmere, alpaca fiber has a hollow core that helps it hold in heat, making it several times warmer than wool. While there's no law stating that you can't knit a sweater out of bulky alpaca, just remember, it's going to be warm, dense, and potentially heavy.

LLAMA

If the alpaca is the gentle, mild-mannered kid in the schoolyard, the **llama**—with its taller stature and more pronounced personality—is the protective big brother. Often used as guard animals for flocks of sheep (and even for alpacas), llamas are also widely used as pack animals in South America.

The llama's coat may look more scraggly and rugged than that of the alpaca because—unlike the alpaca—the llama grows a true dual coat. On the outside, there's a thick, rugged layer of guard hairs. Underneath, there's a softer, more delicate undercoat that some insist is indistinguishable from alpaca.

Because the fibers must be dehaired, many yarn companies avoid llama in favor of its cleaner but more

Stitchwork detail from Norah Gaughan's Cabled Swing Cardi (page 134) knit in an alpaca/wool blend

expensive alpaca cousin. Properly dehaired, baby llama fiber can be just as soft as baby alpaca, however, and far softer than midgrade alpaca. If you do find a yarn with llama fibers, it's well worth pulling off the shelf and examining more closely.

Visually inspect the skein for thick, protruding hairs of a slightly different color than the rest of the yarn. Those would be guard hairs, and if there are too many, your garment will be uncomfortably scratchy. But if you see none and the yarn feels soft and inviting, by all means give it a try.

Quality llama fiber is marvelous to work with, behaving almost exactly like alpaca. The large scales on the fiber surface give it a luminous quality, while the fiber's overall lack of crimp and elasticity produce a relaxed, weighty fabric that drapes beautifully. A hollow core makes llama fiber far warmer than wool.

Because the fibers are long and smooth, with little elasticity, they're often spun worsted—this is when all the fibers are combed together for perfect alignment before spinning. This gives you a lustrous, smooth, long-wearing fiber.

As with alpaca, llama fiber doesn't bleach or felt easily. Manufacturers will often choose the closest shade of natural color and then dye it to achieve the desired results. But some yarns may still look a little dimmer than their highly bleached wool counterparts.

In choosing what to do with your llama yarn, follow the same guidelines you would for alpaca. First and foremost, remember that the fabric will have a heavier, more pronounced drape than standard wool. Also remember that pure llama won't have enough elasticity or fiber memory for patterns where a tight and consistent fit is needed—such as socks or a form-fitting ribbed sweater.

Fortunately, llama is often blended with other fibers that make up for its shortcomings. My favorite llama blend is Montera, a longtime 50 percent llama and 50 percent wool offering from Classic Elite Yarns. As with alpaca, most yarns with llama fiber are spun in Peru.

MUSK OX: QIVIUT

In my version of heaven, all the beds would have qiviut sheets. You wouldn't need much else—no blanket, no nightgown, and certainly no heater—to stay warm on even the most bitterly cold nights. For **qiviut** is one of the softest, lightest, warmest fibers on earth. It's also one of the most expensive.

Qiviut is the downy undercoat of the musk ox, native to the Canadian Arctic and also found in the Arctic areas of Alaska and Greenland. To survive the howling winds, deep snow, and frigid subzero temperatures of the Arctic winter, the animals grow a thick dual coat of fibers that are so insulating that snow falling on them never melts—it just lands on their backs and stays there.

In the spring, the musk ox sheds this winter coat in large clumps, leaving behind five or more pounds (2.3kg) of fiber per animal. Domesticated musk ox are led into a small area or a restraining device (remember, they can weigh upward of 600 pounds [272kg]) and the fibers carefully removed with a large-toothed comb. In the case of animals living in the wild, you can simply walk through the tundra and pick up the clumps by hand. After the fiber is harvested, it has to be carefully and delicately processed, so that the rough guard hairs are removed without damaging the short, delicate, downy undercoat.

All this extra work to procure and process the fiber, coupled with a limited supply of musk ox animals being raised in captivity, makes qiviut a rare and expensive fiber. Over the last few years, a handful of companies have begun offering qiviut yarns and fibers on a limited basis. They are expensive but worth a try just once, so you can say you've experienced qiviut for yourself.

A driving force behind the domestication of the musk ox for fiber production is Oomingmak, the Musk Ox Producers' Cooperative. Begun in 1969, the cooperative is owned by some 250 Native Alaskan women who collectively knit and market their handknitted qiviut scarves to a worldwide audience.

Qiviut is incredibly fine, averaging just 10–13 microns (finer than cashmere or vicuña). But the actual fiber quality can vary depending on the age and gender of the animal. It's always best to buy qiviut in person, so you can touch it and see if it's been properly dehaired.

Qiviut is eight times warmer than wool. It's a smooth fiber surface with few scales and very little elasticity. This smooth surface and lack of scales makes qiviut less prone to felting when subject to agitation. It also takes dye well, although I've found that some dye processes can make the fiber feel harsh.

Because of its cost and rarity, qiviut tends to be sold in laceweight and used for small projects that make efficient use of just one or two skeins. A bulky qiviut yarn would be not only prohibitively expensive but stiflingly hot to wear.

YAK

A member of the bovine family, the **yak** is native to the high-altitude regions of Tibet, Mongolia, and south-central Asia—areas where you need a rugged outer coat to stay warm during the harsh winters.

The animal releases its coat during spring molting, and the fibers are either collected from the ground or combed right off the animal. Next, the rough guard hairs are removed and used for more rugged things such as rope, brushes, and tents. How well these guard hairs were removed, and how fine the down fibers were underneath, will dictate just how soft your yak garment will be. It's often blended with other fibers, such as wool, for greater strength and lower cost.

The fiber comes in varying shades of brown or black, although some white yaks are being bred because the fiber does not take bleach well. It's a relatively short, crimpy fiber of only $1^1/_5$ inches (3cm), with a micron count ranging from 15 to 22.

Because of this short fiber length and good crimp, yak benefits from being spun in the woolen style in which the fibers are allowed to stay jumbled in every which

way. One of the most beautiful examples of this is Karabella Yarns yak/merino blend, Super Yak.

Karabella Yarns Super Yak

OPOSSUM

Only limited quantities of this fiber are available now to handknitters. Most of the yarns are produced in Australia and New Zealand, where the opossum roams wild in extremely large numbers. This cat-sized marsupial is trapped as a predator, and its fur is shaved and dehaired to obtain the soft undercoat. It's a hollow fiber that's extremely warm. But yarn quality can vary dramatically, depending on how well the fiber was dehaired—with the outer hairs being quite prickly to the skin.

SILK

For thousands of years this luminous fiber has been wooing and distracting, prompting espionage, thievery, and the creation of the longest road in the world. Silk production—called **sericulture**—is believed to have begun in China in 2600 BC. China managed to keep its hold on the secrets of sericulture until AD 300 when, legend has it, a precious few silkworm eggs and mulberry seeds were smuggled to India in the headdress of a Chinese princess. In 522, Persian monks smuggled more silkworm eggs to the Roman Empire, and soon China's exclusive hold on silk was lost.

Fast-forward nearly fifteen hundred years to today, when eager knitters across the globe routinely fall prey to seductive skeins of silk and buy them without any idea what they'll do with them.

Where It Comes From

Silk is produced by silkworms, the most common species of which is the *Bombyx mori*. Because the *Bombyx mori* feeds exclusively on chopped mulberry leaves, which have no tannin, the resulting fiber—called **Bombyx** silk—is a brilliant, pure white.

The other kind of silk, **Tussah**, comes from the wild or semicultivated silkworm that feeds indiscriminately on other leaves from the cherry tree, the oak tree, the castor-oil plant, the uncultivated mulberry tree, and others—most of which contain tannin. The resulting fiber tends to have a dimmer color, ranging from ivory to honey brown.

Unlike other animal fibers, silk does not grow, so it has no cellular structure. It's composed of a viscous protein fluid, known as **fibroin**, which consists of digested leaves that are secreted by the silkworm. Viewed up close, the fiber has the smooth, scale-free finish of a rod of glass.

How It's Made

The silkworm (actually more of a caterpillar) starts by feasting on leaves—in the case of the Bombyx, exclusively chopped mulberry leaves. The gluttony continues for some thirty days, during which time the caterpillar grows to ten thousand times its original size. When it stops eating, that's the signal it's ready to spin its cocoon.

The caterpillar begins to secrete a liquid called fibroin from two salivary glands on its head. While secreting the fibroin, the caterpillar rotates its body almost 200,000 times, in the process secreting some 800 yards (732m) of fibroin in one continuous thread. As it is secreted, the thread is coated with another liquid substance called **sericin**, which hardens upon contact with air and serves to seal and protect the cocoon. Once complete, the cocoon is the size of a peanut shell.

At this point silkworkers have two weeks to get the cocoons gathered, sold, and "stifled" before the pupa inside matures and makes its way out of the cocoon. (**Stifling** is the polite term for killing the chrysalis that is slowly metamorphosing into a moth.)

If the cocoon isn't stifled before the moth is ready to escape, the moth will secrete a dark fluid to loosen the cocoon, forming a hole to work its way out. When this happens, the cocoon is broken and the filament no longer continuous, lessening the value of the cocoon for silk production.

Cocoons must then be soaked in warm soapy water to soften the sericin coating and separate the fibers from the chrysalis—a process called **degumming**. Then the individual strand of filament is reeled, like unwinding

The Diamonds and Pearls Shawl (page 202) has a silk foundation punctuated by fine brushed mohair.

a bobbin on a sewing machine. Despite some modernization, reeling is still a labor-intensive, mostly manual process. For this reason, sericulture tends to be practiced in countries with relatively lower-cost workforces, such as China, India, and Korea. Even in areas where the process has been modernized, the finished product still sells at a premium.

Types of Silk
There are three grades of silk for yarn: reeled, spun, and noil.

Reeled silk is the finest grade available and is mostly reserved for industrial weaving and fabric yarns. Reeled silk is composed of those continuous filaments that have been unwound directly from the cocoons, then twisted together. Because of its high cost and premium in the textile market, reeled silk is a rarity among handknitting yarns. It is also somewhat impractical for handknitters because it is extremely slippery and prone to snags.

The second and most common type of silk you'll see in handknitting yarn is called **spun silk** yarn. As the name suggests, spun silk consists of silk fibers that have been cut into standard lengths, carded together, and then spun. They can also be further processed by combing, which removes any shorter fibers and noils (which are set aside for more textured **noil silk** yarns).

Spun silk yarn is generally made using the waste silk from the reeling process. This waste silk could be fibers from a cocoon that was pierced and the moth allowed to escape; fibers from damaged cocoons; the fibers from the beginning and end of the cocoon, which tend to be more irregular; the threads that the silkworm first produces to anchor itself to a nearby secure surface; or, last but not least, the most inner casing surrounding the dead chrysalis—called basin waste.

What It's Like
A warm fiber, silk has similar hygroscopic qualities to wool. It can absorb and release moisture and feel warm against the skin, even when wet. Silk is one of the strongest fibers on the planet. The fiber has what I'll call "slow" elasticity. That is, it'll definitely stretch, but it's slow to recover and may not quite make it back to the original shape. So your garment may stretch out of shape over time. Blocking will bring it mostly back, although eventually you may lose a little tightness.

Bombyx silk is naturally a bright white, with a smooth, translucent, and lustrous surface that accepts dye brilliantly. Tussah tends to be a coarser but stronger fiber with a dull, "raw" appearance that's not nearly as brilliant and shimmery as Bombyx—but it's less expensive.

Knitting with It
The main thing you'll notice when working with pure silk is its smooth, slippery surface and lack of bounce or body. On its own, you have a fluid material with relaxed drape and gorgeous reflective qualities—a dream for lace shawls and slinky tops.

But if you want to make something with a little more body and hug to it—say, a ribbed sweater or a pair of socks—you'll benefit from a yarn that blends silk with more durable, elastic fibers, such as wool. On their own, the smooth silk fibers won't hold ribbing consistently tight. An intriguing example in this category is La Lana Phat Silk, which is spun with a Merino core around which silk seems to float, as if by magic. The result is a yarn that has the durable, elastic body of wool but the shimmer and drape of silk.

La Lana Phat Silk

Visually speaking, the amount of shimmer in your yarn is impacted by the number of twists and plies it has. The less interrupted the fibers, the more intense the shimmer will be. But beware of yarns that have too little twist or ply in them because silk relies on some twist to hold the smooth, slippery fibers together. If you fall in love with a loosely spun, single-ply silk and simply *must* have it, be sure to knit it relatively tight to help hold the fibers together.

If you find the yarn slipping off your needles, try using a needle one or two sizes smaller than you normally would. Check your gauge, of course, but you may notice that these smaller needles introduce no change in gauge. And speaking of gauge, if you're using a smooth pure silk and want to work large bodies of stockinette, you'll need to be very careful about your gauge. There's no crimp or loft to absorb irregular stitches; they'll all appear exactly as you left them. That's another reason to use a silk/Merino blend, since the Merino will help balance out any flubs. We did this with Gina Wilde's Seascape Bolero top on page 79. The yarn has a base of shimmery silk to reflect her hand-dyed colors brilliantly, but it's set against 50 percent Merino for plumpness and body.

Along with sliding *off* your needles, the smoother silk yarns also tend to snag on needles with sharp tips. You may want to experiment with using slightly dull-tipped needles to minimize snags. Likewise, because silk is so slippery, it can be difficult to manage on sleek "high-speed" metal needles. I personally prefer to use bamboo or wood needles when working with silk, because these materials have more surface drag to keep the fibers in check. But this is a personal thing—it's best to practice with all of them and determine your own favorite policy. You'll find over time that your fingers will tell you what to do.

STINKY SILK

FUN FACT

All fibers tend to have their own particular smell when wet, but you may occasionally run across a skein of silk that smells especially nasty when you wash it. Chances are you're smelling remnants of the chrysalis that weren't properly removed during degumming—normally a sign of sloppy processing and low-quality fiber. Sometimes the smell goes away with a few washes in warm soapy water, but other times—especially with Tussah silk—it'll come back every time you wash it.

Another, more dramatic technique is to fill a large pot with 1 gallon (3.7L) water, ¼ cup (60mL) washing soda (also called sodium carbonate, and not to be confused with baking soda), and ¼ cup (60mL) soap, such as Ivory flakes. Boil the solution to dissolve the soda and soap, and then reduce it to just under a simmer. Add the silk and leave it in the solution for 30 minutes, stirring gently once in a while. Remove from heat and let cool before draining and removing the silk. Fill the pot with 1 gallon (3.7L) warm water and ¼ cup (60mL) white vinegar and submerge the silk. This will re-acidify the silk. This also works with finished garments, although you may want to test a small amount of the yarn first.

Cellulose Fibers

Leaving behind the land of fibers grown by animals, we enter the realm of fibers grown by *plants*. Cellulose fibers are derived from the cellulose that naturally occurs in plants. Cotton has the highest percentage of pure cellulose, and the other main cellulose fibers for yarn include linen and hemp. The latter two fibers are often called *bast* because they are derived from cellulose in the stalks of plants.

Whereas protein fibers hold heat close to the body, cellulose fibers tend to do the opposite, pulling heat *away* from the body. This makes them ideally suited for warm-climate garb, not so great for your next trek up Mount Everest.

Behaviorally speaking, cellulose fibers have a capacity to stretch with wear—they just aren't very good at bouncing back to their original shape. Washing and reblocking will revive your garment, but the more times the fiber stretches with wear, the more diminished its ability to bounce back becomes.

Adding to the challenge is the fact that cellulose fibers can be dense and heavy. The bulkier your yarn and the more elaborate your stitchwork, the heavier the garment will be. And the heavier the garment, the more it will stretch with wear. It's a vicious circle from which there is no easy escape except awareness, smart yarn-to-project pairings, and use of yarns that blend cellulose fibers with other, lighter-weight fibers if you simply must have that bulky cable-filled cotton turtleneck.

While moths are the mortal enemies of protein fibers, cellulose fibers have two enemies whose names also start with the letter m: mold and mildew. Normally, we worry about mold and mildew when it comes to towels and washcloths and other cotton-based items that see lots of routine moisture, but this can also be an issue with cotton garments not allowed to dry completely before being placed in storage or with clean garments stored in unusually humid conditions.

COTTON

A beloved staple in Egypt, Asia, and South America for nearly six thousand years, cotton didn't reach Europe until the late Middle Ages. The Europeans were so accustomed to wool that they naturally assumed cotton also came from a sheep. In 1350, traveler John Mandeville described the cotton plant as, "a wonderful tree which bore tiny lams on the endes of its branches." Even today the German word for cotton, *baumwolle,* literally means "tree wool."

While Mandeville's description paints a pretty picture, it's far from the truth. Cotton fibers begin their life as fine, downy fibers growing around the seed pod, or **boll**, of the cotton plant.

As the boll matures (which can take forty to seventy days, depending on the plant and growing conditions), the fibers grow longer and their outer walls thicken. The outer shell of the boll then cracks and the fiber-covered seeds emerge, like giant puffs of popcorn still attached to the plant.

Remember that these are living plant fibers. When the bolls are picked, the cotton fibers dry up and collapse onto themselves. But because of their thick cellular structure (up to 95 percent pure cellulose), they don't collapse flat—rather, they collapse in a twisted, convoluted shape similar to that of a vanilla bean. This natural twist can range from two hundred to three hundred convolutions per inch (2.5cm), depending on the fineness of the fiber, and it is part of what makes cotton such a comfortable and resilient fiber.

After picking, the bolls are quickly taken to a ginnery where the fibers are separated from the seeds using, you guessed it, a **gin**. As much as two-thirds of the picked weight of cotton is lost when the seeds are removed (but these seeds are then used for everything from oil to livestock feed). After the cotton has been ginned and processed, the fibers are then carded and, if desired, combed before being spun into yarn.

The Fiber

Many different types of cotton have been adapted to thrive in different regions of the world. Egyptian and Sea Island cotton are considered the finest and longest-stapled fibers, and they are always clearly labeled (and priced) accordingly. Another prime fiber is Pima cotton, a supersoft cotton named for the Pima American Indians of Arizona, who worked with USDA scientists breeding Egyptian seed-based cotton on an experimental farm in Arizona in the early 1900s. Many other types of cotton exist, all taking dye beautifully but varying in their staple length and overall softness.

Behaviorally speaking, cotton is extremely strong and durable—not as strong as silk but stronger than wool, and even stronger when wet. It is considered ideal for warm-weather climates because it can absorb more than twenty times its weight in water and release it quickly through evaporation. These evaporative-cooling powers make cotton less useful for climates where you need heat held close to your body. But for climates where you need to stay cool, cotton is perfectly suited.

The feel of cotton yarn varies dramatically, depending on how the fibers were prepared. Most cotton is combed to ensure that the fibers are smoothly aligned and are of uniform length. Combed cotton can produce a smooth, firm surface with few pills.

The tightness of spin will substantially impact how the yarn feels. Generally speaking, the tighter the spin, the firmer the yarn and the longer it will wear. The looser the spin, the softer and more comfortable the knitted fabric—but fabric knitted with looser spun yarn will generallly pill and show signs of wear much more quickly. Combed cottons can also be ringspun, a process whereby they are twisted and heat-set for greater durability without sacrificing softness.

Cotton yarn has a split-personality reputation for both shrinking in the wash and stretching out over time. The truth lies somewhere in the middle. Cotton fiber lacks elasticity or "memory," which is required for a fabric to bounce back after being stretched. So, as you wear it, your garment will relax into whichever way it tends to be pulled. The simple fix is to wash and reblock the garment, which will pull the fibers tight again—in a way some people consider shrinking. But over the long term, the fibers gradually lose their ability to shrink in the wash; you'll have to make do with a more relaxed garment. Depending on the yarn, the type of knitting, and the degree of wear, this deterioration could take years—but it's still something to know.

You also need to consider the fiber's innate inelasticity when choosing patterns for your cotton yarn. Be aware that ribbing alone won't consistently draw your knitted garment tight to the body—a tight-fitting top would hang instead of cling. The only way to combat this inelasticity is to choose a cotton yarn that has been blended with a more stretchy fiber, such as wool or even nylon or Lycra.

The way a yarn has been spun will also impact its elasticity. Smoother-spun cottons tend to have less elasticity than the bouncier cabled or corded cottons, which are made up of several strands of multiple-ply yarn that have been plied together.

But all that twist comes at a price. The natural convolutions in cotton fiber give it some crimp and loft, but not always enough to absorb excess twist. For this reason, if a 100 percent cotton yarn isn't balanced precisely when twisted and plied, this excess twist will cause your knitted fabric to **bias**, or tilt, in whichever direction the excess twist leads. Sometimes this bias won't reveal itself until the fabric has been washed, making it extremely important not just to swatch your cotton yarn but to *wash* your swatch.

If your swatch does bias, all is not lost. Simply choose a pattern that incorporates a mix of knit and purl stitches, such as seed stitch. The combination of stitches will balance out your twist and keep your fabric nice and even.

Textured stitches can be lovely in cotton, but be sure to keep in mind the weight of your fabric, especially if you're working with dense, tightly spun yarns with multiple plies. For colorwork and simple patterns, these yarns perform well with their crisp stitch definition. But for complex stitchery, such as all-over cables and bobbles, the finished fabric may be far heavier than you anticipated. If you really want to do that elaborate Aran project in cotton, try to find a more lightweight cotton blend.

Special Treatments

You may see cotton yarn advertised as **mercerized**. This is a special treatment that renders the cotton fiber stronger, more brilliant and lustrous, and more receptive to dye. It can also make the yarn less susceptible to mildew, which is the most common threat to cotton and other vegetable fibers.

Mercerization involves submerging cotton in a caustic soda solution. This causes the fibers to permanently swell and straighten. When spun together, these straightened fibers produce a stronger yarn with a highly reflective, silklike surface. The straightened fibers tend to be denser, with less air trapped within a strand of mercerized cotton yarn—which translates into a cooler, denser fabric with fewer insulating qualities. Cotton isn't a notoriously warm fiber to begin with, but if you want some warmth, you may want to stick with an unmercerized cotton yarn.

FLAX: LINEN

I can understand how our forebears glanced at a sheep or even a cotton boll and said, "Hey, that'd make great fabric!" But how did people figure out that if they ripped the tall stem of the **flax plant** out of the soil, ran it through a rough comb to remove the seeds, soaked it in water for a few weeks to rot out the straw and pith, set it out to dry, beat it against a board, and ran it through another set of rough metal combs, they'd end up with a strong, fluid, and lustrous fiber for clothing? It boggles the mind.

People have been growing flax and transforming it into linen fabric since ancient Egypt ruled the Nile. The fiber is a bit misleading, especially in yarn. I say this because when you first hold a skein of linen yarn in your hands, it can feel rough and limp, almost like twine, and it may be the last thing you'd want to work with. But work with it for awhile, and it'll still feel a bit harsh and unyielding. Yet the more you work with it, the more you abuse it, the more you wash it and wear it, the softer and more lustrous the linen becomes. It absorbs dye deeply and permanently, resisting fading and keeping a true color through wash after wash.

How It Feels

Linen is an extremely durable fiber—several times stronger than cotton. And, as with other cellulose fibers, linen has its own internal evaporative cooling system. It is highly absorbent and wicks moisture away from the skin. As the moisture evaporates along the fiber shaft, the air around it is comfortably cooled.

Drawbacks

Like other cellulose fibers, linen lacks elasticity. The yarn has no real spring to it, nor will the fabric. So if you're considering linen socks, think again. However, if you want something with beautiful drape and durability, linen is perfect. You could use it for a relaxed summer top or even play around with a smaller knitted dish towel or basket liner like the ones shown below.

Ripple and Lace Leaf Basket Liners (page 168)
both knit in 100 percent linen.

HEMP

While some covet the leaves and flower buds of this herb for their medicinal qualities, for almost ten thousand years people have also coveted the stem of the Cannabis sativa plant for its durable fiber. Industrial hemp has been regulated to the point of prohibition in the United States, although, as of this writing, legislators in California were challenging the federal ban. The cultivation of industrial hemp was legalized in Canada in 1998, and it's also legal in other parts of the world, including the European Union. Industrial hemp is grown from a type of Cannabis sativa that has been bred for maximum fiber, seed, and oil production, and it contains very few of the medicinal powers found in the "other" Cannabis sativa—marijuana—which has been bred specifically for those purposes.

Hemp fiber is processed much like flax, producing a rugged fiber that—like linen—grows softer with washing and wearing. It is less susceptible to mold and mildew than cotton, and benefits from being machine-washed and -dried. It has the same lack of elasticity as linen and should be used accordingly.

In the past few years, we've seen more hemp-based knitting yarns on the market. The Girly Tee on page 156 was designed by Lana Hames, the Canadian knit-wear designer and owner of Hemp for Knitting, and it uses her six-ply hemp yarn.

Hemp on its own can be a bit too strong for some knitters, so manufacturers are also coming out with hemp blends. Lana Hames's Hemp for Knitting has a 50 percent hemp/50 percent lamb's wool blend, where the wool gives elasticity and a more comfortable wear. Another company to provide hemp yarns is DZined, which offers hemp/wool and hemp/wool/mohair blends that have been hand-dyed in 3-pound (1.5kg) increments with multiple colors of dye in the same pot.

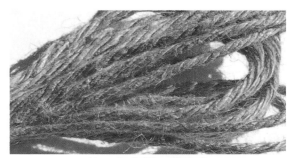

Hemp for Knitting allhemp6

DZined hand-dyed hemp/wool/mohair blend

Cellulosic Fibers

This entire category was born from a longstanding desire to re-create silk without the aid of a silkworm. The Chinese thought about it for thousands of years, but it wasn't until the mid-1800s that serious progress was made in creating so-called **artificial silk**. Its early manufacture *did* mimic the silkworm's method, processing cellulosic plant materials (including mulberry tree bark) into a liquid solution that was then extruded and hardened into fibers. Several different techniques for creating artificial silk evolved simultaneously, and in 1924, in an effort to promote this fiber on its own two feet, it was given the name *rayon*. Development has continued and, even today, efforts are underway to transform the cellulose base of many more plant materials into wearable fibers.

In recent years, increased interest in these kinds of fibers has emerged because they are all derived from renewable resources—trees and plants—and they are all biodegradable. Some of the fibers require more chemical intervention than others, and some may use genetically modified seed stock or materials that rely heavily on fertilizers—but they still are uniformly more environmentally friendly than their petrochemical synthetic counterparts.

As a general group, these fibers tend to have a fluid feel, with a brilliant sheen and a luminous quality (hence the original name, artificial silk). The fibers show good dimensional stability when knit up, although they can shrink with washing. They absorb dyes beautifully and are uniformly highly absorbent, although some weaken significantly when wet.

Just as different tips on a frosting tube produce different designs on a cake, synthetic fibers can have different qualities depending on the shape of the **spinneret** holes through which they're extruded. Slight modifications in the holes can result in a smoother, flatter, rounder, or rougher surface, all of which impact light reflection and wearability.

RAYON

The fiber that launched the manufactured fiber revolution, rayon was originally called all sorts of names, such as *artificial silk*, *fiber silk*, *wood silk*, or even *art silk*, until it was dubbed *rayon* in 1924.

Although there are several ways to produce rayon, most of what you'll find today in knitting yarn was made from wood pulp, using the **viscose process**. (You may come across a skein labeled *viscose rayon*—that's what it means.) The wood pulp is chopped up and soaked in a caustic soda solution, squeezed, shredded, and fermented. It's then treated with carbon bisulphide, which forms a cellulose xanthate compound. This compound is then mixed with a weak solution of caustic soda and aged again before being filtered and finally forced through a spinneret (picture a shower head with microscopic holes) into a coagulating bath of sulfuric acid, where those streams of liquid harden into strands of fiber. Essentially, the materials are broken down into raw cellulose that's regenerated into spinnable fiber.

The fiber feels soft and comfortable against the skin. It's extremely receptive to dye and can have a brilliant, lustrous surface. The fiber can be rendered even more colorfast if the dye pigments are added to the liquid

FLAMING FURS

TAKE CARE

In 2005, several viscose rayon novelty yarns were recalled from the market because of reports that they quickly ignited when held near an open flame. The two biggest recalls were Sirdar Fizz (which has since been rereleased with a different fiber blend) and Bernat Fur Out. While the industry appears to have learned its lesson, do be very cautious of eyelash and textured novelty yarns. Read the label and make sure they don't have a high percentage of viscose rayon.

solution just before being extruded. Manufacturers will sometimes add a material such as titanium dioxide to the solution, which will dull the fiber's luster ever so slightly.

Rayon fibers are smooth and firm, spinning up into a dense yarn with beautiful drape but not as much elasticity as the protein fibers. This means heavy rayon garments may stretch out of shape over time and require more frequent reblocking. Although rayon is highly moisture-absorbent, once wet it loses strength significantly and is less able to recover from stress.

Modal

A subset of rayon, made from the reconstituted cellulose in beech trees, **Modal** has an extremely smooth, soft surface that is comparable to mercerized cotton but almost 50 percent more absorbent. The fiber absorbs dye well and is colorfast in warm water. It doesn't pill, and resists shrinking and fading with wash. Modal is the registered trademark of Lenzing AG, an Austrian company.

Acetate

First developed in the late 1860s, cellulose acetate was originally used as a varnish for military aircraft in World War I and as a nonflammable material for motion-picture film. The first continuous filament for yarn was produced in England in 1912, and then in the United States some twelve years later.

Acetate is made from regenerated cotton or tree pulp cellulose. It differs from viscose rayon in that it is not a *regenerated* cellulose. It begins and ends as cellulose acetate, which is an acid derivative of cellulose.

Acetate creates a breathable, relatively absorbent fabric that is hypoallergenic and resistant to mold and mildew. However, it tends to be weak when wet, and it can be further weakened by strong oxidizing agents, such as bleach.

Acetate requires a different dye process than the one commonly used for cotton and rayon—something you don't need to worry about unless you're doing the dyeing yourself at home.

Lyocell

This is one of the newer fibers in the rayon family, having come to the market in 1992. It is manufactured in the United States under the exclusive trademark name **Tencel**. The FTC considers **lyocell** a subcategory of rayon, but it differs slightly from rayon in that the wood pulp is dissolved into an amine oxide solution and immediately filtered and extruded through a spinneret to form the fibers.

Behaviorally speaking, lyocell has excellent dimensional strength and durability. It can absorb moisture, making it suitable for warm-weather attire, and it has a relaxed weight and drape that are enhanced by its excellent dye absorption and reflective qualities. It has a soft feel that makes it highly suitable for fabrics used in next-to-the-skin wear.

Classic Elite Premiere, a Pima cotton and Tencel blend

SOY

In the 1930s, automobile magnate Henry Ford pushed for the development of a soy-based fiber to help promote the soybean industry. The resulting product, called Azlon, was produced but it never gained widespread commercial adoption, losing out to rayon and nylon. Today the fiber is enjoying a worldwide revival, thanks to the efforts of Shanghai farmer, businessman, and self-taught scientist Li Guanqi. He took the soy pulp that remains after soybeans have been pressed and their oil removed, and developed a process by which the soy proteins are isolated from the pulp, rendered into a liquid state, and wet-spun with polyvinyl alcohol.

Sea Silk from Hand Maiden Fine Yarns, made from 70 percent silk and 30 percent SeaCell

STITCHING WITH SEAWEED

QUICK NOTE

A German company recently added a new spin to lyocell with **SeaCell**, made from 95 percent lyocell fiber and 5 percent seaweed. Manufactured by Zimmer AG under the trademark SeaCell, the yarn has the soft, breathable, comfortable elements of lyocell, infused with trace elements and seaweed extracts. Zimmer AG claims that seaweed's anti-inflammatory properties, as well as trace elements of magnesium, calcium, and vitamin E, will transfer to the skin of the wearer, contributing to an overall sense of well-being. Claims aside, it's a beautiful yarn with the customary shimmer and drape of lyocell.

As of this writing, the only major yarn company to offer SeaCell is Hand Maiden Fine Yarn, which blends it with 70 percent silk for its wildly popular Sea Silk lace-weight yarn.

The fiber itself has the luster of silk and the resilience of wool, with a soft hand, lustrous appearance, and marvelous drape. Keep in mind that this drape may vary depending on how the yarn is spun. Worsted-spun soy yarn will have exceptional drape, but a knitted-tube soy yarn (such as Phoenix from South West Trading Company) sacrifices drape for a thicker body and loft.

Soy fiber feels warm, yet it also wicks moisture away from your skin, making it well-suited to warmer climates. The yarn and fiber are also marketed in the United States as SoySilk, a registered trademark of South West Trading Company.

BAMBOO

A relatively recent addition to the fiber family and primarily coming from China, **bamboo** fiber is derived from the cellulose in the bamboo stalk. The fiber is unique in that it contains an antibacterial and bacteriostasis bioagent that stays in the fiber even after the garment has

Kollage Yarns Cornucopia yarn made from
100 percent corn

Corn fiber has the soft, comfortable feel of nonmercerized cotton. Its light weight and great absorbency make it well-suited to warm-weather garb. Unlike cotton, however, many incarnations of corn fiber will melt under a hot iron. Also, although corn fiber is biodegradable and derived from annually renewable crops, some groups remain concerned because the fiber contains some genetically modified corn.

been washed fifty times, making it unusually good for antibacterial purposes (in hospitals, for example).

The fiber's cell structure is made of microscopic holes that provide for extremely rapid moisture absorption and evaporation, giving it an excellent ability to breathe. You'll find it alone or frequently blended with fibers such as Tencel and cotton. Regia blends it with wool and polyamide in its popular machine-washable sock yarn aptly named Bamboo. I've even seen it blended with cashmere in manufactured garments, but not yet in handknitting yarn.

CORN
Corn fiber, a new biotech development, is based on the large quantities of starch that occur naturally in corn. These starches are broken down into sugars, fermented, and separated into polymers. The resulting pastelike substance is extruded into fine, delicate strands that are processed and spun into yarn. You may eventually see this same technique used on other high-starch agricultural products like wheat, maize, and sugar. Imagine, a pair of socks made out of sugar!

Synthetic Fibers

The advent of rayon proved to chemists that it was, indeed, possible to create wearable fiber from plant cellulose. Their next question: Could they create such a fiber from other materials?

After years of experimenting, members of a DuPont research team developed the first successful synthetic fiber in 1935. They combined carbon, hydrogen, oxygen, and nitrogen—essentially coal, air, and water—to form large, chiplike polymers. When melted, extruded through the tiny holes of a spinneret, air-cooled, and steam-conditioned, these polymers formed a soft, durable, stretchy fiber known today as *nylon*.

Experiments continued, always with the goal of producing easy-care, long-wearing fibers that were invulnerable to moths and mildew and could be inexpensively mass-produced. Over the years, many more synthetic fibers came onto the market, including acrylic, polyester, and spandex (also known under the trademark name **Lycra**) in the 1950s. More recently, production has been refined to create extremely fine synthetic fibers less than 1 **denier** thick and labeled **microfiber**.

We call these fibers *synthetic* because they are the result of chemical synthesis. They can be made to resemble almost any natural fiber—wool, angora, cotton, cashmere, you name it. Behaviorally speaking, these fibers tend to be lustrous, soft, strong, resilient, easy to wash, inexpensive, and resistant to pests and mildew.

But while these materials may look and initially feel somewhat similar to natural fibers, it's important to understand that their underlying structures are dramatically different. To begin with, most synthetic fibers have a uniformly smooth surface like a rod of glass, while animal fibers (with the exception of silk) have scales along their surface.

This can be good for machine-washability because scales are what cause felting. But scales also contribute to the natural hygroscopic qualities of animal fibers, which help the fabric breathe and absorb several times its weight in moisture while feeling warm and dry to the wearer. Synthetic fibers hold far less moisture before they feel wet, which means they don't breathe as well on the wearer. Some pure synthetic garments can feel clammy or uncomfortably warm in hot climates—especially high-moisture items such as socks. This is one reason you'll often find synthetics blended with natural fibers.

This lack of moisture absorption also means that the fiber is much more likely to conduct static electricity. Not only does static electricity cause those annoying zaps and the occasional embarrassing case of static cling, but it also acts as a magnet for microscopic elements of dust and dirt, pulling them deep into the fabric. This means your garment will need to be washed more frequently.

Although you'd think that long-wearing synthetics wouldn't pill, they actually do. Synthetic fibers tend to have a far longer staple length than their natural counterparts. Longer fibers give greater strength and wearability. But without scales to hold the fibers together under friction, they can work their way to the surface of your fabric. There they form pills that are deeply anchored within the other stitches and difficult to remove without damaging the rest of the surface.

Finally, synthetic fibers tend to react to heat and flame differently than natural fibers. While cellulose fibers burn and protein fibers self-extinguish, synthetic fibers react to heat by melting. Some synthetics have especially low melting points, although chemists are working on special chemical treatments to make synthetics more heat-resistant. For this reason, it's important to note the care instructions on your yarn label, especially if it says *Tumble Dry Low* or *No Iron*. If you have the terrible misfortune of being a little too close to an open fire, the melting synthetic fibers may produce serious chemical burns on your skin. They can also emit toxic fumes as they melt.

Recent renewed interest in eco-friendly, biodegradable, nonpetrochemical fibers has lessened the momentum of synthetics just a little, but they still remain a popular choice because of their affordability, widespread availability, and ease of care—especially for baby clothes and charity items where machine-washability is extra important. Synthetics also remain an extremely common ingredient in elaborate novelty yarns, but nearly all these yarns cannot be machine-washed. The research and development of these fibers owe much to the world's largest chemical manufacturers, including DuPont and Monsanto.

NYLON

The word **nylon** is actually a generic term for an entire group of synthetic fiber-forming polyamides. If you see the words *polyamid*, *polyamide*, or *polymid* on a yarn label, it's most likely nylon. Several different materials can be used for the production of nylon, but the most common are petrochemicals.

As already mentioned, nylon was first developed in 1935 by a DuPont research team. The material was first used for toothbrushes and women's stockings (hence, the term *nylons*). During World War II, we needed a synthetic substitute for the Japanese silk originally used in parachutes—and nylon fit the bill. During the 1950s, it was highly touted as the miracle fiber that would free women from the drudgery of washing and ironing.

Today, nylon fiber is still a common component of knitting yarns. Its qualities cannot be overlooked: It is just as strong when wet as it is dry; it is mold- and fungus-resistant; and it's very strong, stretchy, and able to withstand great tension before breaking.

The biggest drawback of nylon is its low moisture uptake. The fiber doesn't easily allow for absorption and evaporation of moisture, resulting in a warm fabric that can become clammy with perspiration. However, the minute you introduce more hygroscopic natural fibers into the mix, the fabric's ability to breathe improves dramatically.

Nylon is often used in small doses to add strength and durability to a natural fiber. The best example is sock yarn, which often features 75 percent wool and 25 percent nylon. You benefit from the hygroscopic qualities of the wool and the durability of the nylon. The more nylon in the mix, however, the stronger its presence—I tend to keep it down to 40 percent or less when possible.

Swirly O Socks (center, pattern on page 140) knit in a wool-blend sock yarn that includes 15 percent nylon.

You'll also find different varieties of nylon fiber used in novelty yarns, such as ribbon and eyelash, where strength, elasticity, and silky shimmer are desired. Nylon is also the common core binder thread for wool yarns such as brushed mohairs.

Nylon has a great wash-and-wear reputation, and most smooth-spun, standard, nylon-based yarns will do fine in the washing machine (but always check your label to be sure). However, the more elaborate novelty nylon yarns almost always require handwashing.

Regardless of what kind of yarn it's in, nylon does *not* like extreme heat. If you put a hot iron on the fabric, it will first start to stick and eventually melt your beloved masterpiece into a sticky chemical mess. So keep your nylon far away from hot dryers and hot irons, just to be safe. Nylon can also weaken with prolonged exposure to sunlight, although—unless you want to knit a pair of nylon curtains or a dashboard cozy for your car—this shouldn't pose too much hardship.

Nashua Cilantro, a blend of 70 percent cotton and 30 percent polyester, was used to make the Cabled Headband (page 186).

POLYESTER

Nearly indistinguishable from nylon, **polyester** was first developed in 1953 and is known in the UK as Terylene. The fiber is made from polymers of polypropylene and polyethylene. It's lightweight and strong, with good dimensional stability, which means your garment will retain its shape after countless wearings. It has the same strength wet as dry, which makes it safe in the washing machine. It also tends to be softer and warmer than nylon.

Polyester suffers from the same pilling problems as other synthetic fibers, however. It is less absorbent than nylon, which means you also have the static and the dust-magnet potential. It also weakens after prolonged exposure to sunlight, although not as much as nylon. And polyester is also susceptible to heat damage, softening at 455 degrees Fahrenheit (235 degrees Celsius) and melting at 500 degrees Fahrenheit (260 degrees Celsius)—although chemists are making progress on chemical additives that raise the melting point. Bottom line: Always check the yarn label and do what it says, especially where heat is concerned.

ACRYLIC

In commercial production since 1950, **acrylic** fiber was born from the wartime development of synthetic rubbers. Technically, acrylic fibers are anything that has a chemical base of 85–90 percent vinyl cyanide or acrylonitrile. It's the remaining 15–10 percent (often called the *minor constituent*) that determines the special characteristics of the fiber and justifies the separate brand name—of which there are many. In 1962 alone, there were already at least thirty on the market, including Orlon and Courtelle.

Acrylic has excellent elasticity (second only to nylon) and, although not as strong as nylon and polyester, it wears better than pure wool. The lightweight, abrasion-resistant fiber also wicks away moisture and is quick-drying. As with other synthetic fibers, acrylic is not prone to moth and mildew damage but it is sensitive to heat and should be treated accordingly. I find acrylic best used in small percentages as a lightweight strengthener for shorter-staple natural fibers such as cotton.

You may also come across fibers labeled *Modacrylic*. From a handknitting standpoint, these fibers are nearly identical to acrylic. The only difference is that they contain 35–85 percent acrylonitrile.

Making Yarn }

WHEN WE THINK OF A YARN COMPANY, WE OFTEN CONJURE UP IMAGES OF A VINE-COVERED STONE BUILDING WHERE HAPPY PEOPLE TEND TO A FEW WELL-MAINTAINED PIECES OF MACHINERY, DIP YARNS INTO STEAMING VATS OF RICHLY COLORED DYE, TENDERLY PUT FINISHED SKEINS IN A BOX, AND SEND THEM OFF WITH A KISS. PERHAPS A FEW DOZEN SHEEP GRAZE PLACIDLY ON A GRASSY HILLSIDE NEARBY.

MILLS AND MICROSPINNERIES

Smaller spinneries—the yarn equivalent of microbreweries—make yarn production accessible to smaller farms, fiber cooperatives, and enterprising individuals who may not otherwise be able to meet the minimum run requirements for larger international mills. This, in turn, gives us a vastly superior range of yarns from which to choose.

page **49**

FARM YARNS AND FIBER FESTIVALS

By supporting local sheep farms and festivals, you're helping sustain an important business and a rapidly disappearing agricultural way of life. You're also helping ensure a richer, higher-quality variety of yarns for all knitters.

page **51**

COLOR IN YARN

page **55**

Natural color, stockdyeing, hand dyeing—part of what makes yarn so endlessly fascinating is the way it responds to the addition of color.

THE ORIGINAL SPIN

page **60**

Before they can be spun into yarn, all fibers need to be prepared for spinning. This is done by running the fibers through a large carding machine. Then, yarn companies can choose to go down one of two paths that will ultimately determine how your project knits up, looks, feels, and lasts.

The truth is that most of today's large yarn companies are located in office parks in which the only piece of machinery you'll find is a forklift by the loading dock. Their role is to pick the best providers for each step of production, negotiate the best price, find designers to create enticing patterns for this yarn, keep their yarn-store customers happy, and stay on top of the cycle until the yarn reaches the customer. The fiber may come from one place, the processing and spinning may happen in two other places, and the dyeing and skeining at yet another place before it makes its way to the warehouse to be labeled, packed up in smaller boxes, and shipped off to the yarn store.

Mill Ends and Copycats

 The irony for consumers is that some competing yarns may come from the very same mill—in some cases using materials from the same source, especially in the alpaca industry. Even more competing yarns were spun on identical machines. Some mills and yarn companies will package up any leftovers from a large production run and offer it to someone else, or sell it themselves, as mill ends. (If you're buying yarn and see a cone of yarn marked *mill end,* don't be afraid—you may be getting quite a nice yarn for a bargain.)

With hand-dyed yarns, you should also know that many of the smaller hand-dyed yarn companies—down to the *really* small, single-person eBay and Etsy operations—get their undyed yarns from the same handful of suppliers (including Henry's Attic and Louet Sales). Because the yarns can be so similar, the major differentiators become the dyer's eye for color, the specific kind of dye used, and the way in which the color is transferred *onto* the yarn. Check to see if the fiber has been rendered too harsh by the dyes, if the yarn is still fluid and lustrous, and if the colors transfer well into knitted form. Sometimes the most spectacular-looking hanks of hand-dyed yarn knit up into a muddled mess of pooling colors and awkward stripes you didn't want.

The issue of copycat yarns occurs most often with novelty yarns. These more elaborate concoctions require digitally controlled core machines to produce—of which only a few machine brands exist. Some mills will even sublease to another mill the specific modular component used to create a yarn when they're done with it.

If yarn companies frequently sell nearly identical yarns, what makes one more distinctive than the next? A few things. First, while yarn companies often get inspiration from one another, not all of them *intentionally* create identical copies of other yarns. Just like people, some yarn companies strive to innovate, while others may be more comfortable improving on the innovations of others—or offering those innovations at a lower price.

Among the duplicators you can still find some significant differences. First, they may use fibers of a slightly higher or lower grade or of a different composition than their competitors—allowing them to sell the yarn for less, or give it a more exclusive branding and a higher price. They may also change the fiber blending in the yarn ever so slightly—more nylon, less silk, a hint of microfiber, you name it. They may use a different dye process and offer different colorways. They may also change the way the yarn is delivered to the customer—in a hank instead of a ball, for example. And they may modify the yardage slightly to make a side-by-side price comparison a little harder for the customer.

And then the yarn company itself could be the differentiator. Some offer notoriously fantastic customer service, some offer notoriously mediocre service, and the vast majority sit somewhere in between. They may offer extensive pattern support, limited pattern support, or none at all, relying instead on their competitors to invest in patterns and then producing comparable substitute yarns, sold for less. It's a jungle out there, but, fortunately, your LYS or favorite online store can be your buffer.

EVALUATING YARNS UP CLOSE

It's rare for any company to have an "exclusive" on any specific kind of yarn. Even if the mill gives one company an exclusive on a certain yarn construction, as I've mentioned already, another mill will easily be able to copy it. This leaves us, the consumers, to decipher the differences for ourselves. If you're trying to decide between two seemingly identical yarns—or you simply want to study one yarn at close range—here are some of my favorite techniques:

- Look at the skeins in the sunlight. Are they equally lustrous? Does one have more shimmer, while the other is more matte? If the fiber shimmers, is it a natural or a brassy shimmer? If matte, is it rich and opalescent or dull and lifeless?

- Study the surface of the skeins. Does one have a slight halo of loose fibers, while the other is still crisp and firm? Try pulling any loose fibers from each skein. Do they come off equally easily or are they more firmly planted in one? What do they look like? Are they equally smooth, or crimpy, or long, or short?

- Pull out a short length of yarn from each skein. Roll it around in your fingers. Does one feel thinner than the other? Firmer? Rougher? Does it stay spun or does it easily come unspun?

- If it's a multiple-ply yarn, untwist the strand and let go. Does one seem to have more bounce than the other? Do they both stay open and unraveled?

- Tug each strand. Do they have equal elasticity or does one stretch more than another? And do they bounce back at the same rate? How hard can you tug each before it breaks? Does one break more quickly than the other?

- If you possibly can, buy a skein of each and knit a sample swatch. Even a 6- by 6-inch (15 by 15cm) stockinette swatch will give you a good idea of how the yarn will behave. I once studied two seemingly identical Merino superwash multiple-ply yarns, finding no difference between them whatsoever until I started swatching. While one of the yarns purred smoothly, the other immediately (and repeatedly) snagged on my needles. The cost of that one skein was well worth it—I was spared the angst of buying twenty skeins and suffering through an entire snag-ridden sweater.

- Wash your swatches! More mysteries can unfold here. Put each swatch in a separate mixing bowl, hopefully either clear glass or white so you can see any bleeding or residue from the wash. How do the swatches behave in the wash? Do they both block to the same measurements, or did one stretch or shrink? Once dry, do they have the same surface texture, or did one bloom more than the other? Some superwash wools can stretch dramatically in the wash, while others manage to keep decent shape. Again, the cost of a single skein will save you far greater angst later on.

MILLS AND MICROSPINNERIES

I said most of today's large yarn companies are located in office parks, and the key word here is *large*. You can still find smaller spinneries—consider them the yarn equivalent of microbreweries—dotted across the continent. These mills are important because they make yarn production accessible to smaller farms, fiber cooperatives, and enterprising individuals who may not otherwise be able to meet the minimum run requirements for larger international mills. This greater accessibility, in turn, gives us a vastly superior range of yarns from which to choose for our next projects.

Some **microspinneries** specialize in processing specific kinds of fiber. One example is Belfast Mini Mills of Prince Edward Island, Canada, which offers small-scale processing equipment (nicknamed *mini mills*) to help smaller cottage industries make their own yarns. This equipment is specially tuned to process the finer, more delicate fibers, such as cashmere, qiviut, and angora. You can also get fibers spun there, and you can buy their mill ends if you visit the mill. However, the company otherwise focuses on helping other people make gorgeous yarns.

Meanwhile, other microspinneries may prefer to scour the globe for all sorts of materials and then make the *blending* their calling card—here I'm specifically thinking of the Fibre Company in Biddeford, Maine. The company was founded in 2003 and quickly moved away from custom fiber processing services to focus on producing its own line of artisanal natural-fiber-blend yarns. For example, the three-ply Road to China blends baby alpaca with camel, cashmere, soy, and yak.

In the Midwest, we have Blackberry Ridge Woolen Mill, Ohio Valley Natural Fibers, and Zeilinger Wool Co., three well-established mills that focus on custom processing for small to midsized sheep farms as well as for individual spinners and knitters. And in the western United States, we have the Taos Valley Wool Mill in New Mexico, which specializes in eco-friendly semiworsted spinning of longwools and exotic fibers. Many of the millspun yarns that Luisa Gelenter offers at La Lana Wools in Taos, New Mexico (including the Phat Silk yarn used in the Honeycomb Hat shown below; pattern on page 76), were spun here.

Honeycomb Hat (page 76) knit in La Lana Wools millspun Phat Silk yarn

Community Spinneries

My favorite kind of microspinnery is the **community spinnery**, often founded by hopeful idealists more concerned about contributing to the community than to

their own coffers. These mills provide a critical market for local farmers whose animals might otherwise be valued only for their meat. Community spinneries will either buy fleeces outright from local farmers and use them for their in-house lines of yarns or they'll custom-process the fleeces and ship them back to the farms. They often work on a barter system, whereby the farmer retains only a portion of the finished materials and the mill keeps the rest as payment for processing.

Perhaps the best-known community spinnery is Green Mountain Spinnery, located in Putney, Vermont, and in operation for more than twenty-five years. In addition to providing custom services for other folks who want to sell their own yarn, the spinnery purchases fibers directly from farmers across New England and transforms them into several marvelous Green Mountain Spinnery–branded yarns. The dyed yarns are among my very favorites, with rich, heathery colors that really do evoke the flowers, berries, soul, and seasons of New England. The spinnery also offers eco-friendly undyed yarns, processed using the Greenspun method in which the fibers have been minimally processed using only biodegradable materials and no chemicals.

Another eco-friendly New England upstart is Hope Spinnery, a wind-powered fiber-processing mill in midcoast Maine. This small mill uses all-natural fiber processing techniques that even extend to its dye operations—all yarns are hand dyed using natural dyestuffs, such as cochineal and madder.

Also in New England, we have Bartlett Yarns, located in Harmony, Maine, and widely distributed in yarn stores around the country. These beautifully dyed yarns have a rich scent of lanolin and are woolen-spun into the warm, hard-wearing, rugged New England wools of yesteryear. As with the other spinneries mentioned here, Bartlett buys fleece from local farmers. But instead of keeping each farm's fibers separate, Bartlett blends them all together and will send some of the *finished* yarns back to individual farms as a portion of their payment. These farms then sell the yarns at festivals and markets, but you're really buying fibers from sheep all across the region, not just from that farm.

Finally, no discussion about New England mills would be complete without mentioning Harrisville Designs of Harrisville, New Hampshire. The proud mill town had been spinning woolen yarn since 1794, but in 1970 Harrisville's last mill closed. Just one year later, Harrisville Designs was founded with the goal of renewing the town economy and preserving its rich textile heritage. You'll find Harrisville Yarns widely distributed across the country and easily available online. Whereas many of the other mills mentioned here source their materials locally, Harrisville obtains its wools from New Zealand and Australia. They are all **dyed in the wool** to achieve a fantastic array of delicate, heathered hues—the New England Shetland line alone has fifty-six different colors.

Many more microspinneries have cropped up in the last five years, a marvelous reaction to the inevitable sense of sameness that globalization has brought us. I enjoy these yarns immensely. They have a tender honesty and sense of soul that you don't always feel in products that are produced on an industrial scale. In Section 3: Ply Me a River (page 66), where patterns are listed, I've tried to include as many options as possible for farm yarns produced by these smaller spinneries. Even if (heaven forbid) one or two of them are no longer in business by the time you read this book, I do hope that more will have sprouted up in their place.

FARM YARNS

You may be visiting a sheep farm or a farmers' market when you spot a basket of yarn for sale. I'm always on high alert for anything indicating small-scale, locally produced yarn. Not only is it a chance to get something totally unique in an age of increasing conformity, but it's a small way to validate and support what these farmers are trying to do. Plus, it's a rare gift to meet the person who tended the sheep whose fleece you'll be working with and wearing for years to come—it takes the connection between artist and material to entirely new heights.

Every knitter should support local sheep farms. Without a market for their yarns, these farmers would have to pile up their fleeces and burn them (as many already do in Ireland and the United Kingdom), and the animals would be sold for breeding stock, or, even worse, soup stock. Carefully maintained bloodlines of sheep bred for fleece quality, luster, staple length, and crimp would be lost forever. But by supporting a sheep farm—by making even one purchase a year—you're helping sustain an important business and a rapidly disappearing agricultural way of life. You're also helping ensure a richer, higher-quality variety of yarns for all knitters.

What do you get when you buy yarn from a farm? Symbolically, you get a bit of the farm. Materially, it depends. In almost all cases, the farm sends the fleeces to a mill to be processed and spun. Some will even have the spinnery do the dyeing, while others will dye the yarn themselves. Be sure to ask, because sometimes there's a good story behind it: What kind of dyes did they use? How did they dye it? Where did they get their color inspirations?

Depending on where the farm sent the fibers for processing, you'll either be knitting with the wool from the farm's own sheep or from the collected "wool pool" of many sheep farms in the area, with the farmer receiving a portion of finished wool as payment for the raw fleeces sent in. The answer shouldn't necessarily determine whether you buy the yarn or not, but it helps to ask, "Is this from your animals?"

Not all farm yarns are appropriate for the same projects. Sometimes you'll get yarn from a small-scale farm in which yarn is only a small element of what they do—and the fibers may not be as soft or delicate as your ideal. Consider them "whole-grain" versions of the highly refined white-bread yarns you'll find in yarn stores. But for colorful winter hats and outerwear, they'll work well.

But then you have the farms that are more serious about their fiber. My favorite such example is Margaret Klein Wilson, owner of Mostly Merino. She carefully sorts all the fleeces from her small Vermont flock, and then blends them with fleeces she has hand-selected from other farms for a perfect pairing of crimp, length, softness, and natural color. She sends them to the Green Mountain Spinnery for minimal processing, but otherwise all the work of sorting, mixing, dyeing, washing, and skeining is done by her and an occasional assistant.

What Does *Minimal* Processing Mean?

When processors say their wool has been *minimally processed*, they generally mean that they've used very little or no chemicals at all during processing. Instead of scouring the fleece with strong chemical detergents, they'll use a readily biodegradable soap. Instead of carbonizing any flecks of vegetable matter in an acid bath, they'll let them stay in the fiber (you can easily remove them while knitting). Instead of bleaching the fibers a bright white, they'll leave the fibers in their natural colors. And instead of spraying the fibers with synthetic oils to tame the static prior to spinning, they'll use a more eco-friendly vegetable- or animal-based oil.

All these steps add up to a pure, raw, just-off-the-sheep's-back material that is ideal for anyone with chemical sensitivities. There tends to be a greater amount of residual lanolin, making the fibers fragrant, fluid, and water-repellant—but perhaps not so ideal for people with lanolin sensitivities.

Beaverslide Dry Goods mulespun wool yarn

One of my favorite larger-scale farm yarns comes from Beaverslide Dry Goods, a family ranch that occupies three thousand acres along Montana's Rocky Mountain Front. They send the supersoft fleeces from their Merino flock to a mill in Alberta, Canada, for minimal processing, dyeing, and spinning on an old-fashioned

spinning mule. This device closely replicates the movements of the handspinner, producing a loftier, "fuzzier" woolen yarn. Not only are Beaverslide yarns inexpensive, they're easy to knit and bloom beautifully in the wash.

Another farm that has its fibers minimally processed, then **mulespun**, is Marr Haven Farm, which raises Merino-Rambouillet sheep in Allegan, Michigan. Theirs is truly an astonishing farm yarn. On the skein, it looks and smells like it came straight from a farm—complete with small flecks of vegetable matter. But after you knit it up (which is easy to do) and wash your garment in warm water, you'll witness a stunning transformation. The yellow cast in the undyed yarn suddenly brightens to a whipped-cream hue, complemented by a frothy surface of fully bloomed fibers (as shown on page 61).

Most of these farms raise specific breeds of sheep, which gives you a rare chance to knit with a pure single-breed wool instead of the jumble that goes into the commercial wool pool. Not all are Merinos, however. Elsa Sheep and Wool Company specializes only in fiber from the Cormo sheep. It's nearly as soft as Merino (I actually think it's softer), but it tends to get overlooked in favor of its older, more aristocratic Merino uncle. The difference is that Cormo retains more of a "moist" feeling after processing, even when the majority of its lanolin has been removed. The yarn is fabulous to work with and wears like a dream. (You can see Elsa's Cormo in action in Amy King's Guernsey Socks on page 106.)

Farm yarns can also change the way you think about a specific fiber. A perfect example is Icelandic wool, which you usually find in the rugged, lopi-style yarns used for traditional Icelandic sweaters. What the large-scale commercial yarn companies miss, however, is the delicacy of the finer, younger Icelandic fleeces. For that you'll need to go to a farm such as Tongue River Farm, which specializes in breeding Icelandic sheep. The Missouri-based farm sorts the fleeces and has them spun at the Taos Valley Wool Mill, and the premium fibers are used for a gorgeous sock-weight yarn as well as a laceweight yarn that's so popular, they even send it to customers in Iceland. Yes, you heard me right. (You can see a pair of Amy King's Guernsey Socks on page 106 in the Tongue River Farm sock yarn, too.)

Even widely mainstream fibers can be different when from the farm. For example, a skein of 100 percent Merino will be vastly different from what you can get from farms such as Morehouse Merino, the famous Milan, New York, farm. First profiled in Melanie Falick's *Knitting in America* before being given their own voice in the book *Morehouse Merino Knits*, this farm is a model lesson not only in producing exquisite materials but in marketing them well. If you come upon a Morehouse Merino booth at New York's Greenmarket or any of the major East Coast fiber festivals,

you'll see colorful shelves filled with simple, portable kits, complete with pattern and plastic tote bag. The yarn itself is fabulous—soft, doughy, begging to be worn directly against the skin.

FIBER FESTIVALS

For every farm mentioned here there are literally dozens more awaiting your discovery. But sometimes your travels don't take you near sheep farms or farmer's markets. You can still touch, see, and

---

Major Fiber Festival **SCHEDULE**

APRIL	MAY	JUNE	JULY
Connecticut Sheep and Wool Festival, Vernon, CT (www.ctsheep.org)	**Maryland Sheep and Wool Festival**, West Friendship, MD (www.sheepandwool.org) **New Hampshire Sheep and Wool Festival**, Contoocook, NH (www.yankeeshepherd.org) **Massachusetts Sheep and Woolcraft Fair**, Cummington, MA (www.masheepwool.org)	**Maine Fiber Frolic**, Windsor, ME (www.fiberfrolic.com) **Estes Park Wool Market**, Estes Park, CO (www.estesnet.com/events/woolmarket.htm) **Black Sheep Gathering**, Eugene, OR (www.blacksheepgathering.org)	**Lambtown Festival**, Dixon, CA (www.lambtown.com)

AUGUST	SEPTEMBER	OCTOBER
Michigan Fiber Festival, Allegan, MI (www.michiganfiberfestival.info)	**Wisconsin Sheep and Wool Festival**, Jefferson County, WI (www.wisconsinsheepandwoolfestival.com) **Vermont Sheep and Wool Festival**, Essex Junction, VT (www.vermontsheep.org) **Finger Lakes Fiber Arts Festival**, Hemlock, NY (www.gvhg.org/fest.html) **Oregon Flock and Fiber Festival**, Canby, OR (www.flockandfiberfestival.com)	**Wool Festival at Taos**, Taos, NM (www.taoswoolfestival.org) **Fall Fiber Festival of Virginia**, Montpelier Estate, VA (www.fallfiberfestival.org) **New York Sheep and Wool Festival**, Rhinebeck, NY (www.sheepandwool.com) **South Eastern Animal Fiber Fair**, Asheville, NC (www.saffsite.org)

smell dozens—even hundreds—of different farm yarns at once by attending a fiber festival.

The number of festivals across the country grows each year—as does the number of exhibitors and workshops you can take. These are joyous weekends. You're surrounded by like-spirited folks who are as crazy about yarn as you are. Depending on the festival, you may have hundreds of vendors rolling out their red carpet just for you—and you may be able to meet all sorts of sheep to see the different fibers up close and on the animal. It's like Woodstock for knitters.

The fiber festival season in the United States tends to run from late April to October. A select list of some of the most well-known and well-established festivals in this country appears on page 53. For more variety and depth, you can peruse the *Knitter's Review* updated calendar of worldwide fiber festivals and knitting-related events online at knittersreview.com/upcoming_events.asp.

GOING ORGANIC

The same interest that has caused organic produce to show up on the shelves of our grocery stores has extended into the yarn store as well. Cotton, a notoriously high consumer of pesticides and insecticides, is a major growth area for organics right now. We used the Organic Cotton from Blue Sky Alpacas for Jennifer Hagan's Baby Soft Cardigan on page 90.

This yarn uses organically raised and harvested fibers in naturally occurring colors (shades of brown, tan, and sage). But the company also offers a dyed version

Blue Sky Alpacas Organic Cotton

(thereby losing the organic stamp) for those who crave the brighter colors only dyes can produce.

USDA organic certification among sheep farms is a more recent and controversial development. Although many farms offer yarn that's essentially organic—minimally processed fibers shorn from sheep raised in an organic manner—not all of them can afford the steep fees and extensive paperwork required to conform to the USDA's rigorous organic standards program for nonedible fibers.

One company that *is* spearheading the organic wool movement is the Vermont Organic Fiber Co., which we used in Tara Jon Manning's Patchwork Carriage Blanket on page 152. Because of insufficient domestic organic wool production in the United States, the company still sources much of its wool internationally.

On a more local scale, the New Mexico–based cooperative Tierra Wools began offering yarn from certified organic New Mexico Rambouillet sheep in 1999. Not only are the animals raised organically and the fibers *processed* organically, but great time and care are taken to hand dye the yarns in small vats using all-natural **dyestuffs** and **mordants**. This is a painstakingly slow process—especially when dyeing indigo, a challenging color to obtain without chemicals—but it shows their commitment to keeping the cycle 100 percent pure. The yarn is then labeled according to the dyestuff and mordant used. Located in Los Ojos, a tiny town 83 miles (134km) northwest of Taos, the Tierra Wools facility is open for visitors year-round. The yarns often end up on looms rather than knitting needles, but the view from the outdoor dyepots is worth the entire trip.

I'm not suggesting that nonorganically raised natural fibers are of different quality behaved differently on the needles, or pose greater hazards to the knitter—and I'm sure many people have strong opinions about this one way or the other. But the move toward organic yarns lets us make a statement with our pocketbooks, while enjoying fibers that are free from as much twenty-first-century muddling as possible.

COLOR IN YARN

Part of what makes yarn so endlessly fascinating is the way it responds to the addition of color. While some fibers immediately soak up all the pigment in the pot, others may require a more leisurely courting period before they'll finally let go and absorb the color. The challenge comes when you want to achieve a uniform color in a yarn that blends both eager and reluctant fibers. But that's exactly what master dyers do, and do well.

Natural Colors

Yarn can get its color from several methods. First and most obvious, it can be made using a material that has its own natural color. While sheep generally grow different colors of fleece, breeding efforts have often focused on animals that produce a bright white fleece. Shetland sheep are a glorious exception to the rule, with one of the widest color ranges of any sheep breed on the planet. You'll find eleven different color variations and some thirty markings with romantic names like moorit, emsket, shaela, and mioget.

While Shetland wool producers used to offer as many as thirty colors of undyed yarn alone, that number has been reduced dramatically in recent years. You can still find undyed Shetland wool at fiber festivals and small-scale Shetland breeders. Yarns International also offers five different colors of undyed Shetland wool under the Shetland 2000 label. Another undyed wool comes from Cascade Yarns and is called Ecological Wool. It is made of 100 percent undyed Peruvian wool and currently ships in fifteen shades. Alpaca and naturally pigmented cottons (including the Pakucho Organic Cotton shown in the photo below) are two other wonderful sources of natural, dye-free color in yarn.

Pakucho Organic Cotton in natural colors

Yarn-Dyed Color

Naturally occurring colors are lovely, but sometimes you want more than varying shades of brown—and that's when you need dye. The most common large-scale commercial dye method is the **immersion method**, in which entire hanks of spun yarn are immersed in large vats of dye. There are many, many variations on how this is done. Yarns can be suspended over the vats on poles that are regularly rotated, or suspended from large covered frames that are then lowered into the dye, or even rolled up on bobbins and placed in large, sealed, metal contraptions that look like enormous pressure cookers. But the important point is that a finished yarn has been uniformly exposed to a single dye.

The smaller the vat, the less yarn you can dye at once and the greater the amount of manual intervention required—all of which can translate into higher-priced yarn. Manufacturers will normally indicate this on the label with terms like *vat dyed* or *kettle dyed*. (We'll overlook the fact that we're given no idea precisely how big that vat was, or how many skeins they managed to fit into it!)

Done on an industrial scale, however, immersion dyeing produces one steady color all the way through. A yarn that blends several different fibers may require several different stages of immersion before all the fibers are equally saturated with dye.

You'll want the intense clarity of immersion-dyed yarns when working on crisp colorwork patterns such as Adrian Bizilia's Norwegian Snail Mittens on page 148. But for greater subtlety in colorwork, where you want to slowly migrate from one hue to the next, you'll need to use many more colors of yarn because each is so distinct from the next.

You can still get some delightfully subtle variations in color from immersion dye done on a far smaller scale, however, such as hanging yarn from a broomstick over a bubbling, wood-fired kettle of dye. Jennifer Hagan's Cabled Tea Cozy, shown on page 56 (pattern on page 72), was knit using one such kettle-dyed wool from Uruguay, called Malabrigo merino.

The kettle-dyed wool in the Cabled Tea Cozy (page 72) shows subtle variations in dye saturation

Dyed in the Wool

Sometimes you may want even more subtlety to your colors, and here's where another technique comes into play. Instead of dyeing the finished product, the raw materials are dyed before they are ever blended and spun into yarn. (If you see a yarn listed as *dyed in the wool*, *fleece dyed*, or *stock dyed*, that's what it means.)

This technique lends itself to far greater color-depth intricacy. Instead of using a yarn dyed solid green, for example, you can use a yarn that's actually made up of yellow and blue fibers. From far away, they create a soft but steady green. But as you get closer, you'll start to see more complexity—rather like when you study a Seurat painting up close.

Some of the most gorgeous dyed-in-the-wool colorways can be found in Alice Starmore Hebridean 2 Ply yarn (as used in Adrian Bizilia's Double-Thick Mittens on page 120). Best known for her exquisite Fair Isle colorwork designs, Alice launched her new yarn company in 2000. Other beautiful fleece-dyed colorways can be found in yarns from Peace Fleece, Green Mountain Spinnery, and Harrisville Designs.

While subtle heathered blends are perhaps the most common way to present dyed-in-the-wool yarns, they

can also be presented in a bolder, more dramatic manner. The Japanese yarn company Noro is notorious for this. Instead of thoroughly blending different colors together to form a continuous mass of one general hue, Noro founder Eisaku Noro tends to blend his fibers in slow-moving successions from hue to hue and even fiber to fiber. When spun into yarn, the colors transition from one to the next in a truly fluid and organic flow.

Delicate heathered hues in Alice Starmore Hebridean 2 Ply Yarn

You can see the contrast between yarn-dyed and fleece-dyed colors up close. The solid is Valley Yarns Amherst; the fleece-dyed is Alice Starmore Hebridean 2 Ply.

Another example of this type of blending can be found in the Forever Random blends from La Lana Wools in Taos, New Mexico.

These must be seen up close in person to be fully appreciated for their vivid essence of life. The fibers are all

Truly random, naturally dyed color blends in La Lana Wools Forever Random yarn

dyed using 100 percent natural dyestuffs, the color repeats are kept closer together, and the yarn is hand-spun to create truly one-of-a-kind blendings. Because they're naturally dyed and handspun, they cost far more than your commercially dunked counterpart—but the sense of rarity is exceptional.

You can see yarns from both Noro and La Lana in the same Maine Morning Mitts on page 70. The contrast between these yarns is fascinating, yet they both have one thing in common—no two mitts are alike.

What Makes a Hand-Dyed Yarn?

We have strict labeling standards to dictate how a yarn's fiber content is listed, but we have nothing to guide how a yarn's *dye process* should be listed. As a result, we have yarns listed as **hand dyed** and **hand painted** and **kettle dyed** and **vat dyed** with very little indication of what these terms really mean—except that the yarns usually cost more.

True hand-dyed yarns convey a sense of personal color artistry that goes beyond simply dunking skeins in a big vat and letting them simmer. For this same reason, the most exceptional **hand-dyed** yarns on the market tend to be driven by a single person: Maie Landra at

Koigu, Gina Wilde at Alchemy Yarns, Beth Casey at Lorna's Laces, Darlene Hayes at Hand Jive Knits, and Iris Schreier at Artyarns. It extends to those who do the dyeing before the fibers are blended, such as Eisaku Noro of Noro and Luisa Gelenter of La Lana Wools. We even have some duos out there, including Leslie Taylor and Diana McKay at Mountain Colors and Missy Burns and Anita Tosten of Wool in the Woods.

Obviously, these people rely on the help of a few trusted individuals to produce yarns on the scale that they do, but I still consider their yarns to be hand dyed. It only becomes questionable when you enter factorylike settings where a dozen or more people carry out someone else's written instructions—and only because this removes the personal, intimate, expressive soul that makes hand-dyed yarn so special.

Another term you'll see used is **handpainted yarn**. This indicates a yarn onto which dye has been manually applied in a painterly fashion, not just dunked into different dye pots to achieve a rainbow of color. Whether the dye was applied with the use of a brush, a sponge, a squeeze bottle, a spray bottle, a fountain pen—as long as it was a handheld device controlled by the dyer and used to carefully place small amounts of color onto fiber, I'd consider it handpainted.

A truly good hand-dyed yarn not only looks beautiful on the skein, but it actually knits up into an equally beautiful, cohesive work of color. Only a few people have mastered the art of applying more than three or four vastly different colors onto a single skein without having it knit into a muddy mess of color overload—the master of them all being Maie Landra with her Koigu Painter's Palette Premium Merino. (You can see this yarn in action in Elanor Lynn's Endpapers Shawl on page 114.) Other hand dyers practice more restraint, using just two or three different colors on the skein. Even then, the colors can vary from intense contrasts to smooth transitions within the same color family.

And then there are the colors themselves to consider. Are they flat reds and blues, straight out of the bottle, or did the dyer slowly build up those hues from other

ALICE STARMORE

A STORY

I asked Alice how she and her daughter Jade came to create the yarn they did.

"Our central decision was that the wool should be dyed in the fleece as opposed to being dyed in the skein after spinning," she told me. "I had worked for years with flat shades dyed in the skein. You need access to a massive palette to achieve a satisfactory effect, and in the end that is all it is—satisfactory. The gold at the end of the rainbow remains elusive. We wanted that gold. We wanted precision blends of fleece-dyed wool that would be spun into yarns of subtlety and depth. This would allow us scope to create beautiful effects in our textiles, where the colors would play off one another and give us the alchemy we sought."

colors? Alchemy Yarns's Gina Wilde tends to take a more circuitous route to her colors. "I love color that has to be thought about," she told me. "Don't just say 'red,' and mix something that comes straight out of the pigment jar. Say 'red' by mixing in a bit of yellow, and a touch of orange, perhaps a spot of violet, and even, to give depth, a bit of black. This makes a red one has to ponder."

As I said, hand-dyed yarns excel when they are an intimate manifestation of one person's color vision. And just as each person is different, so these yarns will vary dramatically from artist to artist. This is part of what makes them so magical.

Color Pooling

With any yarn dyed in multiple colors, whether it was hand or machine dyed, you run the risk of **color pooling**. This occurs when specific colors in the yarn repeat at just the right intervals on the knitted fabric so that they stack on top of one another to form strong "pools" of color. Sometimes the effect can be attractive, with flickering flames and warm patches of color. Some yarn manufacturers even *plan* for color pooling, measuring out their dye intervals precisely so that the yarn will produce a specific pattern when knit up at a certain width. This is what self-patterning sock yarns do.

But sometimes the color pooling can be awkward and splotchy. If you want to work with hand-dyed yarns and avoid color pooling, your best bet is to work from two different skeins simultaneously. Just knit two rows from one skein, then two rows from the other, always stranding the unworked yarn up a side seam as you go.

Color pooling can occur less with handpainted yarns. The dye isn't always applied to a uniform cross-section of the hank, which makes the color repeats more random and sporadic. But if you ever have doubts, knit a sizable test swatch in your intended width to be sure.

Keep in mind that the stitch you use will also impact how hand-dyed colors appear on the fabric. Textured stitches, such as cables, ribbing, and seed stitch, use up more yarn, causing your colors to span shorter sections of fabric. Open, lacy stitches use less yarn, so you'll

Socks That Rock superwash sock yarn from Blue Moon Fiber Arts is a favorite for socks. The skein is a jumble of colors.

But when knit up, the colors often pool dramatically along the narrow circumference of the sock.

have larger strips of color. But remember that the more intense the color combinations in your hand-dyed yarn, the greater the chance those colors may overpower and obscure your beautiful stitchwork. (Even in the two pairs of Swirly O Socks on page 140, both hand-dyed yarns use modest color themes and don't obscure the stitch patterns.)

If you want a hand-dyed effect that doesn't overpower your stitchwork, look for those hand-dyed yarns offered in "nearly solid" colors. A perfect example of this is the gently fluttering velvety green of Alchemy Yarns Synchronicity, used in the nearly solid version of Gina Wilde's Seascape Bolero on page 78. As you can see, there's beauty in restraint.

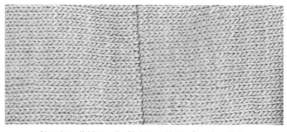

Nearly solid hues in Alchemy Yarns Synchronicity

Evaluating Hand-Dyed Yarns

Want to try a new hand-dyed yarn from a lesser-known source? First, see if the vendor has knitted swatches of the yarn (or pictures of swatches, if you're buying online). This will give you a sense of how the colors will knit up. If the store owner will let you unravel one of the skeins a little, or if you already have a skein at home, here's how you can get a general sense of the color repeats. (It won't work as well with handpainted yarns because the repeats are more random.)

Pull out a few yards of yarn and look at it. How many colors are used in the skein? And how often do they shift? Every few inches? Or do you have longer spans of one color before getting to the next? The shorter the color shifts, the faster your bursts of color will be and the less pooling will occur. The longer the individual colors on the yarn—say 10 inches (25.5cm) or more—the more gradual the color shifts but the greater the potential for pooling.

With lesser-known hand-dyed yarns, it's also important to touch the skein to feel how the fibers have reacted to the dye process. Are they still as soft, or have they been rendered lifeless or rough? Experienced dyers know how to treat fibers properly and minimize the risks of damage, but some smaller cottage dyers haven't quite figured it out yet.

If you can't see a knitted sample and can't play with a skein first, your next best option is to look around on the Web to see if anyone else has had success with that particular yarn. If you're lucky, you'll find a few blogs with pictures of finished projects—or horror stories of why you'd be better served with another yarn.

A Few Words About Dye Lots

Despite yarn companies' best attempts to standardize color formulas and dye processes, you may still encounter two skeins of olive green that aren't quite the same shade of green. If you check the label, chances are you'll discover that the yarns came from two different dye batches, or **dye lots**. Sometimes the difference among dye lots can be indistinguishable; other times, disastrous. The first rule is to always check your labels and make sure the yarns are from the same dye lot.

But despite our noblest intentions, we may occasionally still need to knit with yarns that come from different dye lots. (Say, for example, we found twenty such skeins of pure cashmere on sale for $1 a piece.) The important thing to know is that it *can* work.

The secret is to introduce the new dye lot in small doses. The last thing you want to do is end one skein and abruptly begin a new one. You may not see the difference when you look at the skeins, but, knit up, you may very well see a glaring difference. Instead, try alternating two rows of the old skein and two rows of the new skein, starting as early as you can in the process. The more slowly you can introduce the new color, the more subtle the change will be.

Some hand-dyers find the whole process so quixotic that they don't even bother with dye lots. One such dyer is Gina Wilde of Alchemy Yarns. "Subtle factors influence the creation of a color," she explained. "The temperature of water used in mixing paint, the direction

HELP, I'M BLEEDING!

QUICK NOTE

It's not uncommon for hand-dyed yarns—especially the brightly colored ones—to **bleed** a little in their first few washes. This should not be cause for any great alarm. It's simply the yarn's way of releasing any unexhausted dyestuff that wasn't fully rinsed out during the dye process. Generally you won't see any lessening of the overall color in your garment. A word of caution, however: If you're giving an item as a gift, it's always wise to wash it first and make sure you've gotten out all the excess dye. I once gave my niece a pair of bright fuchsia hand-dyed socks that I *thought* I'd sufficiently rinsed, but I later learned the socks had dyed her feet and her shoes bright pink. While she thought it was delightful, my brother—who had bought her the shoes—wasn't so thrilled. So it's always best to be extra careful with gifts.

the wind is blowing on the day when I steam the fiber to set the color, the characteristics of the fiber being painted—there is always a factor of unpredictability in the making of handpainted fiber." When working with yarns like these, you're generally advised to alternate skeins every two rows, or let go and let the yarn work its magic.

THE ORIGINAL SPIN

Before they can be spun into yarn, all fibers need to be prepared for spinning. This is done by running the fibers through a large **carding machine**. These machines vary in size and sophistication, depending on the facility, but they all rely on several series of large, opposing cylinders lined with tiny teeth. As the cylinders rotate, the fibers move through the carder and the teeth catch the fibers, stripping them from one cylinder and pulling them onto the next. The process loosens up the fibers, opens up any natural lock formations, and removes dirt and unsuitable **neps** of fiber. At the end, you have a thick, lofty, jumbled blend of fibers called a

Fibers spilling off the carding machine at Taos Valley Wool Mill

batt. Consider it the large-scale equivalent of running a soft bristle brush over your hair. These fibers are then pulled into thin continuous strips called slivers.

At this point, yarn companies can choose to go down one of two paths: They can gently twist the slivers into strands of **roving** and spin them into a **woolen-spun** yarn; or they can run the fibers through more machines to remove all the shorter or irregular fibers and comb the remaining fibers into perfect parallel alignment to produce a **worsted-spun** yarn. The path they choose will ultimately determine how your project knits up, looks, feels, and lasts.

Woolen-Spun Yarns

The most common, versatile, and inexpensive technique is to spin yarns woolen—a method suitable for any relatively short fibers that have a natural crimp to them (including, as the name suggests, wool). Woolen spinning simply means that the fibers are pulled out of this jumbled state in thin strips and then twisted. The resulting airy, springy yarn is adaptable to a wide range of needle sizes, forgiving of mistakes, more likely to bloom with wash, and wonderful to wear—as long as you understand its limitations.

If you pull out a strand of woolen yarn from the skein, you may notice that the thickness is not consistent. This is a natural side effect of working with different

Yarn being spun at the Taos Valley Wool Mill

lengths of fibers that are oriented in all directions and only loosely spun. Knit up, those irregularities all but disappear beneath the blurred, spongy surface of the fabric. You end up with a lofty, lightweight material that's extremely warm because of its ability to trap still air and keep the wearer toasty warm.

Woolen preparation is ideal for fibers that already have a natural crimp to them, such as the softer, higher-crimp wools, cashmere, yak, and qiviut. You'll find woolen yarns in all sorts of weights and thicknesses, perhaps the most common one being a DK-weight two- or three-ply.

I find woolen yarns extremely forgiving. Their loft and general disorder conceal any irregular stitches or changes in tension. You can use them for a wide variety of projects because they adapt to a broader range of needle sizes. The fibers will simply expand or contract to fill whatever space they're given.

All those jumbled shorter fibers contribute to what I consider the true magic of woolen yarns: the bloom. Here's how it happens. The crimpy fibers were held under tension during spinning and even during knitting. Once you submerge your finished item in warm soapy water, however, those fibers finally get a chance to relax, move around, and adapt to their new surroundings. Rinse the garment and let those fibers dry, and they'll naturally resume their original crimpy form. This process of relaxing, adjusting, and recrimping creates a gorgeous, cohesive piece of knitted fabric with a surface that literally seems to "bloom" in the wash. With time and wear, the bloom only gets better.

As with all things wonderful, there are a few drawbacks to woolen-spun yarns. The biggest one is durability. The woolen spinning method tends to favor minimal twist. The less force there is holding fibers together, the more quickly they'll come apart under abrasion. For this reason, most people would advise against using a woolen-spun yarn for socks, or reinforcing the heels and toes with a nylon binder thread. You can also gain yarn strength by seeking a woolen-spun yarn with more plies, since each ply adds strength.

While woolen yarns may have a reputation for being scratchy, this depends entirely on the fibers being used. Whenever you have mixed lengths of jumbled fibers that are loosely spun together, you'll have many loose fiber ends sticking out of the yarn. The softer the fiber, the smaller its diameter and the less likely you are to even feel it against your skin. But conversely, the more rugged the fiber and the larger its diameter, the greater the chances you'll feel it rubbing against your skin. This is why I tend to keep an eye out for the softer wools, such as Merino, Cormo, Rambouillet, or Columbia, when considering woolen-spun yarns for next-to-the-skin clothing.

A traditional Shetland pattern, knit in Harrisville New England Highland, a classic two-ply woolen-spun yarn

Woolen-spun yarns also tend to pill a little more than their smoother counterparts because all those loose ends have a greater chance of catching one another, getting enmeshed, and forming a pill on the fabric surface. Because woolen-spun yarns have fibers of shorter lengths, however, these pills can often be easily removed without damaging the remaining knitted fabric.

Marr Haven Farm yarn before (left) and after (right) washing. Can you see the delicate bloom of the fibers?

Knit up, woolen-spun yarns produce a visually soft, matte fabric with minimal stitch definition and almost imperceptible ply structure. While you'd think this makes them unlikely candidates for colorwork, the opposite is true. They can produce gorgeous, subtle color effects, rather like moss growing on a forest floor. Because of the bloom on the fabric surface, you're less likely to see any of the nonworking colors running along the back of your work.

Woolen-spun yarns can also be gorgeous in textured stitchwork. You'll lack the crisp stitch definition of smoother yarns, but you'll make up for it in a softer, more *weathered* look.

The woolen-spun Mostly Merino renders a diagonal ribbing pattern in subtle, low relief.

Finer-gauge woolen-spun yarns can also look exceptionally beautiful in knitted lace patterns, where the yarn's softness and bloom can help bring together openwork and stockinette stitches.

When in doubt, you can also simply relax into the stockinette zone and let the softness and depth of the woolen yarn be the main attraction.

Worsted-Spun Yarns

All that fuzz and jumble is fine, but sometimes you may want a smoother, longer-wearing fabric. That's when you choose a worsted yarn.

The worsted spinning preparation takes woolen one step further by running the carded fibers through industrial combs to remove all the shorter fibers. You end up with a cohesive batch of perfectly aligned fibers, all of uniform length and all lying parallel to one another. Worsted preparation is suitable for most wools,

COMMON CONFUSIONS

Yarn companies may use the word *worsted* to define a yarn's thickness and recommended gauge range. Worsted-weight yarn knits up somewhere between 4 and 5½ stitches per inch (2.5cm); *worsted-spun* yarn, on the other hand, can come in nearly any weight and thickness. So always double-check the context when you hear someone refer to a yarn as *worsted*.

QUICK NOTE

as well as for cotton, silk, linen, Tencel, and even synthetics. Because the combing process produces a great amount of waste, driving up costs, yarn companies normally advertise the fact that a yarn has been worsted spun (and increase the price accordingly). The waste from combing—called **noil**—will often be collected and reused for lower-grade woolen yarns.

Dalegarn Baby Ull is a classic worsted-spun yarn

The first thing you'll notice about worsted yarns is their smoothness and fluidity. The longer fibers tend to spin up into a denser, more compact yarn with greater drape. This lack of abundant air pockets can make worsted-spun yarns slightly less insulating than their woolen counterparts.

Because loft and crimp help balance out excess twist in yarn, you can have a well-balanced single-ply woolen-spun yarn, but it's not as common to find a well-balanced single-ply worsted-spun yarn. Instead, you'll typically find worsted-spun yarns with a minimum of two plies and normally four or more, with each ply having a decent amount of twist.

With longer fibers of uniform length, held together by tighter twist, you end up with a sturdy yarn that has great tensile strength and resistance to abrasion. With fewer fiber ends sticking out, these yarns are less likely to pill or feel irritating against the skin. This is partly why you'll often see worsted-spun yarns used for socks and for baby garments. Worsted-spun yarns do not bloom as dramatically with wash.

With multiple-ply yarns, especially worsted ones, the tightness of the ply will influence how your yarn feels and behaves. If you see that the ply angle is almost perpendicular to the yarn itself, know that the yarn will most likely have a greater spring and bounce to it—especially if it's a crimpy fiber like wool. If the ply angle is almost aligned with the yarn, the yarn will be much softer and smoother to knit, but it may not have as much bounce. Most commercial yarns fall somewhere in between tight and loose, but it's always helpful to look at the degree of the twist and the angle of the ply as you evaluate the yarn.

Ideal Uses

The smoother, more uniform fibers in worsted-spun yarns tend to give the knitted fabric a lustrous, reflective quality—made even more so by the addition of mohair or silk. This is why worsted-spun yarn is the yarn of choice for open lacework where you want to highlight the movement of the stitches. (You can see this in Jackie Erickson-Schweitzer's Raspberry Rhapsody Scarf on page 98, and Shelia January's Optic Waves Shawl on page 94.)

Knit up, worsted-spun yarns tend to have a crisp, clear stitch definition that's ideal for stitchwork in which

you want a vivid, sculptural effect. The effect is slightly muted in two-ply yarns, where the visible ply definition can soften the stitches; but the more plies you add to the yarn, the fuller and more high-relief your stitches become.

The crisp stitch definition of worsted-spun yarns is also ideal for colorwork in which you want precise, almost photographic clarity. The only drawback with colorwork is that you'll need to have far more precise tension to keep your fabric from puckering and the stranded colors on the back side from showing through.

Some yarn companies will also produce a semiworsted yarn that seeks to forge a compromise between the durability of worsted and the loft of woolen. Consider them a midway hybrid between the two types.

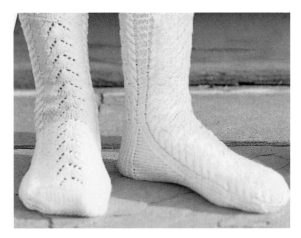

The two plies in this worsted-spun wool soften the textured stitchwork in these Guernsey Socks (pattern on page 106).

Colorwork is rendered more vividly in the worsted-spun Dalegarn Heilo.

Using a fuller yarn with three plies, the cables immediately become more crisp and sculptural (pattern on page 134).

THE POLITICS OF PILLS

You can't make great yarn from lousy wool, but you can make lousy yarn from great wool. —ROBERT DONNELLY

Robert knows his wool, having worked with it in many capacities for more than thirty years. When I visited him at the Taos Valley Wool Mill recently, I asked Robert what made a good yarn, and he gave me the answer above.

After asking him to repeat it a few times, I finally got what he meant. Each fiber has an ideal way to be spun. Respect and work with those innate qualities and— unless the fiber itself is poor—you'll have a great yarn. Work against it, that is, force the fiber to do something against its will, and you'll end up with a potentially lousy yarn—no matter how good the fiber is. It's that simple.

When I say *lousy yarn,* I mean primarily that it won't wear well. It'll start pilling quickly—perhaps even as you work with it on the skein itself. Chances are you've had this happen already, and innately you understood that something wasn't right. Most likely, the fibers were either of a poor grade or not given their optimal spin.

Pills are caused by the tiny ends of fiber that don't get completely tucked in during the spinning process. With normal friction, these tiny ends begin to work their way loose from the fabric. They catch on one another and become increasingly enmeshed until they produce a "pill" of loose fibers on the fabric surface. Shorter fibers need more twist to keep all those ends from working their way out; longer fibers don't need as much twist because they have fewer ends.

But here's the problem: Sometimes we want a fiber to do what we want it to do. I once saw an exquisite single-ply cashmere yarn and had to have it, even though I knew instinctively that it wouldn't wear well. Those short fibers needed far more twist than they'd been given. But it was heavenly, like holding a cloud, so I bought it anyway. That's what I call a calculated pill risk, and every knitter must take one now and then. It's fine as long as you know what you're doing. The problem arises when you expect it to be a durable yarn and it starts falling apart right away.

Some yarn companies may let their need for profits drive their decisions about what grade of fibers to use and how much twist to give them (remember, running their machines costs money). But most companies put great thought and consideration into figuring out a compromise that works for us and for the fiber. For example, they'll take Merino and other similarly delicate, pill-prone fibers and spin them into what I call "cheater" singles. Look closely, untwist the strand for a few inches (centimeters), and you'll see that the yarn actually consists of two or three barely spun strands of fiber twisted together. The yarn looks like a single but has the strength and dimension of a multiple ply. Margaret Klein Wilson does this with the Mostly Merino yarn in her Step Ribbed Stole on page 86, Morehouse Merino does it as well, and it's a smart compromise. This, plus the absorbency of the bouncy fibers, will also help combat any bias in your knitted fabric.

Evaluating the Pill Potential

The most foolproof way to determine a yarn's pilling potential is to knit test swatches, wash them, and subject them to standard wear and tear. But before you buy the skein, you can do some basic reconnaissance at the yarn store simply by picking up a skein and studying it closely. Here's what you want to be thinking about as you study that skein.

Consider the fiber content. This should always be your first key. The shorter the fibers in your yarn—for example Merino, cashmere, qiviut, or angora—the more ends you'll have per inch (2.5cm). Since each end introduces a potential for pilling, short-staple fibers naturally have a greater tendency to pill. The longer the fibers in your yarn—for example, longer-staple wools such as Bluefaced Leicester and English Leicester Longwool, as well as mohair, alpaca, silk, and synthetics— the fewer ends you'll have per inch (2.5cm), and the less your yarn's potential for pilling.

Next, look at how the fibers were spun. Woolen-spun yarns, with their lofty jumble of assorted fibers going every which way, naturally have more ends sticking out. And this means they will be more likely to pill. The trade-off here is that woolen yarns produce a soft, lofty, and extremely warm fabric. The more plies in your woolen-spun yarn, the better its chances of wearing longer.

Worsted yarns, on the other hand, are made of firmly aligned fibers of uniform lengths, leading to fewer protruding ends that will catch and pill. If durability is your number-one priority, you'll want to stick with worsted yarns. However, be aware that worsted yarns tend to have a denser hand, less loft, and not as much warmth.

Count the plies in the yarn. **Plies** are part of the essential energy that holds all your fibers together. Hence, the more plies you have, the less likely it is that your yarn will pill—which is why single-ply yarns have such a reputation for pilling.

Test the twist. The tightness of the spin will also indicate how the yarn may wear. The tighter the spin within each ply of your yarn, the firmer and more durable your yarn will likely be. The looser the spin, the less energy holding all those ends together. But remember that the tighter the spin, the firmer the fabric will be; the looser the spin, the softer and more inviting the fabric. Finding the perfect compromise between softness and durability is the lifelong quest of every yarn lover.

Removing Pills

Pills only show you half of what's going on—the other half is still firmly anchored in the fabric. For short fibers, such as finer wools, cashmere, and some cottons, the pills can be pinched off almost effortlessly. But if your yarn is made up of longer fibers, such as silk, longwools, mohair, and most synthetics, these pills will be harder to remove from the fabric because their anchors run far deeper. As you tug the pill, you'll feel resistance and hear tiny tearing sounds. This is because you're ripping fibers and disturbing others deeper within the fabric—something that may ultimately produce more loose ends that will pill.

For such firmly rooted pills, your best course of action is to snip them off with a pair of scissors. This could be tedious and risky, but technology has come to the rescue. There is a simple "sweater shaver" device that's sold in most drugstores around the country. It functions like a crude electric razor, snipping the pills at the base of the fabric while leaving the rest of your material intact.

The more intact you leave the rest of your fabric, the longer it'll take the rest of those loose ends to work their way out. Be sure to test a small section of your garment first to make sure the shaver snips only the pills and nothing more.

SECTION 3

Ply Me a River }————————

WE'VE EXPLORED THE MOST COMMON FIBERS IN THE WORLD, WHERE THEY COME FROM, HOW THEY BEHAVE, THEIR LIKES AND DISLIKES, FRIENDS AND FOES. WE'VE ALSO DISCUSSED THE WAYS IN WHICH THOSE FIBERS CAN BE PREPARED FOR SPINNING, AND HOW THAT PREPARATION ULTIMATELY IMPACTS THE FINISHED PROJECT AND YOUR EXPERIENCE OF IT.

THAT'S ONLY HALF THE STORY. THE OTHER HALF TAKES PLACE AT THE MILL WHEN THE FIBERS GET THEIR FIRST TWIST AND OFFICIALLY BECOME YARN.

SINGLE PLY

page
68

Yarn purists insist that singles aren't a "true" yarn because they hold pent-up twist that hasn't been balanced by another ply. This hasn't stopped yarn companies from creating all sorts of single-ply yarns. The key is to know how to work with them.

TWO-PLY

If you take two single-ply yarns, line them side by side, and allow them to release their excess twist by untwisting back on one another, you end up with a two-ply yarn. The degree of initial twist and plying twist varies dramatically, depending on the fibers, their preparation, and the intended results.

page
84

page
126

THREE-PLY

By the time that third ply gets added to the mix, you have a yarn that's well-suited for projects that get high abrasion—such as socks and mittens for rugged everyday wear.

FOUR-PLY AND MORE

page
144

The more plies you add to a yarn, the more hard-wearing it will be. However, you may notice with four-ply yarns that the plies don't nest together as completely. If you study your stockinette up close, you'll always be able to trace one extra ply, like the edge of a square box, working its way through the stitches.

The simplest, most basic form of yarn is the single ply. All spun yarns are born this way, but only a special few remain singles all the way to your knitting basket. Single-ply yarn is formed by taking fibers and twisting them under tension into a continuous thread. From here they may be paired up with any number of other single plies and spun together (either in the same or the opposite direction) to form a stronger, more complex and balanced strand of yarn. But in the beginning, they all start as singles.

The main issue with singles is balance. The twisted fibers are like a leaning person. They need something to lean on—normally another ply. Without that ply, the excess twist may work itself out by pulling your knitted fabric in a diagonal direction—just as our leaning person may end up tipping over. When you hear people talk about a fabric *bias,* this is what they mean.

How tightly your yarn is spun, and what fibers it contains, will both impact a single's likelihood to bias. Generally speaking, the smoother your fiber and the tighter its spin—for example, a tight silk, alpaca, or cotton—the more it may bias. This is because the smoother fibers lack the crimp and elasticity necessary to absorb excess twist. (Consider crimpy fibers the yarn equivalent of shock absorbers.) Conversely, if your yarn has a crimpier fiber to it—such as any of the shorter, softer wools—it will absorb the extra twist and give you a more even fabric.

If twist is energy, then the less you have, the less energy is holding your fibers together, right? Yes and no. Short fibers, such as Merino and cashmere, require more twists per inch (2.5cm) to hold together because each fiber is so short. However, these fibers also tend to have more crimp to absorb any excess twist—which means they can even be spun woolen and still hold together. The knitted fabric will age into a soft, fuzzy, yet cohesive fabric surface. Longer-staple fibers, such as alpaca, silk, and longwools, don't need as many twists per inch (2.5cm) to hold together well, because each fiber may span several inches (centimeters).

These types of fibers can be spun worsted to give you a smoother yarn with greater stitch clarity.

Regardless of the fiber type, most single-ply yarns can only be spun so tight for fear of biasing. This looser spin, combined with the lack of protection from other plies, means that singles often may not wear as well as their multiple-ply counterparts. The fibers will come loose and form pills on the surface, and the fabric may lose shape more quickly.

If your knitting may bias, pill, and lose shape quickly, why bother with singles? Because the bias issue can be overcome and because some of the most magical yarns on the market today happen to be singles.

PLY AND THICKNESS

QUICK NOTE

A yarn's ply count may indicate how its knitted fabric will look and wear, but it doesn't tell you anything about the *gauge* or *thickness* of the yarn. This is because a six-ply yarn can knit up at a much finer gauge than a two-ply yarn—it all depends on the thickness of each ply that was used in the yarn. Nevertheless, older knitting patterns sometimes specified yarns in terms of ply count. If you encounter such a pattern, use the ply count to figure out what *kind* of yarn they want you to use, but refer to the pattern's *recommended gauge* to get the right yarn weight.

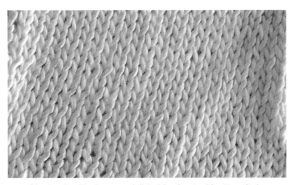

Single-ply silk shows a visible bias in stockinette stitch.

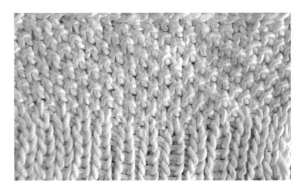

The same single-ply silk shows no bias when knit and purl stitches are introduced.

BEAT THE BIAS

The first thing to do is knit a generous-sized swatch with the yarn, wash it, and see if it does bias. If it doesn't, you're free to do anything you want with it. But if it does bias, here's what to do next.

First, choose a project that incorporates both the knit and purl stitches. Ribbing, seed stitch, moss stitch, or any of the infinite variations on this theme will balance out your twist and give you an even piece of fabric. The other benefit of using textured stitches is that they will give extra body and depth to your fabric.

Second, consider using a needle one-half size smaller than you'd use for a comparable two-ply yarn. The idea here is that the tighter fabric will give the fibers less room to move. As an added bonus, this will also add extra structure to your fabric.

And third, you can bypass the bias by rewinding your yarn. This simple process will help reduce the twist. Examine your yarn to see which way it was spun. Most likely, it was twisted in a counterclockwise direction, called the **S twist.** If that is the case, rewind the yarn into a ball, winding the yarn away from you. If the yarn was twisted clockwise, called **Z twist,** rewind the yarn toward you.

VISUAL EFFECTS

Single-ply yarns tend to produce simple, clear stitches that are undarkened by lines or shadows from a ply structure. (Visualize knitting with tubes of clay or strands of spaghetti.) Some find the unidimensionality of single-ply yarns a little drab when knit up in plain stockinette, especially if the yarn is a solid color to begin with. Others find the smooth simplicity to be calming, in a Zen sort of way. Try it out and see what you think. You can always counter the drabness by introducing more sculptural stitches or by choosing a yarn that brings color complexity to the mix.

MAINE MORNING MITTS

------- details -------

SIZE
To fit a woman's hand, size Medium

CIRCUMFERENCE
8" (20.5cm) stretched

LENGTH
8" (20.5cm)

YARN

Mitt A (close left): Noro Kureyon (100% wool, 110 yds [100m]/50g) 1 skein #148; **Mitt B** (far left): La Lana Wools Forever Random Worsted Obverse (60%

Romney wool, 40% yearling mohair, 70 yds [64m]/57g) 2 skeins Potpourri Glacé. If substituting, use 85 yds (78m) worsted-weight single-ply yarn, the more colorful the better.

NEEDLES
Set of size 7 (4.5mm) dpns, or size to obtain gauge

NOTIONS
Tapestry needle

GAUGE
20 sts + 28 rows = 4" (10cm) in St st
18 sts + 28 rows = 4" (10cm) in rib pattern in the round, slightly stretched

STITCH GUIDE
RIB PATTERN
*K2, p1; rep from * across round.

M1R
Make a right-leaning increase by picking up the bar between stitches from back to front and knitting into the front of the picked-up stitch.

M1L
Make a left-leaning increase by picking up the bar between stitches from front to back and knitting into the back of the picked-up stitch.

------- instructions -------

Many gorgeous artisanal yarns are worsted-weight single ply. They also tend to be pretty expensive. I designed these mitts to show off the exquisite coloring in two favorites—Noro Kureyon and La Lana Forever Random—while using a minimum of yardage. Simple ribbing offsets any bias and keeps the mitts snug on your hands. The real story here is the colors, which will glow like jewels on your hands.

CO 33 sts and divide onto 3 dpns as follows: 12 sts, 9 sts, 12 sts (this keeps your patt repeats even on each needle). Mark beginning and join in round, being careful not to twist sts. Begin Rib Pattern and work until mitt measures 4" (10cm), or desired length, to base of thumb.

THUMB GUSSET
Rnd 1: K2, M1R, p1, M1L, patt to end.
Rnd 2: (K3, p1) twice, patt to end.
Rnd 3: K2, M1R, k1, p1, k1, M1L, patt to end.
Rnd 4: (K4, p1) twice, patt to end.
Rnd 5: K2, M1R, k2, p1, k2, M1L, patt to end.
Rnd 6: (K5, p1) twice, patt to end.
Rnd 7: K2, M1R, k3, p1, k3, M1L, patt to end.
Rnd 8: (K6, p1) twice, patt to end.
Rnd 9: K2, CO 5 sts using backwards loop cast-on, put 9 sts on holder for thumb, and patt to end.
Rnd 10: (K4, p1) twice, patt to end.

Rnd 11: K1, sl1 k1 psso, k1, p1, k2tog, patt to end.
Rnd 12: K1, sl1 k1 psso, p2tog, patt to end.
Next rnds: Work in patt until mitt measures 8" (20.5cm). BO all sts in patt.

THUMB
Place the 9 sts from holder onto 2 dpns. With a third dpn, pick up and knit 4 sts across the top of the thumb opening, then k4, p1, k4. Continue working sts as they appear for 5 rounds or until thumb is desired length. BO all sts loosely.

FINISHING
Weave in all ends. Use the yarn end from the thumb to close any holes around the Thumb Gusset. Both yarns benefit from a final wash in lukewarm water with mild soap. This will release any excess dye and help bring the fibers together into a cohesive fabric.

------- designed by Clara Parkes -------

CABLED TEA COZY

SIZES
4-cup (32 fl oz [or .94L]) pot (6-cup [48 fl oz. (1.42L)] pot)

FINISHED MEASUREMENTS
4-cup: 10" (25.5cm) tall, 10" (25.5cm) wide (6-cup: 10" [25.5cm] tall, 15" [38cm] wide). Shown in 6-cup.

YARN

4 MEDIUM

Malabrigo (100% Merino; 215 yds [196.5m]/100g) 2 skeins each of colors Orchid #34 (A) and Lettuce #37 (B). If substituting, use 465 (580) yds (425 [530]m) single-ply worsted-weight yarn.

NEEDLES
One 24" (60cm) circular needle size 8 (5mm), or size to obtain gauge
Size 8 (5mm) dpns, or size to obtain gauge

NOTIONS
Cable needle, two stitch markers, tapestry needle, two stitch holders (or scrap yarn), fabric for lining (optional)

GAUGE
22 sts + 26 rows = 4" (10cm) in cable patt from chart
18 sts + 27 rows = 4" (10cm) in St st

--------------------------------------- *instructions* ---------------------------------------

You can exploit the smooth roundness of single-ply yarns by using them for sculptural knits, like the high-relief cables and bobbles in this plush tea cozy. You get stitch clarity but also a soft cuddly feel. Plus it shows off the gorgeous kettle-dyed subtlety of those colors beautifully.

Notes: I strongly recommend that you make a photocopy enlargement of the chart (page 75) for easier readability. Work across the chart that corresponds to your desired cozy size.

The cabled sides of the cozy are worked as two flat pieces and seamed. Then the lining is picked up and worked in the round. When complete, only the right side shows. Instead of a knitted lining, the cozy may be lined with fabric. Quilted fabric would work wonderfully. Also, the I-cords may be worked in either stockinette stitch or seed stitch, or any combination, according to your preference.

FRONT
CO 52 (80) sts in A. Work in chart patt for 6" (15cm). Begin decreasing as follows *while working chart*: On RS rows, work ssk decrease after the first 2 sts and then k2tog decrease before the last 2 sts. On WS rows, work

p2tog decrease after the first 2 sts, and p2togtbl before the last 2 sts.

Cont to decrease until piece measures 9" (23cm) from cast-on. BO to middle 6 sts, placing those sts on a holder, and then BO remaining sts.

BACK
With B, work as for Front. Seam the sides, RS together, being careful not to seam together the pairs of 6 sts on holders.

Weave in all ends now so they do not get in the way of the lining.

HANDLES
With RS facing, work handle loops. With dpn and same color yarn as Front, pick up the right 3 sts of the cable, leaving the other 3 on holder. Attach new yarn and work an I-cord approx 4" (10cm) long. Join these 3 sts

instructions continued

with the sts of the same color waiting on the holder with kitchener stitch. Work the loop on Back in the same way, using the same color yarn as Back.

SIDE SEAMS

With dpn and either color, work an I-cord for the trim along the side seams. CO 5 sts and work seed stitch or St st for approx 24 (26)" (60 [66]cm) or length to fit. Sew the I-cord to the side seams. Be sure to attach the I-cord before making the lining so that your seaming will be concealed on the WS. Also, you may wish to secure the loop at the top by stitching the two halves of the loop together.

For the lining, with 24" (60cm) circulars and either color, pick up and knit 43 (66) from the first side, place marker (pm), pick up and knit 43 (66) from the other side of the cozy, pm. Join, and work in the round. Purl the first 2 rounds, knit the next 2 rounds, then purl the next 2 rounds. (This will give the base of the cozy stability and allow it to stand on its own more easily. It will also produce a neat fold.) Work St st without decreasing until piece measures 5" (12.5cm) from the 2 knit rounds between the pairs of purl rounds.

SHAPE LINING

Decrease row: Slip marker (sm), *k1, ssk, knit to 3 sts before marker, k2tog, k1, sm; rep from * to end.

Work decrease round every other round for 2" (5cm). When work becomes too narrow for circular needles, change to dpns. Then work the decrease every row until only 8 sts remain. Cont working in the round on these 8 sts until there is at least a 1" (2.5cm) stem. At desired length, BO 8 sts.

Weave in the ends with duplicate stitch and pull them into the inside to hide them.

If you'd like a little more embellishment, work another I-cord and sew it around the base of the entire cozy, attaching it to the cabled side. Contrast the colors as you like. Tuck the lining inside the cabled cozy, or try it the other way around, depending on your mood.

Chart

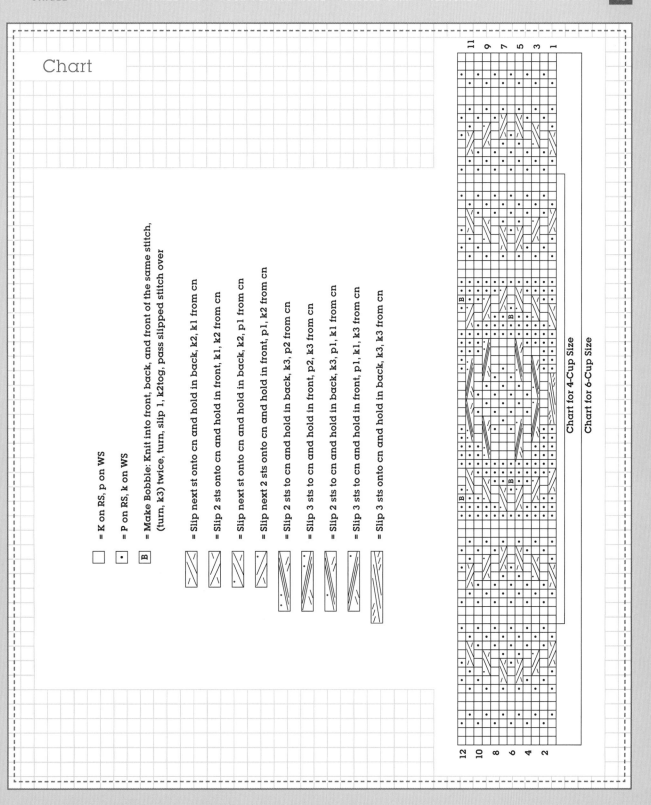

= K on RS, p on WS

= P on RS, k on WS

B = Make Bobble: Knit into front, back, and front of the same stitch, (turn, k3) twice, turn, slip 1, k2tog, pass slipped stitch over

= Slip next st onto cn and hold in back, k2, k1 from cn

= Slip 2 sts onto cn and hold in front, k1, k2 from cn

= Slip next st onto cn and hold in back, k2, p1 from cn

= Slip next 2 sts onto cn and hold in front, p1, k2 from cn

= Slip 2 sts to cn and hold in back, k3, p2 from cn

= Slip 3 sts to cn and hold in front, p2, k3 from cn

= Slip 2 sts to cn and hold in back, k3, p1, k1 from cn

= Slip 3 sts to cn and hold in front, p1, k1, k3 from cn

= Slip 3 sts onto cn and hold in back, k3, k3 from cn

Chart for 4-Cup Size

Chart for 6-Cup Size

HONEYCOMB HAT

---------- *details* ----------

SIZE
Fabric stretches to fit a standard-sized woman's head (size Large given in parentheses). Shown in standard size.

FINISHED MEASUREMENTS
Circumference: 18 (20)" (45.5 [51]cm)

YARN

SUPER BULKY

La Lana Phat Silk Phat (50% wool/50% silk; 98 yds [89.5m]/60g) 2 skeins Magenta. If substituting, use 200 yds (183m) of single-ply bulky-weight yarn.

NEEDLES
One set of size 10 (6mm) dpns, or size to obtain gauge

NOTIONS
Tapestry needle, stitch marker

GAUGE
17 sts + 24 rows = 4" (10cm) in St st
18 sts + 24 rows = 4" (10cm) in Honeycomb st

STITCH GUIDE
HONEYCOMB STITCH
Row 1: *K1, sl1 purlwise with yarn in back; rep from * to end.
Rows 2 and 4: Knit all sts.
Row 3: *Sl1 purlwise with yarn in back, k1; rep from * to end.

---------- *instructions* ----------

You certainly don't have to avoid *all* stockinette with singles. For example, you can compensate for the unidimensionality of single-ply yarns by adding a visually "deep" stitch pattern as I've done around the brim of this hat.

La Lana Phat Silk has more depth and dimension than the average single-ply yarn because it contains wool and silk that haven't been thoroughly blended together. Instead, a plush wool core is literally encased in swirling silk, giving each fiber a distinct presence. When the yarn is dyed (which is done by hand using all-natural dyestuffs), the silk and wool absorb and reflect the dye differently, which gives the yarn even more character.

Note: This hat is sized for a snug fit.

BRIM
CO 80 (90) sts and distribute evenly among three dpns. Join, being careful not to twist. Place marker (pm) to indicate beginning of rnd and work 3" (7.5cm) in honeycomb stitch. This will be the brim.
Turn work inside out so that the wrong side is facing you. Knit in St st for each round until hat measures 7" (18cm) from the brim turn.

SHAPE CROWN
Rnd 1: *K3, k2tog; rep from * to end—64 (72) sts.
Rnd 2 and all even rnds: Knit.
Rnd 3: *K2, k2tog; rep from * to end—48 (54) sts.
Rnd 5: *K1, k2tog; rep from * to end—32 (36) sts.
Rnd 7: K2tog to end—16 (18) sts.

FINISHING
Cut yarn, leaving a generous tail. Run it through the remaining stitches, secure it tightly in the inside of the work, and darn in the ends. Wash and block hat. Fold brim so that it faces out and let dry.

---------- *designed by Clara Parkes* ----------

Single-ply
**Project
#4**

SEASCAPE BOLERO

---------------------------------- *details* ----------------------------------

SIZES

To fit women's size Small (Medium, Large). Shown in size Small.

FINISHED MEASUREMENTS

Bust: 36 (40, 44)" (91.5 [101.5, 112]cm)

Length: 15 (16, 16)" (38 [40.5, 40.5]cm)

YARN

Alchemy Yarns Synchronicity (50% silk/50% Merino; 118 yds [108m]/50g) 2 (3, 3) skeins of Spruce #30W (A); 2 (2, 3) skeins of Silver #42M (B); 2 (2, 2) skeins of Citrine #76E (C) and Fauna #35E (F); 1 (1, 2) skeins each of Topaz #67E (E) and Moonstone #92W (G); and 1 skein of Diamonda #09C (D). (*Total skeins* needed: 11 [12, 15].) Solid-color model on page 83 knit using all Citrine (#76E). If substituting, use 1,300 (1,420, 1,780) yds (1,189 [1,298, 1,628]m) of single-ply worsted-weight yarn.

NEEDLES

One 24" (60cm) circular needle size 5 (3.75mm), or size to obtain gauge

Two 24" (60cm) circular needles size 7 (4.5mm), or size to obtain gauge

One size 7 (4.5mm) dpn for 3-needle bind-off, or size to obtain gauge

Two size 5 (3.75 mm) dpns for I-cord

NOTIONS

Tapestry needle, stitch holders, two buttons
See page 240 for button details.

GAUGE

20 sts + 28 rows = 4" (10cm) in St st using size 7 needles, or size to obtain gauge

STITCH GUIDE

KF&B
Knit through the front loop of a stitch and then, without taking it off the needle, knit through the back loop of the same stitch. You've created two stitches from one.

---------------------------------- *instructions* ----------------------------------

While Phat Silk gave us an energized, complex surface by virtue of the fibers being kept relatively separate, Alchemy Yarns Synchronicity contains a thorough blending of silk and wool. The smooth, reflective surface is the perfect pond onto which designer Gina Wilde tosses a stone to achieve this gently rippling color effect.

Gina loves to drive the backroads of Sonoma County, California, to the Pacific Ocean. The beauty of this place where the elements meet—water and earth and air—is breathtaking, humbling, and truly awe-inspiring. The Seascape Bolero is her attempt to translate that exhilarating and meaningful color palette into knit expression.

This piece is also intended for those of us who ramble into a yarn shop in hopes of selecting one yarn for a project, only to fall in love with a whole group of colors. This piece lets you indulge in many favorite colors while gaining confidence and courage in working with a multicolored palette. Or you can stick with the semisolid, hand-painted colorway, as we did on page 83, to watch the gentle shifts and variations unfold against the smooth, reflective qualities of the silk.

Notes: This garment is knit in two pieces, each a mirror image of the other. Each piece is worked sleeve to sleeve, with only one color in play at all times. The two pieces are joined at the Back center seam in a three-needle BO.

Gauge is very important to this pattern. For the best fit results, make sure you match the stitch and row gauge. To help you work with this multicolored palette, make a simple color card to correlate the colors and the chart.

---------------------------------- *designed by Gina Wilde* ----------------------------------

Color Sequence Chart

COLOR	NUMBER OF ROWS
A	22
F	10
C	2
F	4
E	14
D	2
E	2
C	6
G	18
B	2
G	2
D	2
G	8
B	6
D	16
B	2

Begin shaping right Front and Back. The next row is where all sizing for the Front happens.

COLOR	NUMBER OF ROWS
B	10 (17, 24)
G	4
C	14
F	2
C	4
E	10
D	2
F	12 (End of Front)

For Back: Work 4 additional rows in F, followed by 4 rows in color A.

Cut a length of each color (6" [15cm] or so), tape it to an index card, and write the name and color letter next to each yarn sample.

RIGHT HALF

With larger needle and A, CO 65 sts for sleeve. Work 5 rows in St st.

Turning row for hem (WS): Knit.

Next row: Cont in St st. Follow Color Sequence Chart without shaping for 10" (25.5cm).

SHAPE SLEEVE

Increase row (RS): K1, kf&b, knit to last 2 sts, kf&b, k1. Rep this increase row every following sixth row to 81 sts—118 rows finished, approximately 17" (43cm).

SHAPE RIGHT FRONT AND BACK

At the beginning of the next row, CO 42 (47, 47) sts for Front, work across 81 sts, CO 42 (47, 47) sts for Back— 165 (175, 175) sts. (See note in Color Sequence Chart.) Purl one row.

FOR SIZE SMALL

Decrease row (RS): K1, k2tog, knit to end of row.

Cont in St st and follow Color Sequence Chart, working this decrease row every RS row until piece measures 4½" (11.5cm) from beginning of side edge—150 sts.

FOR SIZE MEDIUM

Cont in St st, work in B without shaping until piece measures 1" (2.5cm) from side edge, ending with a WS row.

Decrease row (RS): K1, k2tog, knit to end of row.

Cont in St st and follow Color Sequence Chart, work this decrease row every RS row until piece measures 5½" (14cm) from beginning of side edge—160 sts.

FOR SIZE LARGE

Cont in St st, work in B without shaping until piece measures 2" (5cm) from side edge.

Decrease row (RS): K1, k2tog, knit to end of row.

Cont in St st and follow Color Sequence Chart, working this decrease row every RS row until piece measures 6½" (16.5cm) from beginning of side edge—160 sts.

DIVIDE FOR NECK

On RS row, and keeping with lower front edge shaping as established, knit across 68 (73, 73) sts. Place remaining 82 (87, 87) sts on holder (for shoulder and Back). Work 2 rows without decreasing at neck edge, but cont lower edge shaping as established.

SHAPE NECK

Cont shaping lower front edge every RS row as established and *at the same time* decrease 1 st at neck edge *every other* RS row as follows: Knit to last 3 sts, sl1 k1 psso, k1. Rep until 42 (47, 47) sts remain. Piece should measure approximately 8 (9, 10)" (20.5 [23, 25.5]cm) from side edge. BO on next row, cont lower edge decreases as established—40 (45, 45) sts.

BACK

Place 82 (87, 87) sts from holder onto needle. With RS facing, BO 4 (5, 5) sts at beginning of row (for neck), then work in St st following Color Sequence Chart to end of row—78 (82, 82) sts. Remember to back up on the Color Sequence Chart to the place where the division was made for the neck, and work color stripes same as for the Front. At the end of the sequence, add 4 rows of F and 4 rows of A. Work until piece measures 9 (10, 11)" (23 [25.5, 28]cm). There is no decrease made on the Back of the jacket as there is for lower front edge. Place 78 (82, 82) sts on holder to be joined later with left half of bolero.

LEFT HALF

With larger needle and A, CO 65 sts for sleeve. Work 5 rows in St st.

Turning row for hem (WS): Knit.

Next row: Cont in St st. Follow Color Sequence Chart without shaping for 10" (25.5cm).

SHAPE SLEEVE

Increase row (RS): K1, kf&b, knit to last 2 sts, kf&b, k1. Rep this increase row every following sixth row to 81 sts—118 rows finished, approximately 17" (43cm).

SHAPE RIGHT FRONT AND BACK

At beginning of next row, CO 42 (47, 47) sts for Back, work across 81 sts, CO 42 (47, 47) sts for Front—165 (175, 175) sts. (See note in Color Sequence Chart.) Purl 1 row.

FOR SIZE SMALL

Decrease row (RS): Knit to last 3 sts, k2tog, k1.

Cont in St st and follow Color Sequence Chart, working this decrease row every RS row until piece measures 4½" (11.5cm) from beginning of side edge—150 sts.

FOR SIZE MEDIUM

Cont in St st, working in B without shaping until piece measures 1" (2.5cm) from side edge, ending with a WS row.

Decrease row (RS): Knit to last 3 sts, k2tog, k1.

Cont in St st and follow Color Sequence Chart, work this decrease row every RS row until piece measures 5½" (14cm) from beginning of side edge—160 sts.

FOR SIZE LARGE

Cont in St st, work in B without shaping until piece measures 2" (5cm) from side edge.

Decrease row (RS): Knit to last 3 sts, k2tog, k1.

Cont in St st and follow Color Sequence Chart, working this decrease row every RS row until piece measures 6½" (16.5cm) from beginning of side edge—160 sts.

DIVIDE FOR NECK

On RS row, and keeping with lower front edge shaping as established, knit 82 (87, 87) sts and place on holder (shoulder and Back), knit remaining 68 (73, 73) sts. Work 2 rows without decreases at neck edge, but cont lower edge shaping as established.

SHAPE NECK

Cont shaping lower front edge every RS row as established and *at the same time* decrease 1 st at neck edge every other RS row as follows: K1, ssk. Rep until 42 (47, 47) sts rem. Piece should measure approx 8 (9, 10)" (20.5 [23, 25.5]cm) from side edge. BO on next row, cont lower edge decreases as established—40 (45, 45) sts.

BACK

Place 82 (87, 87) sts from holder onto needle. With WS facing, BO 4 (5, 5) sts at beginning of row (for neck), then work in St st following Color Sequence Chart to end of row—78 (82, 82) sts. Remember to back up on the Color Sequence Chart to the place where the division was made for the neck, and work color stripes as for the Front. At the end of the sequence add 4 rows of F and 4 rows of A. Work until piece measures 9 (10, 11)" (23 [25.5, 28]cm). There is no decrease made on the Back of the jacket, as there is for lower front edge. Place 78 (82, 82) sts on holder, to be joined later with right half of the bolero.

Join Back seam in 3-needle bind-off or method of your choice.

BORDER

With smaller needle and A, begin at center Back, working along the bottom of the Back and Front, then up the Front to the center of the Back neck, pick up and knit approx 200 (210, 210) sts. Work in St st for 6 rows or 1" (2.5cm), ending with a RS row.

Turning row for hem (WS): Knit.

Cont in St st for 6 rows. BO all sts loosely.

Repeat for other side of bolero.

FASTENER

With A and smaller needle (preferably a dpn), CO 4 sts. Work in I-cord for 12" (30.5cm). BO all sts. With the tapestry needle, join I-cord at both ends to form a circle. Flatten the circle, with sides touching, to form one thick cord, approximately 6" (15cm). With A and tapestry needle, sew the circle together, leaving an opening at each end for buttons approx 1" (2.5cm) from each edge. Sew buttons approximately 2" (5cm) inside front edge and about 1" (2.5cm) below neck shaping, or as desired. Sew one side of I-cord closure to front, and leave the other side free.

FINISHING

With the tapestry needle, sew sleeve and side seams. Sew hems in place for cuffs and border bands. Weave in ends. Block lightly to size only if needed.

The back of the Seascape Bolero knit in a semisolid colorway.

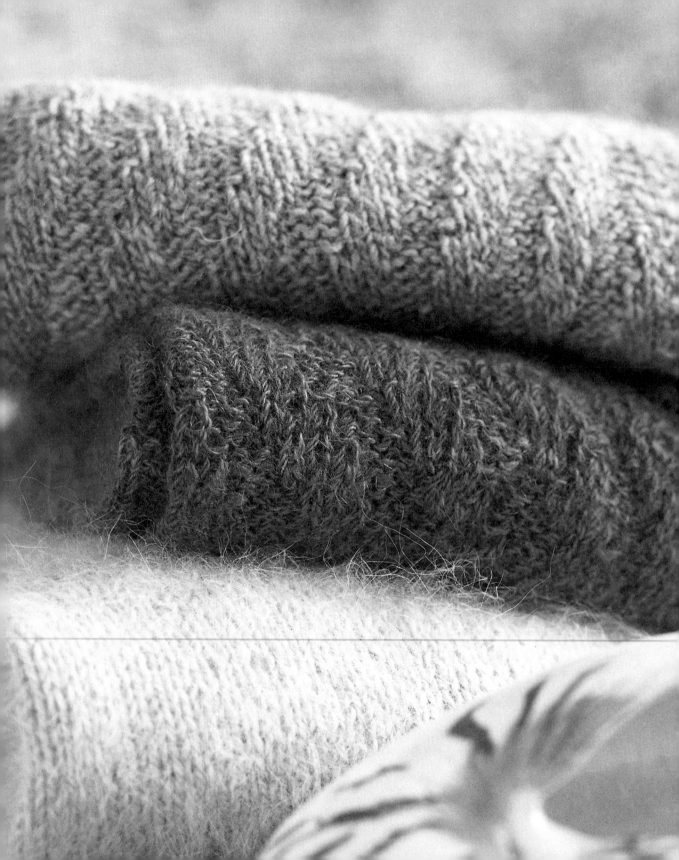

Two-Ply Yarns

If you take two single-ply yarns, line them up side by side, and allow them to release their excess twist by untwisting back on one another, you end up with a two-ply yarn. The degree of initial twist and plying twist varies dramatically, depending on the fibers, their preparation, and the intended results. But the important thing is that you now have a strand of yarn composed of two smaller strands. Because the excess twist on each strand has been released, two-ply yarns tend to be more balanced than singles.

As soon as you introduce a second ply into the mix, your yarn becomes stronger than it would be as a single. This is because you now have the energy and twist of two separate strands—plus the twist that plied them together—to hold all the fibers in place and help them withstand abrasion. Smoother fibers, such as alpaca, angora, and cashmere, benefit from a two-ply spin for added depth, dimension, and strength.

VISUAL EFFECTS

If you study a cross-section of two-ply yarn, you'll see that the yarn is actually oblong, not round. This is because it's made of two round strands of fiber that sit side by side. Their exact position constantly rotates, like a slow-motion airplane propeller, as the plies twist together along the strand.

Knit up, this produces a textured surface with a shadowy three-dimensionality that contrasts with the smooth brightness of single-ply yarns. The yarn's oblong shape helps it hold the fabric open, even in places where there's only air and shadow to be found. This makes two-ply yarns ideal for lace, where the stitches are open and well-defined.

Elsa Sheep and Wool Company two-ply Cormo wool

The Optic Waves Shawl (page 94) in Brooks Farm Primer

STEP RIBBED STOLE

--- details ---

FINISHED MEASUREMENTS

Length: 60" (152.5cm)

Width: **Stole A**: 15" (38cm); **Stole B**: 16" (40.5cm)

Note: If you want to make this a longer stole, you can add 2 more skeins of yarn and continue working until you achieve the desired length.

YARN

LIGHT

Stole A (right): Mostly Merino Fine Vermont Wool (75% Merino/fine wool,

25% kid mohair; 250 yds [229m]/ 125g) 4 skeins Natural Gray

Note: This yarn looks for all the world like a single ply, but it's actually made from two finer plies that are closely stranded together. Many quality "single-ply" yarns are actually spun this way. It gives you the visual benefits of a single ply with the strength, dimension, and durability of a double-ply.

Stole B (left): Buckwheat Bridge Angora (80% mohair, 20% fine wool; 180 yds [164.5m]/57g) 5 skeins Elderberry

If substituting, use 900 yds (823m)

light sport-weight yarn, preferably with some mohair, alpaca, or silk in the mix.

NEEDLES

One 24" (60cm) circular needle size 7 (4.5mm), or size to obtain gauge

NOTIONS

Tapestry needle, stitch markers (2)

GAUGE

23 sts + 24 rows = 4" (10cm) in pattern using Mostly Merino yarn (stole A)

22 sts + 20 rows = 4" (10cm) in pattern using Buckwheat Bridge Angora yarn (stole B)

--- instructions ---

This simple knit and purl diagonal pattern is easy to knit and can be worn with either side facing out. As the pattern flows along, the "steps" give the finished garment a sense of motion and depth, while a narrow seed stitch edge on the sides and ends frames the stole.

The artisanal yarns used for both stoles present a perfect example of what happens when you reverse the fibers in a blend. Stole A (right) is made from Mostly Merino yarn, a blend of 75 percent fine wool and 25 percent kid mohair. In this shawl the wool dominates, with just a subtle hint of shimmer and drape from the mohair. Meanwhile, stole B (left) reverses the proportions. It is made from Buckwheat Bridge Angora and contains 80 percent mohair from the Buckwheat Bridge flock and 20 percent fine wool. Now the drape and shine of the mohair clearly dominate, with the wool only giving a quiet foundation of body underneath. A nice twist: Some of the mohair in Mostly Merino comes from the Buckwheat Bridge angora goats.

Notes: Because this isn't a form-fitting garment, your gauge won't need to be 100 percent exact. But be aware that major changes in gauge may require more (or less) yarn than specified, and that the denser and bulkier your work, the firmer your stole will be and the less drape it may have.

This pattern will have you lay out a border of 5 sts in seed st at the beginning and end of each row. The 18-row pattern rep details just the sts in between those 5 sts at each end.

CO 88 sts and (k1, p1) across row. Knit the next 8 rows in seed stitch ([k1, p1] across the first row, then reverse and [p1, k1] across the second row, always doing the opposite of what you did the row before). Begin the 18-row pattern rep as follows:

Row 1: (RS) Work seed stitch for 5 sts, place marker (pm), (k3, p3) across the next 78 sts; pm, work final 5 sts in seed sitch. Always maintaining the 5-st seed stitch border, work the following patt rep between markers.

--- designed by Margaret Klein Wilson ---

Rows 2–3: *K3, p3; rep from * to end of row.

Row 4: *P1, k3, p2; rep from * to end of row.

Row 5: Knit the knit sts and purl the purl sts as they appear.

Row 6: Rep Row 4.

Row 7: *K1, p3, k2; rep from * to end of row.

Row 8: Rep Row 5.

Row 9: Rep Row 7.

Rows 10–12: *P3, k3; rep from * to end of row.

Row 13: *P2, k3, p1; rep from * to end of row.

Row 14: Rep Row 5.

Row 15: Rep Row 13.

Row 16: *K2, p3, k1; rep from * to end of row.

Row 17: Rep Row 5.

Row 18: Rep Row 16.

Rep this 18-row pattern until you have approximately 30 yds (27.5m) of yarn left, ending with Row 18. Work 9 rows in seed stitch BO in pattern.

FINISHING

Weave in ends, block lightly, and wear your new stole everywhere.

SIZES

3 months (6 months, 12 months, 24 months). Shown in 24 months.

FINISHED MEASUREMENTS

Chest width: 19 (20, 22, 24)" (48 [51, 56, 61]cm)

Length from neck to bottom hem: 8½ (9, 10, 12)" (21.5 [23, 25.5, 30.5]cm)

YARN

Blue Sky Alpacas Organic Cotton (100% undyed organic cotton; 150 yds [137m]/100g) 2 (2, 3, 4) skeins Nut #82. If substituting, use 225 (300, 375, 500) yds (206 [274, 343, 457]m) of 2-ply worsted-weight yarn.

NEEDLES

Size 9 (5.5mm) needles, straight or circular, or size to obtain gauge

NOTIONS

Stitch holders, darning needle, three ¾" (19mm) buttons

GAUGE

16 sts + 20 rows = 4" (10cm) in St st

STITCH GUIDE

BOX STITCH

Rows 1–2: *K2, p2; rep across row.

Rows 3–4: *P2, k2; rep across row.

It doesn't get much easier than this sweet little baby cardigan. Knit in four flat pieces, there are no extra button bands to work—just seam up the shoulders and side seams, sew on the buttons, and you're done. The soft, naturally colored, two-ply organic cotton knits up quickly and has an innate texture that conceals irregular stitches and adds intrigue to simple stockinette. Mission Falls 1812 Cotton is another excellent yarn candidate for this sweater.

Note: The front placket will be slightly asymmetrical.

BACK

CO 38 (40, 44, 48) sts and work box stitch for 8 rows. Change to St st and work for 4¼ (4½, 5, 6)" (11 [11.5, 12.5, 15]cm) from cast-on. Change back to box stitch and work until entire piece measures 7½ (8, 9, 10)" (19 [20.5, 23, 25.5]cm). With RS facing, work 12 (12, 14, 16) sts in box stitch pattern, BO center 14 (16, 16, 16) sts, work across remaining 12 (12, 14, 16) sts in box stitch. Work both shoulders separately in box stitch until piece measures 8½ (9, 10, 12)" (21.5 [23, 25.5, 30.5]cm). Place each shoulder section on holders.

SLEEVES (MAKE 2)

CO 20 (22, 24, 28) sts and work box stitch for 8 rows. Change to St st and increase 1 st each side every third row 7 (7, 8, 10) times (34 [36, 40, 48] sts). Work until sleeve measures 6 (6½, 7½, 8½)" (15 [16.5, 19, 21.5]cm). BO all sts.

LEFT FRONT

CO 18 (20, 22, 24) sts and work in box stitch for 8 rows. Next row on RS, work first 6 sts in box stitch, and the rest of the 12 (14, 16, 18) sts in St st. Work this way until piece measures 4¼ (4½, 5, 6)" (11 [11.5, 12.5, 15]cm) from cast-on edge. Change to box stitch across entire row, work until entire piece measures 7½ (8, 9, 10)" (19 [20.5, 23, 25.5]cm). On RS, BO first 6 (8, 8, 8)

------- *designed by Jennifer Hagan* -------

------------------------------------ *instructions continued* ------------------------------------

sts for neck, and cont in box stitch until entire piece measures 8½ (9, 10, 12)" (21.5 [23, 25.5, 30.5]cm), place remaining sts on holders.

RIGHT FRONT

CO 18 (20, 22, 24) sts and work in box stitch for 8 rows. Next row (RS), work in St st to last 6 sts, which will be worked in box stitch. Work this way until piece measures 4¼ (4½, 5, 6)" (11 [11.5, 12.5, 15]cm) from cast-on edge. Change to box stitch for entire row. At end of the first RS row, use backward loop to CO 6 extra sts to create the buttonhole tab. Work across these 24 (26, 28, 30) sts in box stitch, adding 3 buttonholes evenly over length of tab.

Work buttonholes as follows: On RS row, work to last 4 sts. BO 2 sts, work 2 sts in patt. Next row, work 2 sts in patt, CO 2 sts using backward loop cast-on. Remember to work these sts in patt. If on WS, work to last 4 sts. BO 2 sts, work 2 sts. On the next RS row, work 2 sts, CO 2 sts. Work until entire piece measures 7½ (8, 9, 10)" (19 [20.5, 23, 25.5]cm). On WS, BO first 12 (14, 14, 14) sts for neck, and cont in box stitch until entire piece measures 8½ (9, 10, 12)" (21.5 [23, 25.5, 30.5]cm), place the remaining sts on holders.

FINISHING

For best results, block each piece to measurement prior to assembling. You can seam the shoulders together using a 3-needle BO, or sew a seam across using running stitch or backstitching. Set in the sleeves and sew the side seams, from cuff to hem. Weave in all ends, attach buttons, and reblock.

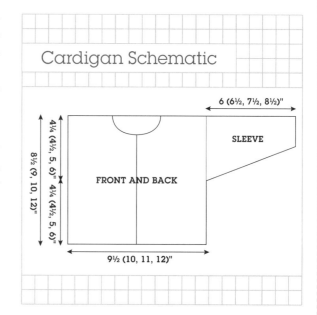

Cardigan Schematic

6 (6½, 7½, 8½)"

SLEEVE

4¼ (4½, 5, 6)"

4¼ (4½, 5, 6)"

8½ (9, 10, 12)"

FRONT AND BACK

9½ (10, 11, 12)"

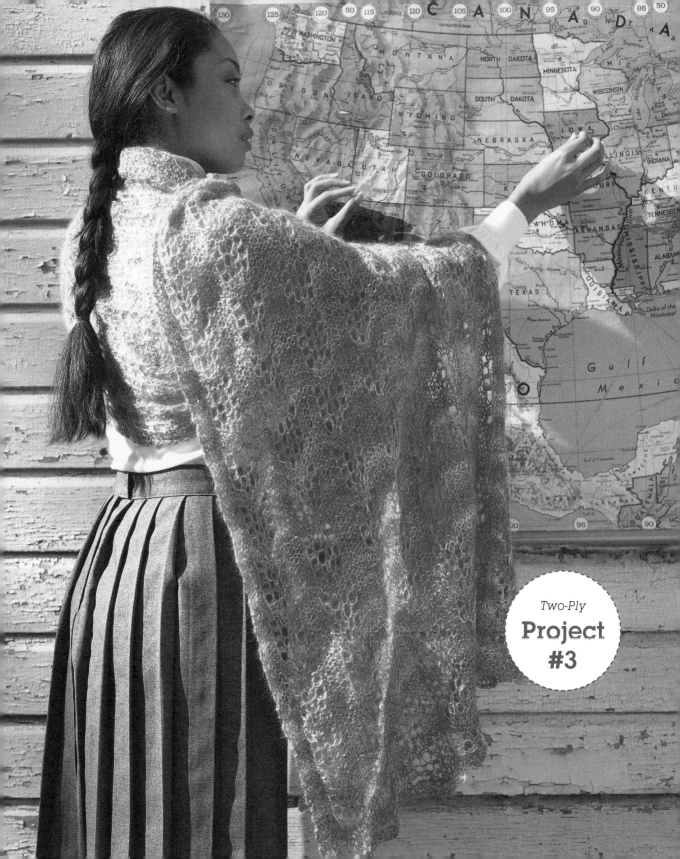

OPTIC WAVES SHAWL

-------------------------------- *details* --------------------------------

**FINISHED MEASUREMENTS
(AFTER WASHING AND BLOCKING)**
Width: 29" (73.5cm)
Length: 80" (203cm)

YARN

Brooks Farm Yarn Primero (100% kid mohair; 500 yds [457m]/227g) 2 skeins Orangeade. If substituting, use 800 yds (732m) of 2-ply DK-weight yarn.

NEEDLES
Size 8 (5mm) needles, choice of 14" (35.5cm) straight or 26–29" (66–74cm) circular, or size to obtain gauge

NOTIONS
Stitch markers

GAUGE
14 sts + 16 rows = 4" (10cm) in Optic Waves pattern

-------------------------------- *instructions* --------------------------------

If you've been to any of the major fiber festivals on the East Coast, chances are you've seen the crowds swarming the Brooks Farm Yarn booth. This Lancaster, Texas–based farm works magic with the mohair from its flock of angora goats. Instead of the normal bouclé or brushed effect, they keep it fluid and smooth—and are one of the few companies to do so. The yarn comes in massive 500-yard (457m) hanks that are dyed all sorts of bright, warm, clean hues. It's an irresistible yarn that can sometimes be tricky to match to a pattern because of its inelasticity, drape, and weight. This shawl was designed specifically to take advantage of those three features and to highlight the shifting waves of color with a simple series of increases and decreases.

Notes: If you prefer to work from a chart rather than from row-by-row written instructions, you can follow the Optic Waves Shawl chart.

Be aware that the first 3 and last 2 stitches of each row will always be worked in garter stitch and are not *represented in the chart.*

*You may also want to place stitch markers at the * of each repeat section to help keep the stitch counts correct for the motifs. Another visual aid is to "read" your knitting. When working the final k1 of each motif, check to see that (except for the garter bumps from Rows 1–4) the only knit stitches are below that stitch, all the way down your knitting.*

CO 101 sts using a flexible cast-on, such as long-tail or knitted cast-on (page 237).

Rows 1–4: Knit all sts.

Row 5: K3, *k2tog twice, (YO, k1) three times, YO, (sl1 k1 psso) twice, k1; rep from * to last 2 sts, k2.

Row 6: K3, purl to last 2 sts, k2.

Rows 7–12: Rep Rows 5–6 three times.

Rows 1–12 make up one rep of the Optic Waves pattern. These 12 rows are repeated until the shawl measures 56–60" (142–152.5cm), or approximately 27 pattern reps.

If you are a tight knitter, you may want to test-block a section of the shawl at this point to make sure that you

-------------------------------- *designed by Shelia January* --------------------------------

--- *instructions continued* ---

will be able to block out a full 25 percent additional length. While doing the test-blocking, there's no need to remove the live stitches from the needle. With mohair, the less transferring of stitches, the better. If you haven't achieved the length that you want, keep repeating the pattern until you are satisfied.

After finishing the pattern repeats, rep Rows 1–4. Bind off all stitches very loosely.

FINISHING

Wet-block (page 239) to size (80x29" [203x73.5cm]). You can use other blocking methods, but you'll need to be able to stretch the shawl out somewhat aggressively. It is also a good idea to weave in the yarn ends *after* blocking to ensure that they don't come out during the stretching process. If scalloped edges are desired, pin the garter stitch sections of the pattern out on both ends, either rounded or pointed.

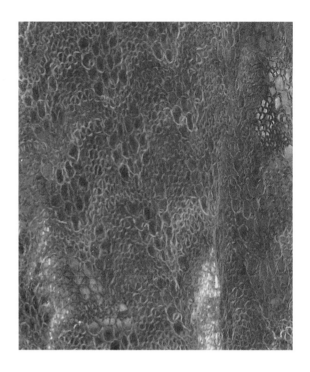

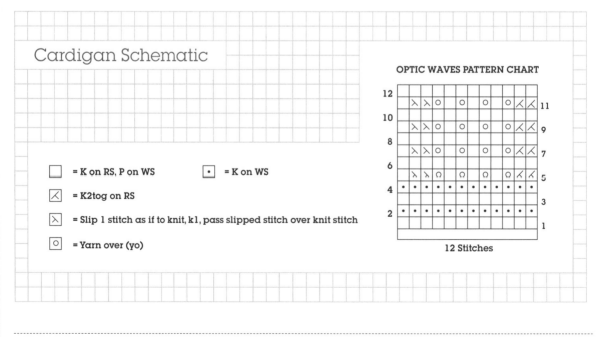

Cardigan Schematic

☐ = K on RS, P on WS   ⊡ = K on WS

╱ = K2tog on RS

╲ = Slip 1 stitch as if to knit, k1, pass slipped stitch over knit stitch

⊙ = Yarn over (yo)

OPTIC WAVES PATTERN CHART

12 Stitches

-- *details* --

FINISHED MEASUREMENTS
(BEFORE WASHING AND BLOCKING)
Width: 8" (20.5cm)
Length: 50" (127cm)

(AFTER WASHING AND BLOCKING)
Width: 9" (23cm)
Length: 52" (132cm)

YARN

SUPER FINE

Lorna's Laces Helen's Lace (50% silk, 50% wool; 1,250 yd [1,143m]/113.5g) 1 skein Pink Blossom. If substituting, use 300 yds (274m) of 2-ply laceweight yarn

NEEDLES
Size 5 (3.75mm) straight or circular needles, or size to obtain gauge

NOTIONS
Tapestry needle

GAUGE
Before blocking: 24 sts + 24 rows = 4" (10cm) in Raspberry Lace Pattern
After blocking under moderate tension: 20½ sts + 21¼ rows = 4" (10cm) in Raspberry Lace Pattern

STITCH GUIDE
KTBL-YO-K1
Knit 1 stitch through the back loop, wrap the yarn over your RH needle, then knit through the front loop of the same stitch.

K2TOG-K3TOG-PSO
Decrease 5 stitches at once by knitting 2 stitches together, then knitting 3 stitches together, then passing the first decrease stitch over the one you just made and off your needle.

CDD
Center double decrease. Slip 2 stitches as if to knit, knit 1 stitch, then pass both slipped stitches together over that stitch and off the right-hand needle.

RASPBERRY LACE PATTERN
6-st multiple plus 1; 8-row repeat.
Row 1 (RS): P3, ktbl, *p5, ktbl; rep from * to last 3 sts, p3.
Row 2: K3tog, *YO, ktbl-YO-k1, YO, k2tog-k3tog-pso; rep from * to last 4 sts, YO, ktbl-YO-k1, YO, k3togtbl.
Row 3: Ktbl, *p5, ktbl; rep from * to end.
Row 4: *P1, k5; rep from * to last st, p1.
Row 5: Rep Row 3.
Row 6: K1, M1, YO, *k2tog-k3tog-pso, YO, ktbl-YO-k1, YO; rep from * to last 6 sts, k2tog-k3tog-pso, YO, M1, k1.
Row 7: Rep Row 1.
Row 8: K3, *p1, k5; rep from * to last 4 sts, p1, k3.

-- *instructions* --

The first thing I ever knit with Helen's Lace was a scarf designed by Jackie Erickson-Schweitzer. When it came time to write this book, I knew I wanted to feature this yarn. And who better to create the design than Jackie? Here, she details her creative process for us.

Helen's Lace yarn is always a delight to use when designing knitted lace. The yarn's fine wool makes a soft and supple fabric, while the silk content imparts added drape and a touch of shimmer that is good for highlighting the texture in lace designs.

I have recently been attracted to designing lace with added textural and dimensional effects. This yarn's shimmer and subtle color shifts of flaming pink suggested a raspberrylike design.

I chose a scarf as my canvas for this project. The trellis lace border evokes the latticework of a basket in which the raspberries are placed. The target knitting gauge is loose enough to open up the lace nicely and make a gossamer fabric, yet firm enough to preserve the purl texture and slight puffing of the Raspberry Lace.

The completed scarf is lusciously soft and light, using not even 1 ounce (28g) of yarn. You can knit it as short or long as you want. Helen's Lace comes in huge 4-ounce (113.5g) skeins, leaving you plenty of leftovers for another scarf or whatever else the yarn tells you it wants to become. **—JACKIE ERICKSON-SCHWEITZER**

-- *designed by Jackie Erickson-Schweitzer* --

Notes: Because this isn't a form-fitting garment, your gauge doesn't need to be 100 percent exact. But be aware that major changes in gauge may require more (or less) yarn than specified. Too dense of a gauge will not retain the open, airy look of the lace. Too loose of a gauge can cause the texture of the raspberries to be lost.

BEGINNING BORDER

Cast on 49 sts loosely.

Row 1 (RS of outer border): Sl1 purlwise wyif, k1, (YO, ssk) 11 times, k1, (k2tog, YO) 11 times, k2.

Row 2: Sl1 purlwise wyif, p to last st, k1.

Row 3: Sl1 purlwise wyif, YO, (ssk, YO) 11 times, CDD, (YO, k2tog) 11 times, YO, k1.

Row 4: Rep Row 2.

Rows 5–8: Rep Rows 1–4.

Row 9: Rep Row 1.

Row 10 (Establish inner border pattern while maintaining 7 sts at each edge of scarf in the established outer border pattern): Sl1 purlwise wyif, p6, k35, p6, k1.

Row 11: Sl1 purlwise wyif, YO, (ssk, YO) 2 times, ssk, k35, k2tog, (YO, k2tog) 2 times, YO, k1.

Row 12: Rep Row 10.

MAIN AREA

Row 1 (RS—Establish main pattern while maintaining 9 sts at each edge of scarf in the established border patterns): Sl1 purlwise wyif, k1, (YO, ssk) 2 times, k3, p3, ktbl, (p5, ktbl) 4 times, p3, k3, (k2tog, YO) 2 times, k2.

Row 2: Sl1 purlwise wyif, p6, k2, k3tog, (YO, ktbl-YO-k1, YO, k2tog-k3tog-pso) 4 times, YO, ktbl-YO-k1, YO, k3togtbl, k2, p6, k1.

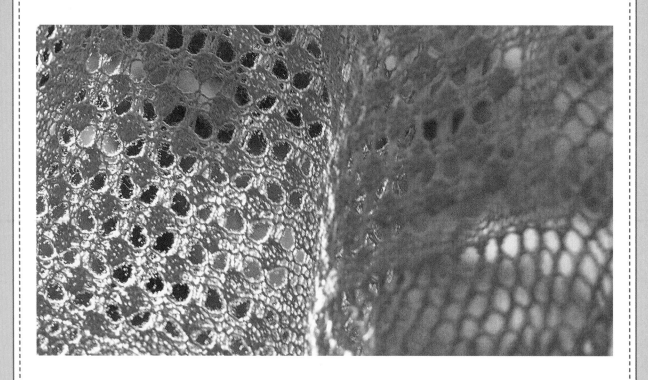

Row 3: Sl1 purlwise wyif, YO, (ssk, YO) 2 times, ssk, k2, ktbl, (p5, ktbl) 5 times, k2, k2tog, (YO, k2tog) 2 times, YO, k1.

Row 4: Sl1 purlwise wyif, p6, k2, (p1, k5) 5 times, p1, k2, p6, k1.

Row 5: Sl1 purlwise wyif, k1, (YO, ssk) 2 times, k3, ktbl, (p5, ktbl) 5 times, k3, (k2tog, YO) 2 times, k2.

Row 6: Sl1 purlwise wyif, p6, k2, M1, k1, YO, (k2tog-k3tog-pso, YO, ktbl-YO-k1, YO) 4 times, k2tog-k3tog-pso, YO, k1, M1, k2, p6, k1.

Row 7: Sl1 purlwise wyif, YO, (ssk, YO) 2 times, ssk, k2, p3, ktbl, (p5, ktbl) 4 times, p3, k2, k2tog, (YO, k2tog) 2 times, YO, k1.

Row 8: Sl1 purlwise wyif, p6, k2, k3, (p1, k5) 4 times, p1, k3, k2, p6, k1.

Rep Rows 1–8 until scarf measures approximately 40" (101.5cm) in a relaxed state, or about 50" (127cm) stretched to simulate blocking, *and completing Row 7.* If adjusting length, work until stretched length of 2" (5cm) less than desired finished blocked size.

ENDING BORDER

Row 1 (WS): Sl1 purlwise wyif, p6, k35, p6, k1.

Row 2: Sl1 purlwise wyif, k1, (YO, ssk) 2 times, k1, k35, k1, (k2tog, YO) 2 times, k2.

Row 3: Rep Row 1.

Work Rows 3–4 of Beginning Border, then Rows 1–4 of Beginning Border, then Rows 1–3 of Beginning Border again.

Bind off all sts loosely.

FINISHING

Weave in ends invisibly, either before blocking or afterward. If before, be sure to leave enough tail to allow for stretching and then trim any remaining ends after blocking has been completed.

Fill container with lukewarm water and a small amount of mild detergent. Mix thoroughly. Submerge scarf into water gently and soak at least thirty minutes (silk takes longer than you might think to become thoroughly wet). Drain and gently press out the majority of the water. Refill the container with water at the same temperature and rinse scarf gently. Again press out the majority of the water. Press the scarf between two thirsty bath towels (do not rub or wring) to remove even more water.

Block under tension by pinning the still-damp scarf on a flat surface while gently stretching it into shape and opening up the lace pattern nicely. Use as many pins as it takes to keep the edges as straight as possible. Let it dry thoroughly before removing the blocking pins.

VINES CARDIGAN

-- *details* --

SIZES
To fit women's size Small (Medium, Large, Extra-Large). Shown in size Medium.

FINISHED MEASUREMENTS
Bust: 34 (38, 42, 46)" (86.5 [96.5, 106.5, 117]cm)
Length: 19 (20, 21, 22)" (48 [51, 53.5, 56]cm)

YARN

Anny Blatt Angora Super (70% angora, 30% extra-fine wool; 116 yds [106m]/25g) 8 (9, 10, 11) skeins Loukhoum #641. If substituting, use 928 (1,044, 1,160, 1,276) yds (849 [955, 1,061, 1,167]m) of 2-ply DK-weight yarn.

NEEDLES
Two pairs of size 5 (3.75mm) straight needles, or size to obtain gauge
Two sets of size 5 (3.75mm) dpns, or size to obtain gauge

NOTIONS
Darning needle for seaming, scrap yarn for provisional cast-on and holding sleeves, clasp for the closure. Rhinestone clasp shown from Windsor Button (more information on page 240).

GAUGE
22 sts + 32 rows = 4" (10cm) in St st

STITCH GUIDE
LEAF PANEL PATTERN
Row 1 (RS): P2, k1, p2.
Row 2: K2, p1, k2.
Row 3: P2, YO, k1, YO, p2.
Row 4: K2, p3, k2.
Row 5: P2, k1, YO, k1, YO, k1, p2.
Row 6: K2, p5, k2.
Row 7: P2, k2, YO, k1, YO, k2, p2.
Row 8: K2, p7, k2.
Row 9: P2, k2, sl1 k2tog psso, k2, p2.
Row 10: K2, p5, k2.
Row 11: P2, k1, sl1 k2tog psso, k1, p2.
Row 12: K2, p3, k2.
Row 13: P2, sl1 k2tog psso, p2.
Row 14: K2, p1, k2.

-- *instructions* --

I challenged Amy to design this cardigan to prove a point: You *can* use angora for an entire sweater. You just have to think it through carefully. First, we chose a yarn that blends angora with wool for stability, durability, and a little cooler wear. To compensate for the fabric's natural warmth, we chose a cropped styling with three-quarter-length sleeves and an open front that's secured with a single rhinestone clasp. The airy leaf pattern along the raglan line adds another element of open ventilation. It's a delicate garment that may require slightly gentler wear than your average woolen, but every time you wear it, you're wrapping yourself in a bit of heaven.

Notes: Alternatives to a provisional cast-on (page 238): If you aren't yet familiar or comfortable with the provisional cast-on, you can also cast on for this project in your preferred method and simply sew up the hem as part of your finishing. Or you can cast on in your preferred method and, when instructed to undo the provisional CO and put those sts on another set of dpns, *simply go back to the cast-on row and pick up one loop that corresponds to each cast-on stitch and place them on another set of dpns instead.*

Be sure to read ahead in this pattern so you don't miss anything—it has several instances where you're given additional instructions to complete at the same time as you're following other instructions.

-- *designed by Amy King* --

instructions continued

SLEEVES (MAKE 2)

Using dpns, CO 46 (48, 50, 54) sts using a provisional cast-on. Join in the round, being careful not to twist. Mark the beginning of the round and knit 6 rounds. Purl 1 round. Knit 6 more rounds. Undo the provisional CO, putting those stitches on another set of dpns. Next round, knit 1 st from working needle with the corresponding stitch from the needle holding the CO sts. This creates a folded hem. Knit 2 rounds.

SLEEVE INCREASES

Rnd 1: Place marker (pm), k1, M1, knit to the last st, M1, k1.

Rnds 2–7: Knit all sts.

Rep Rnds 1–7 until there are 66 (72, 78, 84) sts. Then work in St st until sleeve measures 12½ (13, 13½, 14)" (32 [33, 34, 35.5]cm) from the beginning. Put the last 6 sts of round just completed and the first 6 sts of the next round together on one holder for the underarm— 12 sts total. Hold the rest of the sts on a scrap piece of yarn.

BODY

Using straight needles, CO 188 (210, 232, 254) sts using a provisional cast-on. Work St st for 6 rows. Purl 1 row. Work St st for 6 more rows. Undo the provisional CO, putting those stitches on another needle. In the next row, knit together one stitch from working needle with the corresponding stitch from the needle holding the CO sts. (You're creating a folded hem.) Cont working in St st until the body measures 12 (12½, 13, 13½)" (30.5 [32, 33, 34]cm) from the beginning. End by finishing a purl row.

YOKE

Body: K39 (45, 50, 56) sts, pm, p2, place the next 12 body sts on holder for underarm, p3 from the sleeve, pm, k48 (54, 60, 66) sts from the sleeve, pm, p3 from the sleeve, p2 from body, pm, k78 (88, 100, 110) sts for the Back, pm, p2, place the next 12 body sts on holder for underarm, p3 from the sleeve, pm, k48 (54, 60, 66) sts from the sleeve, pm, p3 from the sleeve, p2 from the body, pm, knit the last 39 (45, 50, 56) sts—272 (306, 340, 374) sts. At this point you will begin to work the Leaf Panel Pattern *at the same time* as you are working the raglan decreases.

Next row (WS): *Purl to marker, insert Leaf Pattern (*starting with Row 2*) between markers; rep from * across, end with p39 (45, 50, 56) sts. Cont to work body in St st, inserting the Leaf Panel as written between markers. *At the same time,* decrease for raglan sleeves every RS row as follows: *Knit to 2 sts before marker, k2tog, slip marker (sm), work Leaf Pattern, sm, ssk; rep from * across to end of row. On WS rows: Work sts as established, placing leaf panel between markers. Work a total of 21 (26, 28, 32) decreases as written. Then work rows as follows, corresponding to the size you are making.

FOR SIZE SMALL

RS: *Knit to 2 sts before the marker, k2tog, sm, p5, sm, ssk; rep from * across, work to the end of the row. **WS:** *Purl to marker, k5; rep from * across, work to end of row.

FOR SIZE MEDIUM

RS: *Knit to marker, sm, work corresponding row in leaf panel, sm; rep from * across, work to end of row. **WS:** Work sts as established, placing Leaf Panel between markers. Work these 2 rows one more time to complete the Leaf Panel.

instructions continued

FOR SIZE LARGE

No extra rows.

FOR SIZE EXTRA-LARGE

RS: *Knit to marker, sm, work corresponding row in Leaf panel, sm; rep from * across, work to end of row.

WS: Work sts as established, placing Leaf Pattern between markers. Work these 2 rows two more times to complete your leaf insertion.

ALL SIZES

At the same time when you have completed 2½ (3, 3¼, 3½)" (6.5 [7.5, 8, 9]cm) of Yoke, begin neck decreases as follows.

RS: K1, ssk, work across as written above to the last 3 sts, k2tog, k1.

WS: Work as established. Work the neck decrease every 4 rows 6 (7, 8, 9) times, then every RS row until you have worked all the rows as described for the corresponding size.

Put all the sts on a holder or length of scrap yarn for finishing.

FINISHING

Starting at the bottom hem on one side, work an applied 4-stitch I-cord up the front of the cardigan, around the neck (using the live neck stitches), and down the other side of the Front. An applied I-cord is worked like a standard I-cord (page 237) except that on every other row you pick up one stitch along the cardigan edge and knit it together with the first stitch of your I-cord. This creates an I-cord that is attached to your work. Bind off. Graft the underarm stitches. Weave in all ends. Block and attach the clasp.

GUERNSEY SOCKS

-- *details* --

SIZE
To fit women's size Medium foot. (Knit the foot shorter or longer to fit your specific size.)

FINISHED MEASUREMENTS
Cuff length: 7¼" (18.5cm)
Foot length: 9" (23cm)

YARN

Sock A (left): Elsa Sheep and Wool Company Cormo Wool (100% wool; 213 yds [195m]/71g) 2 skeins white.
Sock B (right): Tongue River Farm Sock Yarn (100% Icelandic wool; 600 yds [549m]/227g) 1 skein Creamy White (undyed). If substituting, use 330 yds (302m) of worsted-spun 2-ply sport-weight yarn.

NEEDLES
One set of size 3.25 (3mm) dpns, or size needed to obtain gauge

NOTIONS
Tapestry needle

GAUGE
28 sts + 40 rows = 4" (10cm) in St st

-- *instructions* --

Two-ply yarns tend to produce a pebbly surface similar to uncooked rice. It looks especially interesting in stitch patterns that incorporate stockinette with openwork and movement. Guernsey styling typically doesn't include the lacy openwork, but it certainly does have texture and movement—as evidenced in these socks.

Here we also have a perfect example of how wool fibers can vary from breed to breed. Sock A (left) was knit using Elsa Sheep and Wool Company's Cormo wool, a plush, short-staple fiber with great crimp and bounce. Sock B (right) was knit using Tongue River Farm's Icelandic wool, a far smoother, more durable, and lustrous fiber.

CO 60 sts and join in the round, making sure you don't twist the sts. Place a marker to indicate the beginning of the round. Work Rows 1–4 of the Rib Pattern Chart 4 times. After the ribbing is complete, knit one full round and purl one full round.
Next rnd: Start the Guernsey Cable Cuff Chart. Work 7 full repeats of the 8-row chart.

START HEEL
Row 1 (RS): K28, turn work.
Row 2 (WS): P2tog, p29, turn work. (You'll have 30 working sts.) Save the remaining 29 sts on a holder for the top of the foot.
Row 3: *Sl1, k1; rep from * across. Turn work.

Row 4: Sl1, purl across. Turn work.
Work Rows 3–4 until your heel flap measures 2½" (6.5cm) and the next facing row is a RS row.

TURN HEEL
Row 1 (RS): K17, ssk, k1. Turn work.
Row 2: Sl1, p5, p2tog, p1. Turn work.
Row 3: Knit to 1 st before the gap from the previous row's decreases, ssk, k1. Turn work.
Row 4: Purl to 1 st before the gap, p2tog, p1. Turn work.
Cont in this manner until you have 18 heel sts remaining.
The needle that holds your heel flap sts will be needle 1. Knit all sts on needle 1. Pick up and knit 18 sts along

-- *designed by Amy King* --

instructions continued

the left edge of the heel flap. Using needles 2 and 3, take 29 sts from the holder and work the first row of the Guernsey Cable Foot Chart. Using needle 4, pick up and knit 18 sts along the right edge of the heel flap, then knit the first 9 sts from needle 1. This is now the beginning of your round—83 sts.

GUSSET

Rnd 1: Knit all sts on needle 1. Work across needles 2 and 3 in the corresponding row of Guernsey Cable Foot Chart. Knit all sts on needle 4.

Rnd 2: Needle 1: Knit to the last 3 sts, k2tog, k1. Work across needles 2 and 3 in the corresponding row of Guernsey Cable Foot Chart. Needle 4: K1, ssk, knit to the end of round.

Work Rounds 1–2 of the Gusset until you have 59 sts.

Next rnd: Needle 1: Knit to the last 3 sts, k2tog, k1. Work across needles 2 and 3 in the corresponding row of Guernsey Cable Foot Chart. Needle 4: Knit to the end of the round—58 sts.

Work even, keeping needles 1 and 4 in St st and keeping needles 2 and 3 in the Guernsey Cable Foot until the foot of your sock measures 1½" (3.8cm) less than the overall desired length.

Next 2 rnds: Work all needles in St st.

SHAPE TOE

Rnd 1: Needle 1: Work to the last 3 sts, k2tog, k1. Needle 2: K1, ssk, knit to the end of the needle. Needle 3: Work to the last 3 sts, k2tog, k1. Needle 4: K1, ssk, knit to the end of the needle.

Rnd 2: Knit all sts.

Work Rounds 1–2 until 30 sts remain. Finish by knitting all sts on needle 1. Break yarn, leaving about 12" (30.5cm) of length. Kitchener the toe sts together and weave in all ends.

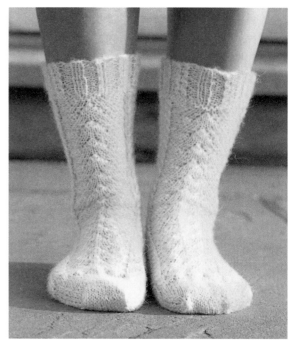

Sock B, in Tongue River Farm's lustrous Icelandic wool

Sock Charts

 = K on RS

• = P on RS

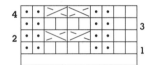 = P2tog

○ = Yarn over (yo)

= Slip next st onto cn and hold in back, k1, k1 from cn

= Slip next st onto cn and hold in front, k1, k1 from cn

= Slip 2 sts onto cn and hold in back, k2, k2 from cn

= Slip 2 sts onto cn and hold in front, k2, k2 from cn

RIB PATTERN CHART

10-Stitch Repeat

GUERNSEY CABLE CUFF CHART

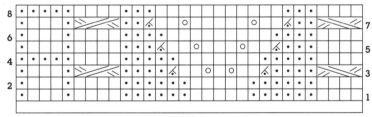

30 Stitches

GUERNSEY CABLE FOOT CHART

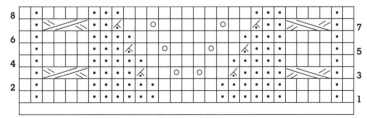

29 Stitches

LITTLE SHELLS SOCKS

----- details -----

SIZES
To fit women's size Medium (Large).
Shown in size Medium.

FINISHED MEASUREMENTS
Cuff length: 7½ (8½)" (19 [21.5]cm)
Foot length: 8 (9)" (20.5 [23]cm)

YARN

Satakieli (100% wool; 360 yds
[329m]/100g) 2 skeins #441.
If substituting, use 440 yds (402m)
fingering-weight yarn.

NEEDLES
One set of dpns size 1 (2.25mm)

NOTIONS
Tapestry needle, stitch marker

GAUGE
32 sts + 44 rows = 4" (10cm) in St st

STITCH GUIDE
LITTLE SHELLS LACE PATTERN
Rnds 1–2: Knit all sts.
Rnd 3: *K1, YO, p1, p3tog, p1, YO, k1;
rep from * to end of round.
Rnd 4: Knit all sts.

----- instructions -----

These socks were designed originally with handspun sock yarn using fiber of different wool types that had been dyed and blended together to make a heathery yarn. The originals were prizewinners at the Maryland and New York State Sheep and Wool festivals. The design emphasizes a tight gauge on the foot to ensure good wear—since this is a two-ply yarn—without the need for reinforcement. The cuff gives a lacy effect while remaining warm.

TOE
CO 10 sts using the long-tail cast-on method.
Knit flat in St st for ½" (13mm), ending with a RS row. *Do not turn work.*
Place marker to indicate the beginning of the round. Using the second needle, pick up and knit 4 sts, working counterclockwise along the edge immediately to the left of the last stitch knitted. *Do not turn work.*
Continue counterclockwise to the cast-on edge, and pick up and knit 10 sts along this edge.
Continue to the last side, pick up and knit 4 sts.
You now have a small rectangle, with a needle on each of the 4 sides—28 sts. The working yarn is back to the marker, indicating the beginning of the round.
Rnd 1: Knit.
Rnd 2: Needle 1: K10 sts across. Needles 2 and 4: K1, M1, k2, M1, k1. Needle 3: Knit all sts.

Rnd 3: Knit all sts—32 sts.
Rnd 4: Needles 1 and 3: Knit all sts. Needles 2 and 4: K2, M1, k2, M1, k2.
Rnd 5: Knit all sts—36 sts.
Rnd 6: Needles 1 and 3: Knit all sts. Needles 2 and 4: K3, M1, k2, M1, k3.
Rnd 7: Knit, rearranging sts on the needles so that the 2 middle sts of needles 2 and 4 become the last sts on needles 1 and 3. Move the stitch marker to the new beginning point of needle 1—40 sts.
Rnd 8: Needles 1 and 3: Knit to last st, M1, k1. Needles 2 and 4: K1, M1, knit to end.
Rnd 9: Knit all sts—44 sts.
Rep Rounds 8–9 until you have 56 (64) sts total. The toe is now complete.

----- *designed by Shelia January* -----

INSTEP

Cont knitting in the round in St st until the foot measures $5\frac{1}{2}$ ($6\frac{1}{2}$)" (14 [16.5]cm), including the toe, or approx $2\frac{1}{2}$" (6.5cm) shorter than desired foot length.

HEEL

In preparation, remove the stitch marker. Position the sts so they are all evenly distributed across the needles. The sts on needles 1 and 4 will be the heel/sole sts, and those on needles 2 and 3 will be the instep. Move 3 sts from each of the instep needles to the adjacent heel needles. There will now be 17 (19) sts on needles 1 and 4, and 11 (13) sts on needles 2 and 3. Combine the sts from needles 1 and 4 onto one needle. These are all of the working sts for the heel. The sts on needles 2 and 3 will rest and can be put on a stitch holder if desired until the heel is completed.

SHORT ROW HEEL (WORKED ON HEEL STS ONLY)

Row 1: Knit 33 (37) sts, turn work and bring yarn over your working needle, from back to front. (This will create a yarn-over loop at the beginning of the next row.)

Row 2: Purl 32 (36) sts, turn work and bring yarn from back to front.

Row 3: Knit 31 (35) sts, turn work and bring yarn from back to front.

Row 4: Purl 30 (34) sts, turn work and bring yarn from back to front.

Rep in same manner, working 1 loop at each row and bringing yarn from back to front each time until 10 stitches remain unworked.

Next row: K10. Do not knit the yarn-over loop, but turn work and bring yarn from back to front. (This will create a second yarn-over loop next to the first.)

Row 2: P10. Do not purl the yarn-over loop, but turn work and bring yarn from back to front. (This will create a second yarn-over loop next to the first.)

HEEL DECREASE ROWS

Note: Make sure to correct the mount of your yarn-over loops so that the right leg of the st is on the front of the left needle when you work the sts.

Row 1: Knit across sts until the next 2 sts are yarn-over loops, k3tog (the 2 loops with the next st). Turn work and bring yarn from back to front.

Row 2: Purl across sts until the next 2 sts are yarn-over loops, p3tog (the 2 loops with the next st). Turn work and bring yarn from back to front.

Rep Rows 1–2, working in the yarn-over loops and bringing yarn from back to front each time until you have 2 rows left with double yarn-over loops.

Next row: K32 (36), k3tog (last 3 sts on the needle), turn.

Last heel row: YO, p33 (37), p2tog (last 3 sts on the needle), turn.

You will now begin knitting in the round again, including the instep stitches that have been sitting idle while the heel was worked.

Next rnd: YO, k17 (19), pm, which will mark the back of the heel, k17 (19) sts. Knit the yarn-over loop together with the first st of the instep needle, which resumes the round. If there is a hole forming at the intersection of the heel and the instep sts, pick up and knit an additional st, which can be decreased away in the next round. K21 (25) sts, to 1 st before the end of the instep sts. Ssk the last instep stitch with the yarn-over loop on the next needle. Another st can be picked up and knit if a hole is noted, again to be decreased away in the next round. Knit to marker—55 (63) sts.

instructions continued

CUFF

Knit 4 rounds. (For size Medium, increase 1 st in the fourth round for a total of 56 sts.)

Begin Little Shells Lace Pattern (page 111) and work for 5 (6)" (12.5 [15]cm), or until the desired cuff length less 2½" (6.5cm) is reached, ending with Round 4 of Little Shells Lace Pattern. (For size Large, increase 1 stitch in the fourth round for a total of 64 sts.)

Switch to (k1, p1) rib for the next 2½" (6.5 cm). BO in rib extremely loosely using a needle 2 sizes larger to achieve a stretchy cuff.

FINISHING

Weave in the loose ends and enjoy.

ENDPAPERS SHAWL

-------------------------------------- *details* --------------------------------------

FINISHED MEASUREMENTS (LIGHTLY BLOCKED)
Width: 64" (162.5cm)
Depth: 41" (104cm)

YARN

Color A: Koigu Premium Painter's Palette Merino (100% Merino, 175 yds [160m]/50g) 3 skeins #P621 (multicolored, with fuchsia and red tones). If substituting, use 525 yds (480m) multicolor 2-ply fingering-weight yarn.

Color B: Koigu Premium Merino Solid (100% Merino, 175 yds [160m]/50g) 1 skein each (#2233 medium rose pink), (#2120 cherry red), and (#1170 fuchsia). If substituting, use 175 yds (160m) each of three solid colors in 2-ply fingering-weight yarn.

NEEDLES
All 24" (60cm) circulars
One size 11 (8mm), or size to obtain gauge
One size 10½ (6.5mm), or size to obtain gauge
One size 9 (5.5mm), or size to obtain gauge

One size 7 (4.5mm), or size to obtain gauge

NOTIONS
Different-colored stitch markers

GAUGE
20 sts + 30 rows = 4" (10cm) in St st using size 7 needles

STITCH GUIDE
CDD
Center double decrease. Slip 2 stitches as if to knit, knit 1 stitch, then pass both slipped stitches together over that stitch and off the right-hand needle.

-------------------------------------- *instructions* --------------------------------------

Hand-painted yarns tend to create horizontal lines of color as you work with them. Here we tilt that horizontal tendency on the diagonal with undulating increases and decreases along the border. This two-ply, Canadian hand-painted Merino has extraordinary color groupings, long-wearing strength, and a surprising amount of spring and cohesion. Watching the colors unfold, Elanor was reminded of the Italian marbled endpapers in sleek, leather-bound classics—hence, the name of this shawl.

Notes: Pay attention on Row 5 of the border. On this row you will work decreases to form unit shaping at the edges of units B and C only. On all other RS rows, you will be working both the unit shaping and the stitch pattern decreases.

BORDER
With size 11 needles and A, CO 315 sts. Change to size 10½ needles and knit two rows. These will be your foundation.

Begin st patt on next row as follows: K3, work Chart B once over 21 sts, work Chart A 11 times over 111 sts, work Chart C once over 21 sts, YO, CDD, work Chart B once over 21 sts, work Chart A 11 times over 111 sts, work Chart C once over 21 sts, k3.

Each RS row will decrease your stitch count by 4 sts. *Tip: Use a different colored marker to set off repeats within the units. For example, use a red marker between units and green markers within the repeats. This will help you keep track of where to work the garment decreases.*

At the same time, after the first 12 patt rows, change to size 9 needles and work the next 12 patt rows. Change to size 7 needles for the final 18 rows, 44 rows total, including 2 foundations rows—235 sts.

MIDDLE
With RS facing, and using size 7 needles and the darkest solid in color B group, you'll begin working short rows, incorporating 1 border stitch at the end of every row.

-------------------------------------- *designed by Elanor Lynn* --------------------------------------

--- *instructions continued* ---

Slip stitches so that you have 5 sts before the CDD on the border (between units B and C).

Using short rows, work the next 10 rows as follows, adding 1 st at each end by working 1 additional stitch from border (in St st).

Row 1: K2tog, k3, YO, k1, YO, k3, ssk.

Row 2 and all even rows: Purl.

Row 3: K1, k2tog, k3, YO, k1, YO, k3, ssk, k1.

Row 5: K2, k2tog, k3, YO, k1, YO, k3, ssk, k2.

Row 7: CDD, k2tog, k2tog, k1, YO, k1, YO, k1, ssk, ssk, CDD.

Row 9: K1, CDD, k3, YO, k1, YO, k3, CDD, k1.

Row 10: Purl. (There are now a total of 14 sts being worked in this row.)

Work the Fir Cone Chart, beginning on Row 11. Cont to add 1 st at the end of each row, working the newly incorporated sts in St st until there are enough stitches to start a new rep. In this way, you will gradually eat up all the border sts. The patt shift of Fir Cone will cause the number of sts being worked to increase only every other row. The st count will increase by 15 sts in the next 10-row patt rep, and by 20 sts every 2-patt rep, or 20 rows.

At the same time, after working 100 rows, switch to the second-darkest solid in color B group (medium color) and work the entire skein, then switch to the lightest solid in color B group to work the remainder of the middle of the shawl. If needed, switch back to A for the remainder of the middle. When all the border stitches are gone, change to size 10½ needles to bind off. This is to ensure that your cast-off edge is not too tight, which would draw your shawl into a horseshoe shape.

TOP EDGE

With RS facing and using size 9 needles and A, work k1, YO, k1 in the very first st of the Chart B edge. Then work another k1, YO, k1 as close as possible to the next garter ridge. Cont across the Chart B edge, work k1, YO, k1 in or next to each garter ridge, for a total of 7 times—21 sts. Work the last of the 7 reps at the intersection of the Border and Middle sections. Cont picking up over the Fir Cone middle section by working k1, YO, k1 in the center stitch of the Chart A motifs, and in the last YO between motifs, across the entire middle section—144 sts. Work the final Chart B Border section as you did for the beginning of row, rep the k1, YO, k1 7 times, with the last rep in the last stitch—21 sts. This gives you a total of 187 sts for the top border.

Knit 3 rows, ending with WS row.

Next row (RS): K21, then work eyelet row as follows: *Double yarn over (wrap yarn twice around needle), k3; rep from * across to the last 21 sts, double yarn over, k21.

Next row (WS): Knit the next row, working each double yarn over from the previous row as follows: Knit into the first loop, purl into the second.

Knit 2 rows, ending with the WS. BO all sts with size 11 needles.

Weave in all ends.

FINISHING

Dampen or wash the shawl in mild soap and roll in towels to remove excess water. Lace looks best stretched to emphasize the holes, but Merino will only take so much blocking before bouncing back to its original crimpy shape. Lay flat to dry, stretching to finished measurements. If you find that the shawl stretched too much with wash, you can always put it in the dryer on a low setting for a few minutes before blocking.

Shawl Charts

☐ = K on RS, p on WS

• = P on RS, k on WS

⟋ = K2tog on RS, p2tog on WS

⋏ = Slip 2 stitches as if to knit, k1, pass both
   slipped stitches together over knit stitch

○ = Yarn over (yo)

FIR CONE PATTERN CHART

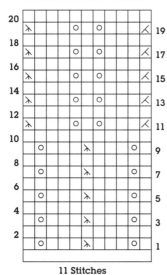

11 Stitches

RAZOR SHELL PATTERN

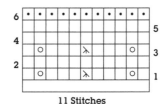

11 Stitches

Shawl Charts

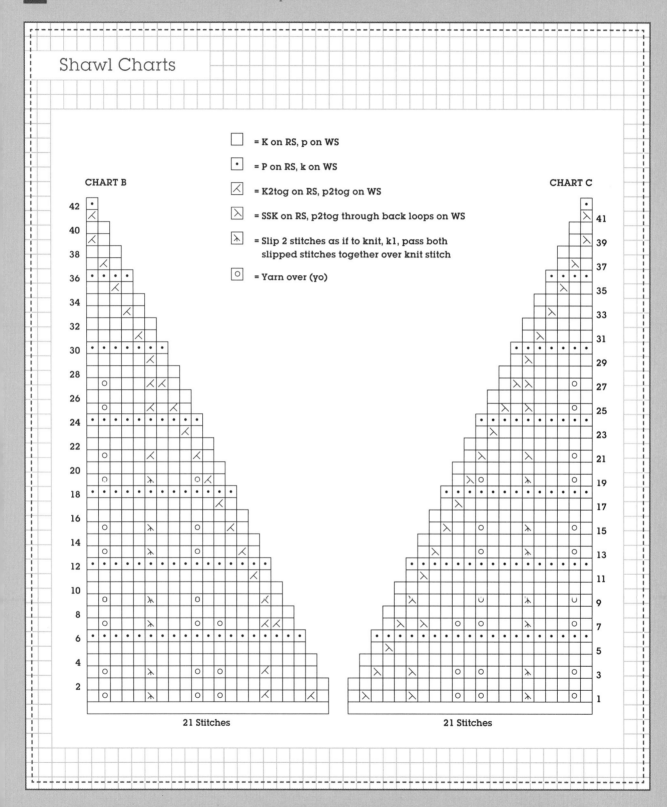

☐ = K on RS, p on WS

· = P on RS, k on WS

⟋ = K2tog on RS, p2tog on WS

⟍ = SSK on RS, p2tog through back loops on WS

⅄ = Slip 2 stitches as if to knit, k1, pass both slipped stitches together over knit stitch

○ = Yarn over (yo)

CHART B

CHART C

21 Stitches

21 Stitches

DOUBLE-THICK MITTENS

-- *details* --

SIZE

Adult women's Medium. This pattern is for one size only, but just a small adjustment of gauge will allow the mitten to fit a larger or smaller hand. Aim for a mitten with a circumference of about ½" (13mm) larger than the palm of your hand.

FINISHED MEASUREMENTS

Cuff: 4½" (11.5cm)
Hand circumference: 8" (20.5cm)
Length: 10" (25.5cm)

YARN

Alice Starmore Hebridean 2 Ply (100% new wool; 93 yds [85m]/25g) 3 skeins Fulmar (brown) (A) and 1 skein Red Rattle (red) (B). If substituting, use 270 yds (247m) of A and 93 yds (85m) B in 2-ply fingering-weight woolen-spun yarn.

NEEDLES

Set of five size 0 (2mm) dpns, or size to obtain gauge

NOTIONS

Tapestry needle, scrap yarn of the same weight, a spare dpn for hemming

GAUGE

34 sts + 36 rows = 4" (10cm) in 1x1 stranded knitting

STITCH GUIDE

1X1 STRANDING

This pattern is double-stranded throughout, even the solid body of the mitten, to create a mitten that's thick and warm even though it's knit from fingering-weight yarn. The single-color stranded section can be knit from two balls of A, or from both ends of the same ball. You will be alternating one knit stitch from each ball of yarn. I found it very easy to keep one strand in the left hand, picking that with the needle, Continental style, and throwing one strand with the right hand, English style. Knitting moves along quickly with this method, and it guarantees that the strand in the left hand is carried under and the strand in the right hand is carried over, creating a lovely vertical ridging to the St st.

LEFT-POINTING BRAID

Rnd 1: With two strands of B, holding both strands in front of the work, purl around, alternating each strand over the other for every st.

Rnd 2: Purl around, alternating strands, this time bringing each strand under the other for every st.

RIGHT-POINTING BRAID

Rnd 1: With two strands of B, holding both strands in front of the work, purl around, alternating each strand under the other for every st.

Rnd 2: Purl around, alternating strands, this time bringing each strand over the other for every st.

-- *instructions* --

The details are what make these mittens. They have a hemmed picot edging, Latvian braids at the cuff, tasseled ties to keep them together when not in use, and a "beaded" edge at the top decreases. There's just enough patterning to make them an interesting knit, and the patterning itself is bold and a bit modern, which is a fun contrast to the classic techniques and yarn (with delicate heathered hues only Alice Starmore could create). The flared cuff is created by the slight difference in gauge between the charted stranded sections and the 1x1 stranding, and can be blocked to further flare, according to taste.

Notes: These mittens are knit in the round with 5 dpns, with sts arranged so there are 17 sts on each of the 4 needles. You will use the 5th needle for knitting. Needles are referred to by number, with the first needle of the round as needle 1 and so on.

The charts for this pattern, which appear on page 125, are for stranded knitting with all stitches knit in stockinette (knit every round). Additionally, these charts are read from right to left on all rows, since the mitten is worked in the round.

-- *designed by Adrian Bizilia* --

RIGHT MITTEN

HEM AND BRAID

With B, single stranded, cast on 68 sts. Join in the round, being careful not to twist. Divide sts evenly onto four dpns. Knit 8 rounds in St st.

Next rnd: *YO, k2tog; rep from * around. Knit two rounds even. Add in second strand of B and knit Left-Pointing Braid. Cut second strand of B leaving 6" (15cm) tail for weaving in. Knit 4 rows even and pause to weave in all ends. Fold up the hem with the crease at the YO, k2tog row to create the picot edge. With a spare dpn, pick up a loop from the cast-on edge that directly corresponds to the first st on the left-hand needle, and place it to the right of that st. Knit the two sts together. Go onto the second st and knit it together with the corresponding st from the cast-on row in the same manner. Cont around, making sure the sts you are knitting together are perfectly vertically aligned or you will create a bias to the fabric.

CUFF DETAIL

Add in 1 strand of A and begin Chart A, working the chart once on each needle.

BODY OF MITTEN

Cut B strand and add in second strand of A. Work 1x1 stranding until work measures 5" (12.5cm) total.

Next rnd: K35 sts, knit in scrap yarn for thumb placement over 14 sts. Slip those 14 sts back onto left-hand needle and knit across them in 1x1 stranding. Cont knitting in this manner until work measures 9" (23cm) total. (Now is the time to add or subtract a little length if your hands are larger or smaller than the mittens shown in the schematic.)

MITTEN TOP

Cut 1 strand of A and add 1 strand of B. Begin Chart B, knitting it once over needles 1 and 2 and again over needles 3 and 4. At the end of needles 2 and 4, bring B over A before beginning to knit needles 3 and 1. This creates a little "bead" of the B between the decreases. After finishing Row 14 in Chart B, cut A and arrange first 8 sts on 1 needle, held in front, and second 8 sts on second needle, held behind. Use 3-needle BO to close hole.

THUMB

Go back and remove scrap yarn and place the 14 lower sts on one needle and the upper 14 sts on two needles. Knit around in 1x1 stranding, picking up 1 st between needles 1 and 2 and another st between needles 3 and 1. Close the hole created by these picked-up sts by knitting into the back of the stitch. You'll now have 30 sts on the needles. Knit even to 2¼" (5.5cm), then begin thumb decrease as follows, still in 1x1 stranding:

Needle 1: Ssk, knit across to last 3 sts, k2tog.

Needle 2: Ssk, knit across.

Needle 3: Knit to last 3 sts, k2tog.

Cont in this manner until 14 sts rem. Cut one strand and do 3-needle BO as for mitten top.

LEFT MITTEN

Work as for Right Mitten, except substitute Right-Pointing Braid on this side and place the 14 thumb sts after the 53rd st.

FINISHING

TIES AND TASSELS

Cut one strand of each color, 45" (114cm) long. Thread them on tapestry needle and put through hem of mitten

at outside edge (the side without the thumb) in one picot hole and out the next. Pull so yarn is the same length on both sides. Take both strands of B in one hand and both strands of A in the other hand and twist in opposite directions. Pause and let one strand twist onto itself to see if you like how it looks. If it needs more twist, continue until you're satisfied with the results.

Grasp all 4 yarn ends in one hand and pull on the mitten to make sure the strands are still of even lengths. Hold the mitten up in the air by the ties and allow them to twist. Tie overhand knot at 11" (28cm). Cut 5 strands of A 6" (15cm) long and thread them onto a tapestry needle. Push them through the tie, just above the knot. Fold them down over to create a tassel and tie it around the knot with another strand of A. Tie off and, with the tapestry needle, pull thread down into the center of the tassel. Trim ends evenly. Repeat these same steps with the second mitten.

Wash and block to size. Flare the cuff as desired. Enjoy how the yarn softens and blooms.

Double-Thick Mittens

A = K on RS with A

B = K on RS with B

◸ = K2tog on RS

◹ = SSK on RS

CHART A

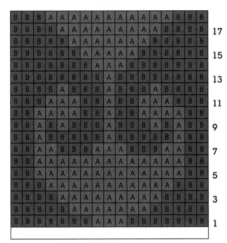

17 Stitches

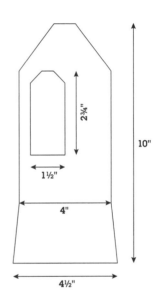

CHART B

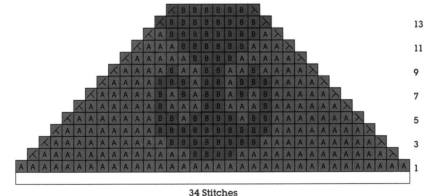

34 Stitches

Just as a three-legged stool is perfectly balanced and will never wobble, three-ply yarns have marvelous stability, balance, and a rounded shape that produces well-defined stitches that fill up their space beautifully. But whereas the stool may lose its balance as you add more legs to it, a yarn becomes stronger and more cohesive with each ply you add. By the time that third ply gets added to the mix, you have a yarn that's well-suited for projects that get high abrasion—such as socks and mittens for rugged everyday wear.

Generally speaking, the more plies you have, the greater the tendency for the yarn to be worsted. This is because woolen-spun wants to be lofty and open. Add more plies, and you need a bulkier yarn to hold it all. But worsted-spun yarns love more plies.

Crystal Palace three-ply worsted-spun Aran

From three plies onward, many of these yarns will start to look alike. Many times they are alike, but sometimes you'll be able to decipher differences by studying the fiber content, tightness of the twist, and angle of the ply. The only generally accepted rule is that the more plies you have in the yarn, the stronger it will be—keeping in mind that each ply adds density to your yarn and more weight to the finished garment. So, while an eight-ply worsted-spun yarn may be ideal in terms of durability, it will also be quite dense. But by the time that third ply gets added to the mix, you have a yarn that's well-suited for projects that get high abrasion—such as the Rhinebeck Mitts (pattern on page 128) and Swirly O Socks (pattern on page 140).

Worsted- and most woolen-spun three-ply yarns have more visible ply lines than their two-ply counterparts.

But these lines and shadows tend to be finer and more subtle, blending more readily into the yarn's overall surface. Three-ply yarns have a more rounded surface in which each ply always has something to lean against. While they may not be as perfectly round as single-ply yarns, they make up for this by having far greater balance and strength.

On the commercial market, woolen-spun yarns rarely exceed three plies. This structure gives you the strength and durability of three plies while still maintaining a decent degree of loft and openness, since the more plies you add, the more compressed the fibers may become. Three-ply woolen-spun yarns produce soft stitches that fill up their space beautifully. They render a mellow colorwork with a surface cohesion that conceals any colors being stranded along the back side of your work.

Meanwhile worsted-spun yarns, with their smoother, more compressed fibers, thrive in the presence of multiple plies. They're just getting started when they have three plies, and they don't really reach their pace until they have five, six, or sometimes even more plies in the mix. In Norah Gaughan's Cabled Swing Cardi on page 134, you can see how a three-ply worsted-spun yarn renders cables and texture stitchwork with crisp clarity and sculptural definition.

RHINEBECK HAT AND MITTS

SIZES

To fit head size Small (Large): 20 (22)"
(51 [56]cm). Shown in size Small.

FINISHED MEASUREMENTS

Circumference: 17½ (19½)" (44.5
[49.5]cm)

YARN

Spirit Trail Fiberworks Bluefaced
Leicester (100% Bluefaced Leicester
wool; 200 yds [183m]/68g) 1 skein
Plum and 1 skein River. If substituting,
use 200 yds (183m) of 3-ply sport-
weight yarn in solid for A and 60 yds
(55m) variegated for B. (Note: Lorna's
Laces Shepherd Sport is an excellent
over-the-counter substitution.)

NEEDLES

One 16" (40cm) circular needle size 5
(3.75mm)
One set of dpns size 5 (3.75mm)

NOTIONS

Tapestry needle, stitch markers

GAUGE

22 sts + 32 rows = 4" (10cm) in St st

STITCH GUIDE

REV ST ST
Reverse Stockinette stitch (rev St st in
pattern) achieved in the round by
purling all rounds.

This set was originally done in handspun yarn from Tunis sheep wool, which was the featured breed at the 2005 New York State Sheep and Wool Festival in Rhinebeck, New York. The design was specifically chosen to coordinate a solid yarn with a variegated yarn in a Fair Isle pattern. This differs from the traditional Fair Isle style of using several yarns for the colorwork. But it's still done in the traditional manner, with only two yarns used in each row. Only the random changes in the contrast color yarn create a pattern that is more interesting than a single solid contrast would be.

With A, CO 96 (108) sts. Place marker and join in the round, taking care not to twist the stitches.

Work in reverse stockinette stitch (rev St st) for 5 rounds.

On Rnd 6, switch to St st, knitting every rnd, for 3 (5) rnds.

Next rnd: Join B and work Chart A for one round. Knit 3 rounds in A.

Next rnd: Using A and B, work the 3 rounds of Chart B. Knit 3 rounds in A.

Next rnd: Using A and B, work the 13 rounds of Chart C. Knit 3 rounds in MC.

Next rnd: Using A and B, work the 3 rounds of Chart D. Knit 3 rounds in A.

Next rnd: Using A and B work Chart A for one round. You are now finished with B. All remaining work will be done in A.

Work the next 2 (3) rounds in rev St st. These three rounds are the corner edge between the brim and crown of the hat.

instructions continued

CROWN

Row 1: *K10, k2tog; rep from * around—88 (99) sts.

Row 2 and all even-numbered rows: Knit all sts.

Row 3: *K9, k2tog; rep from * around—80 (90) sts.

Row 5: *K8, k2tog; rep from * around—72 (81) sts.

Row 7: *K7, k2tog; rep from * around—64 (72) sts.

Row 9: *K6, k2tog; rep from * around—56 (63) sts.

Row 11: *K5, k2tog; rep from * around—48 (54) sts.

Row 13: *K4, k2tog; rep from * around—40 (45) sts.

Row 15: *K3, k2tog; rep from * around—32 (36) sts.

Row 17: *K2, k2tog; rep from * around—24 (27) sts.

Row 19: *K1, k2tog; rep from * around—16 (18) sts.

Row 21: K2tog around—8 (9) sts.

FINISHING

Break yarn and, using a tapestry needle, run the end of the yarn through the 8 (9) sts and pull tight. Weave in this and all other yarn ends. If necessary, the hat can be steam-blocked over a form or a towel folded and rolled to the appropriate shape.

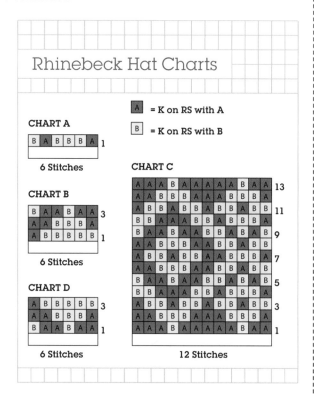

Rhinebeck Hat Charts

---

rhinebeck mitt details

SIZES
To fit size Small (Large). Shown in size Small.

FINISHED MEASUREMENTS
Length: 6 (7)" (15 [18]cm)
Palm circumference: 6 (7)" (15 [18]cm)

YARN

Spirit Trail Fiberworks Bluefaced Leicester (100% Bluefaced Leicester wool; 200 yds [183m]/68g) 1 skein Plum (A) and 1 skein River (B). If substituting, use 200 yds (183m) of 3-ply sport-weight yarn in solid for A and 60 yds (55m) variegated for B.

NEEDLES
One set of dpns size 4 (3.5mm), or size to obtain gauge

NOTIONS
Tapestry needle, stitch markers

GAUGE
24 sts + 33 rows = 4" (10cm) in St st

---

rhinebeck mitt instructions

The following instructions are for one mitt—the second is worked identically to the first. Since the color charts are nearly identical, and the Thumb Gusset is symmetrical, each mitt will fit either hand.

Notes: These mittens are designed for sizes Small and Large (Large size given in parentheses) based on the length of the hand from the base of the thumb to the end of the index finger. If the measurement is 7" (18cm) or longer, knit the Large. If it's shorter than 7" (18cm), knit the Small.

Cast on 36 (42) stitches. Place marker (pm), and join in a circle to begin working in the round.

Work in reverse stockinette stitch (rev St st) for 4 (5) rounds. Rev St st in the round is achieved by working purl rounds rather than knit rnds.

Change to (k1, p1) ribbing and work 12 rounds.

Knit 1 round, increasing 1 st in that round—37 (43) sts.

GUSSET INCREASES

K18 (21) sts, pm, M1, k1, M1, pm, knit to the end of the round. These markers indicate the placement of the Thumb Gusset (detailed in the Thumb Gusset Chart), which will be worked between the markers as the palm stitches are being worked. You will now have a total of 3 markers in the mitten, one indicating the beginning of the round, and 2 marking the Thumb Gusset.

Knit 1 rnd.

Rnd 1: Knit until reaching first thumb marker, slip marker (sm), M1, knit to the second marker, M1, sm, knit to the end of the round.

Rnd 2: Knit across round.

Rep Rnds 1–2 until you have completed Row 7 of the Thumb Gusset Chart and there are 9 sts between the Thumb Gusset Markers. Knit to the end of the rnd and back to first marker. Work Row 8 of Thumb Gusset Chart, sm, and begin Hand Chart. This is the pattern for all 36 (42) stitches of the hand, and it begins and ends on either side of the Thumb Gusset. (Note that you will be working an additional set of Thumb Gusset increases for the Large size.)

When all 21 rows of the Thumb Gusset Chart have been worked and you have reached the beginning of Row 15 of the Hand Chart, place the 9 (11) sts between the Thumb Gusset markers on a stitch holder and arrange the 36 (42) remaining hand sts on 3 needles and cont working the Hand Chart.

After all rows of the Hand Chart have been completed, drop B and continue knitting 4 (5) rounds in A alone. You will not be using B again.

Switch to k1, p1 ribbing and work 3 (5) rounds.

Begin rev St st. In the first purl round, decrease 6 stitches evenly around the row, for a total of 30 (36) stitches. Work 4 (5) rounds of rev St st.

BO purlwise on the next round.

THUMB

Pick up the 9 (11) thumb sts from the holder and place on 2 dpns. With A and a third dpn, pick up and knit 5 sts across the gap. Don't be overly concerned about small holes between the sts here, as any holes can be filled in when weaving in the end of the yarn that was attached.

Next rnd: Knit the sts that were taken from the holder. When you reach the needle with the 5 picked-up sts, knit the first and last st on that needle with the first and last st next to them on the adjacent needles—12 (14) sts.

Knit St st for 2 (3) rounds. Work rev St st for 2 (3) rounds, or until thumb reaches the knuckle line. BO all sts knitwise.

FINISHING

Weave in all ends with a tapestry or yarn needle. Wet and block to desired shape.

Rhinebeck Mitts Charts

A = K on RS with A

B = K on RS with B

M = Make 1 with A

SMALL HAND CHART

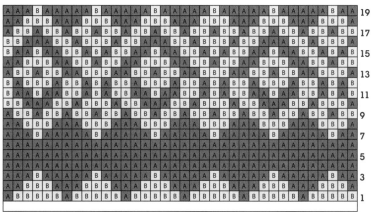

36 Stitches

LARGE THUMB

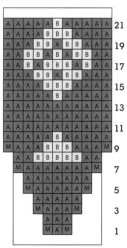

SMALL THUMB

LARGE HAND CHART

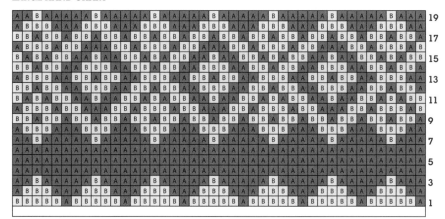

42 Stitches

-- *details* --

SIZES
To fit women's size Extra-Small (Small, Medium, Large [Extra-Large, XXL]). Shown in size Small.

FINISHED MEASUREMENTS
Bust (closed): 34 (38, 42, 46 [50, 54])" (86 [96.5, 106.5, 117 (127, 137)]cm)
Length: 28 (28½, 29, 29½ [30, 30½])" (71 [72, 73.5, 75 (76, 77.5)]cm)

YARN

Berroco Ultra Alpaca (50% alpaca, 50% wool; 215 yds [196.5m]/100g) 8 (9, 10, 12 [13, 14]) skeins Pumpkin Purée #6226. If substituting, use

1,720 (1,935, 2,150, 2,580 [2,795, 3,010]) yds (1,573 [1,769, 1,966, 2,359 (2,556, 2,752)]m) of 3-ply worsted-weight yarn.

NEEDLES
Size 6 (4mm) straight needles, or size to obtain gauge
Size 8 (5mm) straight needles, or size to obtain gauge
One 29" (73.5cm) size 6 (4mm) circular knitting needle, or size to obtain gauge

NOTIONS
Crochet hook, size 1 4.50mm G/7, stitch holders, one 1½" (3.8cm) button

GAUGE
20 sts + 26 rows = 4" (10cm) in St st on size 8 needles

STITCH GUIDE
CROCHET DOUBLE CHAIN OPTION FOR TIE
Make 2 chain, insert hook into first stitch, *wool round hook draw through loop, wool round hook draw through both loops on hook*. Insert hook into left loop, then work from * to *.

MOSS STITCH (ON EVEN # OF STS):
Rows 1–2: *K1, p1; rep from * to end.
Rows 3–4: *P1, k1; rep from * to end.
Rep Rows 1–4 for pattern.

WOOL ROUND HOOK
A crochet term for wrapping the yarn around your crochet hook to form a stitch.

-- *instructions* --

The 50/50 blend of ultrafine alpaca and soft fine wool in Berroco Ultra Alpaca makes a round, fluid yarn that's perfect for highlighting cable stitches. Who better to create those cables than the mistress of cables herself, Norah Gaughan?

At five stitches per inch (2.5cm) in stockinette, the yarn is light enough to wear comfortably without adding unneeded bulk to your silhouette. The fabric also has perfect drape—thanks to the alpaca—when this cardigan is worn open. Norah placed the cable panel on one side only to avoid the extra bulk when worn closed and to be quirkily asymmetrical when worn open.

Notes: Beginning with the right Front is the best way to start this pattern. It will guarantee that your Armholes line up for the Back and Left Front.

RIGHT FRONT
With smaller straight needles, CO 74 (78, 82, 90 [94, 98]) sts.

Row 1 (RS): K2, *p2, k2; rep from * to end.
Row 2: P2, *k2, p2; rep from * to end. Rep these 2 rows until piece measures 3" (7.5cm) from the beginning, end on RS. Change to larger needles and purl the next row, decreasing 4 (3, 2, 5 [4, 3]) sts evenly spaced across—70 (75, 80, 85 [90, 95]) sts. CO 4 sts at the beginning of the next RS row—74 (79, 84, 89 [94, 99]) sts.

-- *designed by Norah Gaughan* --

Set up patt (RS): 4 sts garter (knit every row); 60 sts according to Cable Chart; work the remaining sts in St st. Work even in patt until piece measures 4" (10cm) from cast-on, end on WS.

Next row, decrease row (RS): Cont in cable patt as established, knit to last 5 sts, ssk, k3. Rep decrease row every 14 rows 4 times more—69 (74, 79, 84 [89, 94]) sts. Work even until piece measures 15" (38cm) from the beginning, end with a WS row. BO 4 sts, knit, decreasing 5 sts evenly over next 52 sts, knit to end—60 (65, 70, 75 [80, 85]) sts. Knit 5 rows. On last row increase 0 (1, 0, 1 [0, 1]) st(s)—60 (66, 70, 76 [80, 86]) sts. Change to moss stitch and work even for 2" (5cm), ending with a RS row. (The rest of the Right Front in moss stitch.)

SHAPE NECK

Next row (RS): BO 5 sts, work to end—55 (61, 65, 71 [75, 81]) sts. BO 4 sts at beginning of the next 2 RS rows, then 3 sts at beginning of the next 2 RS rows, then 2 sts at beginning of the next 6 RS rows. End with a WS row.

Decrease row (RS): K1, k2tog, work to end. Rep this decrease every RS row 6 (7, 6, 7, 6, 7) times more, then every other RS row 4 times. *At the same time*, when piece measures 20" (51cm), shape Armhole.

SHAPE ARMHOLE

BO 4 sts at the beginning of the next 1 (1, 1, 1 [2, 2]) WS row(s). BO 3 sts at the beginning of the next 1 (1, 2, 2 [2, 2]) WS row(s). BO 2 sts at the beginning of the next 1 (2, 2, 3 [2, 2]) WS row(s).

Decrease row (RS): Work to last 3 sts, ssk, k1. Rep this decrease every other RS row 0 (1, 0, 1 [1, 1]) time(s) more—8 (10, 13, 15 [18, 20]) sts. Work even until piece measures 28" (71cm) from the cast-on row and bind off.

BACK

With smaller needles, CO 106 (118, 126, 138 [146, 158]) sts.

Row 1 (RS): K2, *p2, k2; rep from * to end.

Row 2: P2, *k2, p2; rep from * to end. Rep these 2 rows until piece measures 3" (7.5cm) from the beginning, end on RS. Change to larger needles, purl the next row and decrease 10 (12, 10, 12 [10, 12]) sts evenly spaced across—96 (106, 116, 126 [136, 146]) sts. Work in St st until piece measures 4" (10cm) from the beginning, end on WS.

Next row, decrease (RS): K3, k2tog, knit to last 5 sts, ssk, k3. Rep decrease row every 14 rows 4 times more—86 (96, 106, 116 [126, 136]) sts. Work even until piece measures same as right front to garter ridges, ending with a WS row. Knit 6 rows. Change to moss stitch and work even for 5" (12.5 cm). (The rest of the Back is worked in moss stitch.)

SHAPE ARMHOLE

BO 4 sts at the beginning of the next 2 (2, 2, 2 [4, 4]) rows. BO 3 sts at the beginning of the next 2 (2, 4, 4 [4, 6]) rows. BO 2 sts at the beginning of the next 2 (4, 4, 6 [4, 4]) rows.

Decrease row (RS): K3, k2tog, work to last 5 sts, ssk, k3. Rep this decrease every other RS row 0 (1, 0, 1 [1, 1]) time(s) more—66 (70, 76, 80 [86, 90]) sts. Work even until Armhole measures 5 (5½, 6, 6½ [7, 7½])" (12.5 [14, 15, 16.5 (18, 19)]cm), ending with a WS row.

SHAPE NECK

Next row (RS): Mark center 26 sts, knit in patt to marker. Join another skein of yarn and BO center 26 sts, knit in patt to end. Working both sides at once, BO 4 sts at each neck edge once, BO 3 sts once, BO 2 sts twice, then BO 1 st at each neck edge once—8 (10, 13, 15 [18,

20]) sts each side. Work even until piece measures 7½ (8, 8½, 9, [9, 9½])" (19 [20.5, 21.5, 23 (23, 24)]cm) from beginning of Armhole. BO all sts for shoulders.

LEFT FRONT

With smaller straight needles, CO 74 (78, 82, 90 [94, 98]) sts. Work in ribbing same as for Back. Change to larger needles and purl the next row decreasing 9 (8, 7, 10 [9, 8]) sts evenly spaced across—65 (70, 75, 80, [85, 90]) sts. CO 4 sts at the beginning of the next WS row. Work the new sts in garter and work the remaining in St st. When piece measures 4" (10cm) from beginning, end on WS.

Next row decrease row (RS): K3, k2tog, knit to end. Rep decrease row every 14 rows 4 times more—60 (65, 70, 75 [80, 85]) sts. Work even until piece measures same as right Front to garter ridges, ending with a WS row. Knit 1 row. BO 4 sts at the beginning of the next row, and knit remaining sts. Knit 4 rows.

Last row: Increase 0 (1, 0, 1 [0, 1]) sts—60 (66, 70, 76 [80, 86]) sts. Change to moss stitch and work even for 2" (5cm), ending with a RS row. (The rest of the Left Front is worked in moss stitch.)

SHAPE NECK

Next row (WS): BO 5 sts, work to end—55 (61, 65, 71 [75, 81]) sts. BO 4 sts at the beginning of the next 2 WS rows, 3 sts at the beginning of the next 2 WS rows, then 2 sts at the beginning of the next 6 WS rows. End with a WS row.

Decrease row (RS): Knit to last 5 sts, ssk, k3. Rep this decrease every RS row 6 (7, 6, 7, [6, 7]) times more, then every other RS row 4 times. *At the same time,* when piece measures same as back to Armhole, shape Armhole.

SHAPE ARMHOLE

BO 4 sts at the beginning of the next 1 (1, 1, 1 [2, 2]) RS row(s). BO 3 sts at beginning of the next 1 (1, 2, 2 [2, 2]) RS row(s). BO 2 sts at the beginning of the next 1 (2, 2, 3 [2, 2]) RS row(s).

Decrease row (RS): K3, k2tog, work to end. Rep this decrease every other RS row 0 (1, 0, 1 [1, 1]) time(s) more—8 (10, 13, 15 [18, 20]) sts. Work even until Armholes measure same as Back to shoulder bind-off.

SLEEVES (MAKE 2)

With smaller straight needles, CO 54 (54, 58, 62 [62, 66]) sts. Work in ribbing same as for Back. Change to larger straight needles and purl the next row decreasing 2 (0, 0, 2 [0, 2]) sts evenly spaced across—52 (54, 58, 60 [62, 64]) sts.

Set up patt (RS): K17 (18, 20, 21 [22, 23]) sts in St st, work 18 according to Cable Chart, k17 (18, 20, 21, [22, 23]) sts in St st. Cont working in patt. When piece measures 4" (10cm) from beginning, end on WS.

Next row, increase row (RS): K3, M1, cont cable patt as established, work to last 3 sts, M1, k3. Rep increase row every 16th (12th, 10th, 8th [8th, 6th]) row 5 (7, 7, 9 [11, 12]) times—64 (70, 76, 80 [86, 90]) sts. Work even until piece measures 18" (45.5cm) from the beginning, end with a WS row.

SHAPE SLEEVE CAP

BO 3 sts at the beginning of the next 2 rows. BO 2 sts at the beginning of the next 2 rows.

Next RS row, decrease row: K3, k2tog, work to last 5 sts, ssk, k3. Rep dec row every RS row 4 (4, 5, 5 [6, 7]) times, then every fourth row 3 (4, 4, 4 [4, 4]) times, then every RS row 4 (5, 5, 5 [6, 7]) times. BO 2 sts at the beginning of the next 2 (2, 2, 4 [4, 4]) rows. BO 3 sts at the beginning of the next 2 rows. BO rem 20 (22, 26, 26 [28, 28]) sts.

instructions continued

FINISHING

Block pieces with steam or wet-block. Sew shoulder seams. Sew in sleeves. Sew underarm and side seams.

NECKBAND

With right sides facing and using smaller circular needle, pick up and knit 68 sts along right Front neck edge, 58 sts across Back neck edge, then 68 sts along left Front neck edge—194 sts. Work ribbing as for Back until ribbing measures 3" (7.5cm). Bind off.

LEFT FRONT AND RIGHT FRONT

Fold garter sts to inside and sew down.

TIES

With crochet hook, attach yarn to right Front at edge in the middle of the garter ridges. Work double chain for 9" (23cm), tie off. Repeat on left Front and inside right side seam. If you aren't familiar with crochet, you can work a 2-stitch I-cord instead. Sew button to left Front on garter ridges 3½" (9cm) from the side seam. Wrap tie around button to fasten. Tie inside ties to secure left Front.

Cabled Swing Cardigan

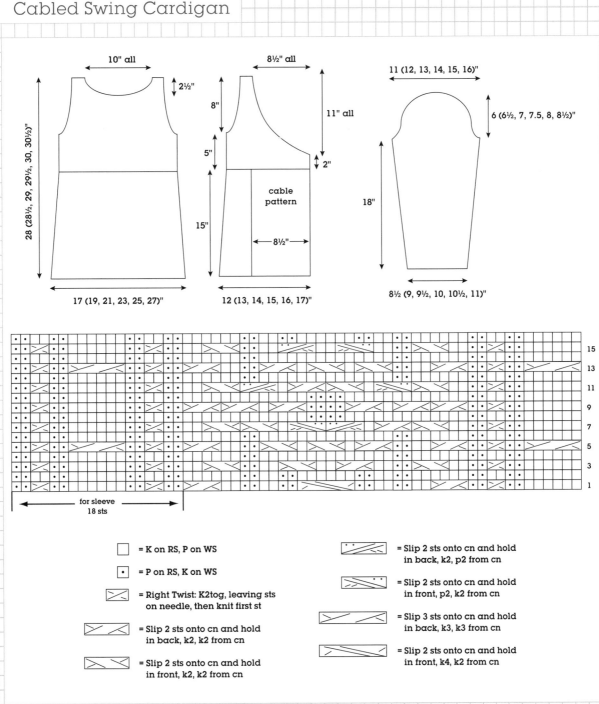

= K on RS, P on WS

• = P on RS, K on WS

= Right Twist: K2tog, leaving sts on needle, then knit first st

= Slip 2 sts onto cn and hold in back, k2, k2 from cn

= Slip 2 sts onto cn and hold in front, k2, k2 from cn

= Slip 2 sts onto cn and hold in back, k2, p2 from cn

= Slip 2 sts onto cn and hold in front, p2, k2 from cn

= Slip 3 sts onto cn and hold in back, k3, k3 from cn

= Slip 2 sts onto cn and hold in front, k4, k2 from cn

Three-Ply

Project #3

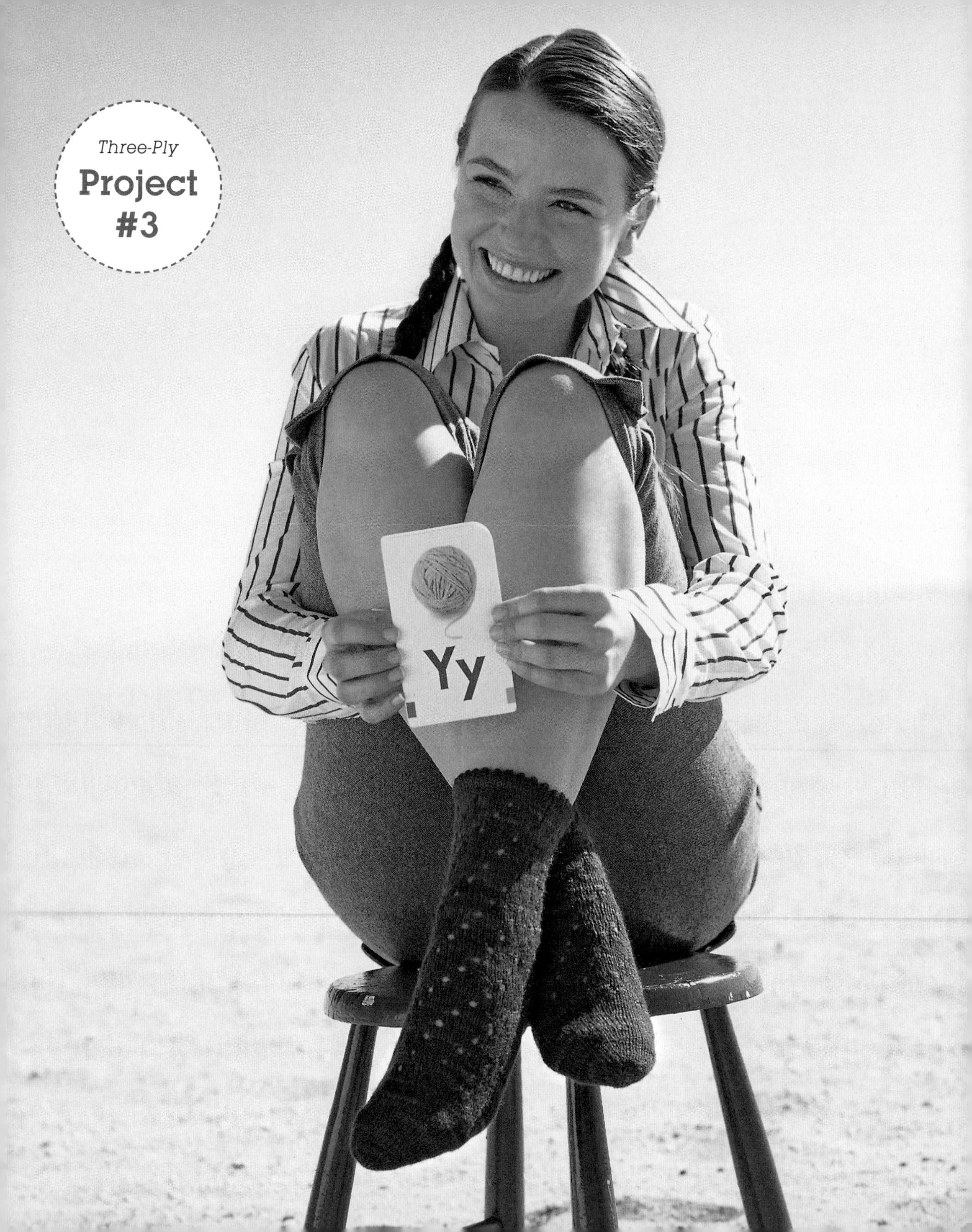

SWIRLY O SOCKS

-- details --

SIZE
To fit women's size Medium

FINISHED MEASUREMENTS
Foot length: 9" (23cm)
Cuff length: 6" (15cm)

YARN

FINE

Version A (left): Mountain Colors Bearfoot (60% superwash wool, 25% mohair, 15% nylon; 350 yds, [320m]/100g) 1 skein Wild Raspberry.
Version B (page 143): Spunky Eclectic Super Sport (100% superwash Merino wool; 180 yds [164.5m]/50g) 2 skeins

Chasing Dreams. If substituting either, use 350 yds (320m) of 3-ply sport-weight yarn.

NEEDLES
Two sets of size 3 dpns (3.25mm), or size to obtain gauge

NOTIONS
Tapestry needle, stitch marker

GAUGE
28 sts + 32 rows = 4" (10cm) of St st

STITCH GUIDE
W&T
Wrap and turn. On the knit side, bring yarn to the front of your work as if to purl. Slip the next stitch, then bring yarn to the back of your work as if to knit, and slip the slipped stitch back onto the left-hand needle. Now turn your work. On wrong side rows, simply reverse the directions of the yarn.

SWIRL STITCH PATTERN
Rows 1–3, 5–7, 9–11: Knit all sts.
Row 4: *K4, k2tog, YO; rep from * around.
Row 8: *K2, k2tog, YO, k2; rep from * around.
Row 12: *K2tog, YO, k4; rep from * around.
These 12 rows make up the lace pattern.

-- instructions --

Hand-dyed sock yarns abound these days. Here's an example of how the depth of colors will impact the finished result. In this sock, simple eyelet patterning creates swirling Os around the leg and instep. Knit in a color that contrasts with your skin tone, the holes will form windows into the foot, with your skin becoming an integral part of the overall effect. Knit in a color that blends more smoothly with your skin, the larger overall swirl pattern of the stitches will become the focal point.

Note: This pattern uses a provisional cast-on (page 238). After you knit the foundation rows you will want to pick up the first row of stitches on a second set of needles so that you can knit the foundation row and the working row stitches together.

LEG
CO 54 sts using a provisional cast-on. Join in the round. Place marker (pm) to mark your beginning. Knit 5 rows even.

Next row: *K2tog, YO; rep from * across. Knit the next 5 rows even. Unravel the provisional cast-on and place those sts on the second set of needles. Fold this together so that the RS is showing to create a folded hem with a picot edge.
Next row: Knit together 1 stitch from your cast-on row with 1 stitch from your working row—54 sts.
Start working in Swirl Stitch Pattern. Work until the leg of your sock measures a total of 6" (15cm) from picot edge.

-- designed by Amy King --

HEEL

Separate the sts for your heel and foot. There will be 30 sts on needles for the heel and 24 sts placed on a holder for the foot. Knit over 29 sts, wrap and turn (w&t) the last st. Slip this wrapped st before working your next row. Purl across 28 sts, w&t the last st. *Knit to 1 st before your last wrapped stitch, w&t. Purl to 1 st before your last wrapped stitch, w&t. Rep from *, working 1 fewer stitch each row, always working a wrapped st before turning. Cont this way until 10 sts rem without wraps and the RS row is facing. Knit across the 10 unwrapped sts to the first unworked, wrapped stitch. Work this st by picking up the wrap and knitting it together with your stitch. Wrap the next stitch twice, then turn. Slip the first, double wrapped st and purl across to the first unworked, wrapped st. Pick up the wrap and purl it together with your st, w&t. Cont in this manner, knitting and purling in all the wraps and working one more st each row until you have worked all 30 sts. Your next row is a RS row.

FOOT

You will now begin knitting in the round again, working the 30 heel sts in St st and the 24 held sts in the Swirl Stitch Pattern. Cont in this manner until the foot is 3½" (9cm) less than the desired finished foot length.

TOE (WORKING IN ST ST):

Decrease rnd 1: *K7, k2tog; rep from * around—48 sts. Knit 6 rounds even.

Decrease rnd 2: *K6, k2tog; rep from * around—42 sts. Knit 5 rounds even.

Decrease rnd 3: *K5, k2tog; rep from * around—36 sts. Knit 4 rounds even.

Decrease rnd 4: *K4, k2tog; rep from * around—30 sts. Knit 3 rounds even.

Decrease rnd 5: *K3, k2tog; rep from * around—24 sts. Knit 2 rounds even.

Decrease rnd 6: *K2, k2tog; rep from * around—18 sts. Knit 1 round even.

Decrease rnd 7: *K2tog; rep from * around—9 sts.

Break yarn and thread tail through the remaining sts with tapestry needle. Pull tightly and fasten well. Weave in ends and block.

The more plies you add to a yarn, the more hard-wearing it will be. However, you may notice with four-ply yarns that the plies don't nest together as completely as they do with three-ply yarns. If you study your stockinette up close, you'll always be able to trace one extra ply, like the edge of a square box, working its way through the stitches.

Because of the hard-wearing nature of these yarns, paired with their excellent stitch definition, they were traditionally used for Aran and Guernsey patterns, where the fuller yarn gives cables and stitchwork an almost sculptural quality. In smooth, worsted-spun yarns, they render colorwork with crisp detail.

The four plies in Dalegarn Baby Ull help lend crisp detail to the colorwork in Adrian Bizilia's Norwegian Snail Mittens (page 148).

Dalegarn Baby Ull is a classic four-ply worsted spun wool.

Looking very closely, you can see hints of that fourth ply sticking out of the otherwise smooth stitches in Classic Elite Premiere, a four-ply cotton/Tencel blend used in the Iris Side-to-Side Sleeveless Top (page 164).

FOOLPROOF BABY HAT

details

SIZE
Fits newborn

FINISHED MEASUREMENTS
Circumference: 6½" (16.5cm)
Length: 8" (20.5cm)

YARN

Knit Picks Swish Superwash (100% superwash wool, 110 yds [100m]/50g) 1 skein Wisteria #23892. If substituting, use 110 yards (100m) worsted-weight 4-ply yarn.

NEEDLES
Size 8 (5mm) needles of your choice, or size to obtain gauge

NOTIONS
Tapestry needle

GAUGE
20 sts + 26 rows = 4" (10cm) in St st

MISTAKE RIB PATTERN
All rows: (K2, p2) across, end with k2, p1.

---

instructions

Mistake rib, or farrow rib as it's often called, is one of my very favorite stitches. It looks beautiful in so many different yarns, from frothy two-ply angoras to smooth singles. But I especially love how it adds depth, texture, and interest to the otherwise smooth, worsted-spun three- and four-ply yarns.

This simple pattern comes from a knitter in my small Maine town. She and her friends have used it to make hundreds of hats for babies in hospitals and shelters. It uses one of the most readily available types of yarn on the market—the machine-washable four-ply worsted—and knits up extremely fast. I modified it slightly for even greater speed and ease. Working steadily, you'll be able to finish one of these in just a few hours.

A note about yarns: When knitting for a hospital, clinic, shelter, or anyone who is too overwhelmed with motherhood to deal with "handwash-only" instructions, you'll want to stick with a soft but machine-washable yarn such as Swish. Other great candidates include Cascade 220 Superwash or Rowan Cashsoft, a slightly more luxurious but well-wearing blend of Merino, microfiber, and cashmere.

Cast on 55 sts. Work Mistake Rib pattern until piece measures 6" (15cm).

SHAPE CROWN
Row 1: (K1, p3tog) across, end with k1, p2tog—28 sts.
Row 2: (K1, p1) across.
Row 3: (K2 tog, p2tog) across—14 sts.
Row 4: (K1, p1) across.

FINISHING
Cut a tail at least 8" (20.5cm) long, run it through the stitches remaining on your needle, then seam up the edge of the hat. Darn in ends and wash the hat in a gentle soap to prepare it for its new recipient.

---

designed by Clara Parkes

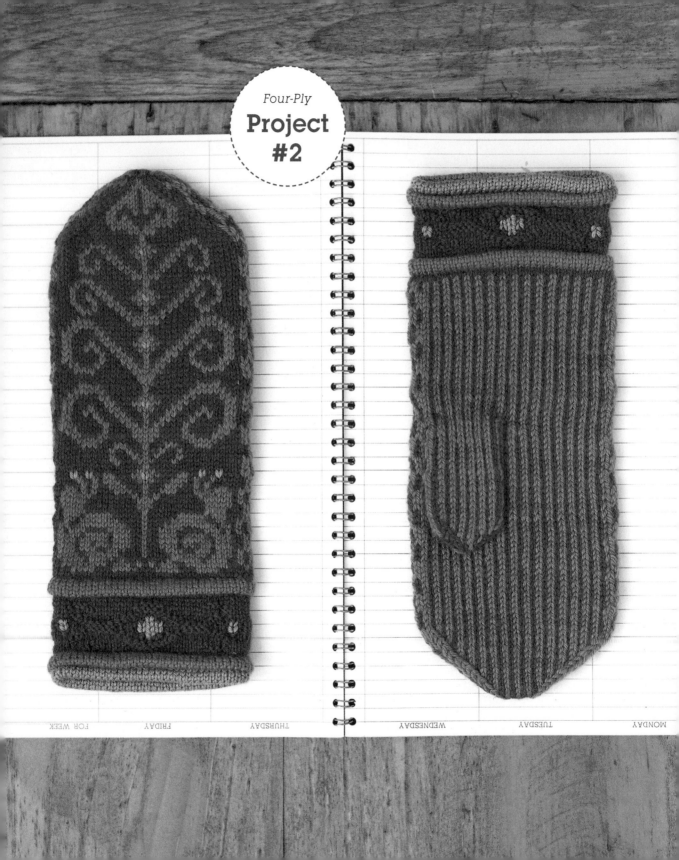

-- *details* --

SIZES

To fit an adult woman's hand, size Medium. A small adjustment of gauge will allow the mitten to fit a larger or smaller hand. Aim for a mitten with a circumference about ½" (13mm) larger than the palm of your hand.

FINISHED MEASUREMENTS

Hand circumference: 8" (20.5cm)
Length: 10" (25.5cm)

YARN

SUPER FINE

Dalegarn Baby Ull (100% superwash Merino wool; 192 yds [176m]/50g) 1 skein each of Deep Blue #5545 (A), Bright Blue #5726 (B), and Kiwi #9436. If substituting, use 570 yds (521m), divided into 3 contrasting colors of 4-ply worsted-spun fingering-weight yarn.

NEEDLES

One set of 5 size 0 (2mm) dpns, or size to obtain gauge

NOTIONS

Tapestry needle, scrap yarn, a nice, pointy spare dpn for creating welts

GAUGE

36 sts + 40 rows = 4" (10cm) in pattern

STITCH GUIDE

KF&B

Knit through the front loop of a stitch and then, without taking it off the needle, knit through the back loop of the same stitch. You've created two stitches from one.

WELT

There are 3 welts on each mitten. They're all created in the same way with a stitch called the Tuck Stitch, which is done by knitting a stitch together with the horizontal purl strand from the back side of a stitch directly in line below it. These welts are done over 8 rows.

HOW TO MAKE WELTS

Knit in St st for 8 rows. On the next row and with the spare pointy dpn, pick up the horizontal strand from the back of the first row (for the first welt at the edge of the mitten, this would be the horizontal strand from the back of the cast-on row) that is straight down from the st that's first in line on the left-hand needle and place it to the right of that st. Knit the two sts together. Repeat this procedure around, being sure that the stitches are directly in line with each other, or your welt will bias and ripple. Since the welts on these mittens are knit in different colors, you can easily spot the purl bar you should be picking up because it will be a purl bar of the color you were previously knitting.

-- *instructions* --

Dalegarn Baby Ull is a worsted-spun yarn with a great array of strong, crisp colors. Worsted yarns are smooth, which makes them great for color knitting. Designs are as graphically striking as you wish. Since there is no blurring to the edges of the stitches, colorwork can be very intricate. The shape and some of the motifs in these mittens are borrowed from the Scandinavian tradition. The use of this soft, machine-washable yarn and some of the motifs (snails!) lend them a very modern feel.

Notes: This pattern is double-stranded throughout and, with the exception of the cuff purl details, is knit in St st. There are a few rows in which you will be required to carry the Contrast Color (B) over a long stretch. Weave it in once or twice by bringing B over A and then knitting the next st in A. I was pleasantly surprised to discover that woven-in floats do not show in this yarn.

I find that carrying B in my left hand and A in my right hand causes the B sts to be slightly raised and stand out from the background in a pleasing manner.
These mittens are knit in the round with 5 dpns, with sts arranged so there are 18 sts on each of 4 needles, with a fifth needle for knitting. Needles are referred to by number, with the first needle of the rnd as needle 1, and so on.

-- *designed by Adrian Bizilia* --

--- *instructions continued* ---

Charts are for stranded knitting with all knit sts and are read from right to left on all rows, since the mittens are worked in the round.

RIGHT MITTEN

CO 66 sts in Kiwi and create welt (page 149), knitting the two rows together with B. Create second welt with B, knitting welt rows together with A. Knit one round plain and then begin Chart A for cuff, knitting chart once over 33 sts and then repeating over the next 33 sts. After Chart A, knit 4 rounds plain in A. Switch to B and create welt, knitting welt rows together with A.

Next rnd: Begin Chart B on needles 1 and 2 for back of mitten and Chart C on needles 3 and 4 for palm. Be sure to kf&b on the first 3 sts for needles 1 and 3. Shift sts so that 18 sts rest on each needle—72 sts.

On Row 26 of Chart C, knit in a bit of scrap yarn over the sts marked by the red line on the right-hand side of chart for thumb placement. Place these sts back onto the left hand needle and knit them in pattern.

Continue knitting from Charts B and C to last row. Slip first st on needle 1 to needle 4 and last st on needle 2 to needle 3. Turn mitten inside out and BO using the 3-needle BO.

Go back and remove scrap yarn and place the 13 lower sts on one needle and the upper 13 sts on two needles. Knit around in vertical stripe pattern as set up on palm, picking up 1 st between needles 1 and 2 and another between needles 3 and 1. Pick them up by knitting into the back of the st, both in B. You'll now have 28 sts on the needles. Knit even for 2¼" (5.5cm), then begin thumb decrease as follows (still in 1x1 vertical stripe stranded knitting):

Needle 1: Ssk in A, knit across to last 3 sts, k2tog in A.

Needle 2: Ssk in A, knit across.

Needle 3: Knit to last 3 sts, k2tog in A.

Cont in this manner until 8 sts remain. Cut both yarns, leaving 6" (15cm) tails. Using a tapestry needle, thread MC through remaining stitches. Push both tails through to inside of thumb and weave in ends.

LEFT MITTEN

Work as for Right Mitten, but placing thumb at red line on left side of Chart C.

FINISHING

Taking about 10" (25.5cm) of Kiwi, duplicate st over the areas marked in Chart A. Weave in all ends. Do this for both mittens. Handwash and block mittens to size.

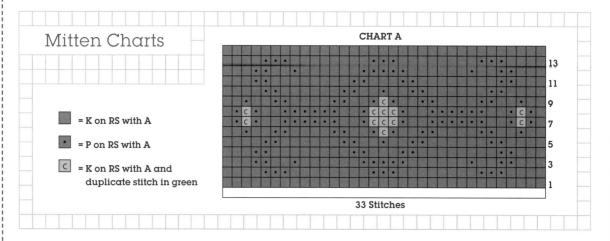

Mitten Charts

CHART A

■ = K on RS with A

• = P on RS with A

C = K on RS with A and duplicate stitch in green

13
11
9
7
5
3
1

33 Stitches

Mitten Charts

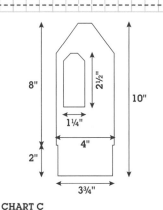

- ▨ = K on RS with A
- ⊡ = P on RS with A
- Ⓑ = K on RS with B
- Ⓒ = K on RS with A and duplicate stitch in green
- ◿ = SSK on RS
- ◺ = K2tog on RS
- ▽ = Increase 1 st by knitting into the front and then into the back of st
- ■ = No stitch
- ─── = Thumb placement

8"   2½"   10"

1¼"

4"

2"

3¾"

CHART B

CHART C

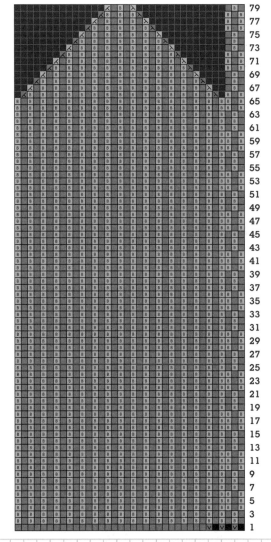

PATCHWORK CARRIAGE BLANKET

---------------------------------- details ----------------------------------

FINISHED MEASUREMENTS

Approximately 36" (91.5cm) square

Note: To make the blanket larger, make additional strips and add squares. This increases the blanket in size by 6" (15cm) in both directions when you add each strip/square. Adding one strip/square makes the blanket 42" (106.5cm) square.

YARN

Vermont Organic Fiber Co. O-Wool Classic (100% organic Merino; 198 yds [181m]/110g) 2 skeins each Mulberry #5201 (A), Sky #2300 (B), and Willow #4302 (C). If substituting, use 1,150 yds (1,052m) total of 4-ply worsted-weight yarn, equally divided among three different colors.

NEEDLES

Size 7 (4.5mm), or size to obtain gauge

NOTIONS

Measuring tape, tapestry needle, scissors, straight pins, crochet hook size J/10 (6mm), stitch markers (optional)

GAUGE

20 sts + 28 rows = 4" (10cm) in St st

Note: Each strip is 30 sts wide (6" [15cm]) and is composed of combinations of 4 basic squares. The instructions for each of these squares are as follows:

SQUARE 1: STRIPES

Rows 1–2: With A, work 2 rows in St st.

Rows 3–4: Change to C, work 2 rows in St st.

Rows 5–6: Change to B, work 2 rows in St st.

Rep Rows 1–6 a total of 6 times.
Rep Row 1.

SQUARE 2: STOCKINETTE STITCH

Row 1 (RS): Knit all sts.

Row 2 (WS): Purl all sts.

Work even in St st in color specified for 6" (15cm). If transitioning from a texture st, you may be instructed to work a transitional row between the texture st and the St st.

SQUARE 3: SEED STITCH (WORKED OVER AN EVEN NUMBER OF STITCHES)

Row 1 (RS): *K1, p1; rep from * to end of row.

Row 2 (WS): *P1, k1; rep from * to end of row.

Rep these 2 rows until work measures 6" (15cm).

SQUARE 4: SIX-STITCH CABLE SQUARE

See chart.

---------------------------------- instructions ----------------------------------

Four-ply yarns are wonderful all-around options for colorwork, stockinette, and textured stitches—all of which Tara Jon Manning has incorporated into this warm and colorful, carriage-sized blanket. The wool is certified organic from Vermont Organic Wool Company.

STRIP 1

With A, CO 30 sts, work Square 1. Join B to RS and work Square 2, ending with RS row. Join A to WS, work 1 purl row across WS, work Square 3, ending with WS row. Join C to RS, work Square 2, ending with RS row. Join B to WS, work 1 purl row across WS, work Square 4. Join A on RS, work Square 2. BO all sts loosely when final square is complete.

STRIP 2

With B, CO 30 sts, work Square 2. Join A and work Square 1. Join C and work Square 2, ending with RS row. Join B to WS, work 1 purl row across WS, work Square 3, ending with RS row. Join A and work Square 2. Join C on WS, work 1 purl row across WS, work Square 4. BO all sts loosely when final square is complete.

---------------------------------- *designed by Tara Jon Manning* ----------------------------------

instructions continued

STRIP 3

With A, CO 30 sts, work Square 4. Join C to RS, work Square 2. Join A and work Square 1. Cont with A and work Square 2, ending with RS row. Join C to WS, work 1 purl row across WS, work Square 3. Join B to RS, work Square 2. BO all sts loosely when final square is complete.

STRIP 4

With C, CO 30 sts, work Square 2. Join B, work Square 4. Add A, work Square 2. Starting with A, work Square 1. Join B, work Square 2, ending with RS row. Add A to WS, work 1 purl row across WS, work Square 3. BO all sts loosely when final square is complete.

STRIP 5

With B, CO 30 sts, work Square 3. Join A, work Square 2, ending with RS row. Join C, work 1 purl row across WS, work Square 4. Join B, work Square 2. Join A, work Square 1. Join C, work Square 2. BO all sts loosely when final square is complete.

STRIP 6

With A, CO 30 sts, work Square 2. Join C, work Square 3. Join B to RS, work Square 2, ending with RS. Join A to WS, work 1 purl row across WS, then work Square 4. Join C, work Square 2. Join A, work Square 1. BO all sts loosely when final square is complete.

FINISHING

Sew strips together in order knitted and as shown on chart. Pin strips together, matching lower edges and corners. Ease selvedge edges as needed. If you find it helpful, lightly steam-block the strips first to minimize rolling of edges. Invisibly stitch strips together across long edges, sewing seams 1 st in from the edge. Weave in all ends.

Wet-block blanket by washing and laying flat in exact shape and size in which you wish it to dry. If further blocking or easing is required, lightly steam-block with a damp iron.

EDGING

Using crochet hook, work a single crochet around outer edge in color of choice (color C shown). Weave in ends.

CORNER TIES

Strand all 3 colors together through a tapestry needle. At each intersection of 4 color blocks, pull all 3 strands through 2 diagonal square corners, leaving about 3" (7.5cm) of yarn on both sides. Tie ends in a square knot. Complete this at each intersection—25 corner ties in all.

Blanket Charts

ASSEMBLY DIAGRAM

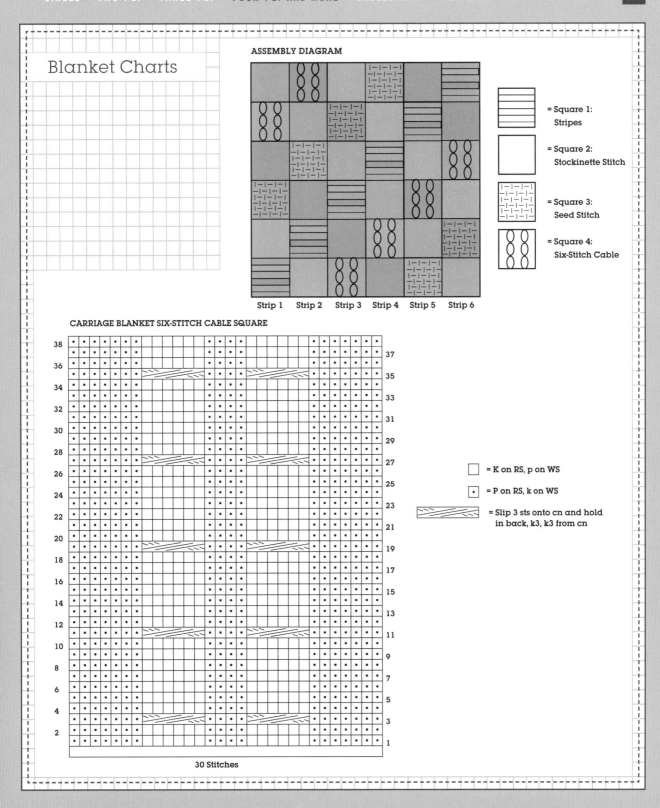

= Square 1:
Stripes

= Square 2:
Stockinette Stitch

= Square 3:
Seed Stitch

= Square 4:
Six-Stitch Cable

Strip 1   Strip 2   Strip 3   Strip 4   Strip 5   Strip 6

CARRIAGE BLANKET SIX-STITCH CABLE SQUARE

= K on RS, p on WS

= P on RS, k on WS

= Slip 3 sts onto cn and hold
in back, k3, k3 from cn

30 Stitches

GIRLY TEE

SIZES

To fit women's sizes Extra-Small (Small, Medium, Large). Shown in size Small.

FINISHED MEASUREMENTS

Chest: 30 (32½, 36, 40)" (76 [82.5, 91.5, 101.5]cm)
Length: 17½ (18½, 20½, 21½)" (44.5 [47, 52, 54.5]cm)

YARN

Hemp for Knitting allhemp6 (100% hemp, 165 yds [151m]/100g) 4 (4, 5, 6) skeins Dusty Rose. If substituting, use 580 (660, 825, 910) yards (530 [603.5, 754, 832]m) 6-ply DK-weight yarn.

GAUGE

22 sts + 30 rows = 4" (10cm) in St st

NEEDLES

One 32" (80cm) circular needle size 2 (2.75mm), or size to obtain gauge
One 32" (80cm) circular needle size 5 (3.75mm), or size to obtain gauge
One set of size 2 (2.75mm) dpns, or size to obtain gauge
One set of size 5 (3.75mm) dpns, or size to obtain gauge

NOTIONS

Stitch holders (4), stitch markers (4)

DECORATIVE BIND-OFF

*K2togtbl, place new st back on left needle; rep from * to end.

Lana Hames is on a mission to show the world that hemp makes an exceptional yarn. She is the founder of Lanaknits Designs and has her own line of hemp yarns, Hemp for Knitting. I wanted a garment that reflected hemp's best qualities, and I knew Lana was the one to design it. This charming and oh-so-girly tee is the result. It'll feel firm at first, but the more you wash it, the softer it gets.

BODY

With smaller needle, CO 140 (168, 182, 210) sts. Join sts and work in round, being careful not to twist stitches. Place marker (pm) at beginning of round.

BODY BAND

Rnds 1–4: *K1tbl, p1; rep from * to end.
Rnd 5: *P1, k1; rep from * to end.
Band is now complete.
Next rnd: Change to larger needle and knit, increasing 20 (12, 18, 10) sts evenly across the row—160 (180, 200, 220) sts.

SHAPE WAIST

K80 (90, 100, 110), pm, knit to end.

Cont to knit all rounds except as follows:
On every sixth row 6 times, knit to 2 sts before marker, k2tog, knit to last 2 sts before marker, ssk.
Next: On every sixth rnd 6 times, knit to 1 st before marker, M1, knit to last st before marker, M1.
Cont to knit each round until work measures approximately 13 (14, 15, 16)" (33 [35.5, 38, 40.5]cm) from beginning, or to desired length to underarm.

SHAPE ARMHOLE

K6 (6, 8, 8) sts and place on holder; k80 (90, 100, 110) sts and place the last 12 (12, 16, 16) sts worked on holder, knit to end, place last 6 (6, 8, 8) sts worked on holder. Leave remaining sts on needle and set aside for now.

SLEEVES (MAKE 2)

With dpns, CO 56 (56, 70, 70) sts. Join, being careful not to twist sts.

Rnds 1–5: Work same as for body band.

Next: Change to larger dpns and knit, increasing 4 (6, 0, 0) sts evenly across round—60 (62, 70, 70) sts.

Knit every round until work measures 3" (7.5cm) or to desired sleeve length.

Next: Place last 6 (6, 8, 8) sts of round and first 6 (6, 8, 8) sts of next round on holder for underarm—48 (50, 54, 54) sts.

YOKE

With larger circular needles, knit 68 (78, 84, 94) sts from body, pm, knit 48 (50, 54, 54) held sts from first sleeve, pm, knit 68 (78, 84, 94) sts from body, pm, then knit 48 (50, 54, 54) held sts from second sleeve, pm—232 (256, 276, 296) sts.

FOR SIZE MEDIUM

Decrease 1 st on next round—275 sts.

FOR SIZE LARGE

Increase 1 st on next round—297 sts.

ALL SIZES

Knit 7 (7, 6, 6) rounds St st.

First decrease: *K6 (6, 9, 9), k2tog; rep from * to end—203 (224, 250, 270) sts.

Knit 6 (6, 5, 5) rounds St st.

Second decrease: *K5 (5, 8, 8), k2tog; rep from * to end—174 (192, 225, 243) sts.

Knit 6 (6, 5, 5) rounds St st.

Third decrease: *K4 (4, 7, 7), k2tog; rep from * to end—145 (160, 200, 216) sts.

Knit 6 (6, 5, 5) rounds St st.

Fourth decrease: *K3 (3, 6, 6), k2tog; rep from * to end—116 (128, 175, 189) sts.

FOR SIZES EXTRA-SMALL AND SMALL

Knit 1 round and proceed to neckband.

FOR SIZES MEDIUM AND LARGE ONLY

Knit 5 rounds.

Fifth decrease: *K5, k2tog; rep from * to end—M150 and L162 sts.

Knit 5 rounds.

Final decrease: *K4, k2tog; rep from * to end—M125 and L135 sts.

NECKBAND

Rnds 1–2: With smaller circular needle, *k1tbl, p1; rep from * to end.

BO all sts loosely using decorative bind-off.

FINISHING

Put underarm sts on dpns. Using tapestry needle and yarn, graft underarm sts together, using kitchener stitch. With tapestry needle, weave in all loose ends. Hand- or machine-wash, lay flat, and block to measurements.

JELLYFISH The moon jellyfish, very common, is washed up on all our beaches. Its pink and orange, varying from white to pink radiating canals and a thin indented fringe. Tentacles are very short. Pink jellyfish, of colder waters, is larger—1 ft. or more wide, with long, trailing tentacles. Specimens 6 ft. across with tentacles over 100 ft. long are reported. It swims by opening and closing its disc.

1. *Moon Jellyfish 3"–9"*

2. *Pink Jellyfish 1'–4'*

45

-------------------------------------- *details* --------------------------------------

FINISHED MEASUREMENTS

OCTOPUS
Height: 9" (23cm)
Width: 3¼" (8cm)

GOLDFISH
Height: 3" (7.5cm)
Width: 6¼" (16cm)

YARN

Lily Sugar 'n Cream (100% cotton; 120 yds [109.5m]/70g) 1 skein Hot Purple for Octopus, 1 skein Pumpkin for Goldfish. If substituting, use 60 yds (55m) for each toy in a 4-ply, worsted-weight yarn.

NEEDLES
One set of size 7 (4.5mm) dpns, or size to obtain gauge

NOTIONS
Tapestry needle, 2 yds (2m) contrasting yarn for duplicate stitch, sachets of catnip (see Notes) or materials for stuffing (polyester fiberfill, wool roving, cotton batting, etc.)

GAUGE
20 sts + 29 rows = 4" (10cm) in St st

STITCH GUIDE
kf&b:
Knit through the front loop of a stitch and then, without taking it off the needle, knit through the back loop of the same stitch. You've created two stitches from one.

-------------------------------------- *instructions* --------------------------------------

While I won't say that *all* knitters have cats, we do seem to have a high proportion of feline companions in our midst—hence these two cat toys. Both knit up quickly, using colorful Lily Sugar 'n Cream, a four-ply, machine-washable cotton that knits up easily, is available everywhere, and costs next to nothing. You can also make these *sans* catnip and give them away as baby toys.

Note: Catnip sachets can be made out of old socks. Simply cut off the toe of an old sock and fill it with catnip. Sew it tightly closed. Put this inside either catnip toy for your favorite feline companion.

OLLIE THE OCTOPUS
BODY
CO 3 sts, join in the round, being careful not to twist sts.
Kf&b into each st around—6 sts. Knit 2 rounds even.
*Kf&b, k1; rep from * 3 times—9 sts.
Note: If you find it too difficult to maneuver with so few sts on your dpns, you can work all sts up to this point on one dpn. Then distribute them evenly over 3 dpns and seam up any holes when finishing.

Knit 1 rnd even.
Rnd 1: (Kf&b, knit all sts to end of dpn) 3 times.
Rnd 2: Knit 1 rond even.
Rep Rnds 1 and 2 until you have 30 sts total.
Cont knitting in the round until body measures approximately 4" (10cm).

DECREASE ROUNDS
*K2, ssk, k2, k2tog, k2; rep from * 3 times—24 sts.
Knit 1 round even.
*K2, ssk, k2tog, k2; rep from * 3 times—18 sts. Purl 1 round even.
*K2, k2tog, k2; rep from * 3 times—15 sts.
*K2tog, k1, k2tog; rep from * 3 times—9 sts.
Cut yarn, leaving 8" (20.5cm) tail. If desired, place

-------------------------------------- *designed by Amie Gavin Glasgow* --------------------------------------

small catnip sachet inside body. With a tapestry needle, thread through remaining sts and pull tight.

I-CORD LEGS

At the ridge of purl sts, pick up and knit 3 sts. Without turning work, slide sts to the other end of dpn and knit them. Rep until leg measures 4–5" (10–12.5cm) or desired length. BO all 3 sts and bury tail of the yarn through center of leg.

Rep this leg on the opposite side of the body, then again halfway between these two legs on both sides, so that you have 4 legs. Make 4 more legs, placing them evenly between the 4 established legs—8 legs total.

FINISHING

Using any comparable yarn in a contrasting color, sew eyes with duplicate st approximately 1" (2.5cm) above the legs. Weave in all ends.

SCARLETT THE GOLDFISH

TAIL

With Pumpkin, CO 18 sts.

Row 1: *K1, p1; rep from * to end.

Row 2: K2tog, *p2tog, k2tog; rep from * to end—9 sts.

Row 3: K2tog, p2tog, k1, p2tog, k2tog—5 sts.

Row 4: K1, p1, k1, p1, k1.

Row 5: P2tog, k1, p2tog—3 sts.

BEGIN GOLDFISH BODY

K3. Slide sts to right side of dpn (as in I-cord) so that working yarn is coming from farthest st on left. Kf&b into each st, add dpns as needed to begin knitting in round.

Knit 1 round—6 sts.

*K1, M1, k1; rep from * 3 times—9 sts.

Knit 1 round.

*K1, M1, k1, M1, k1; rep from * 3 times—15 sts.

Knit 2 rounds.

*K1, M1, k1, M1, k1, M1, k1, M1, k1; rep from * 3 times—27 sts.

Knit 3 rounds.

Begin to work flat by turning and purling 27 sts.

Cont to work in St st flat for 18 more rows.

Begin to work in the round again, knit 3 rounds.

*K1, k2tog; rep from * around—18 sts.

Knit 2 rounds.

K2tog around—9 sts.

Knit 2 rounds.

*K1, k2tog; rep from * 3 times—6 sts.

Knit 1 round.

Cut yarn, leaving an 8" (20.5cm) tail. With a tapestry needle, thread through remaining sts and pull tight.

SIDE FINS (MAKE 2)

CO 18 sts.

*K1, p1; rep from * across.

K2tog, *p2tog, k2tog; rep from * across—9 sts.

K2tog, p2tog, k1, p2tog, k2tog—5 sts.

*K1, p1; rep from * across, ending with k1.

P2tog, k1, p2tog—3 sts.

K3, then BO all sts.

FINISHING

Sew fins to sides of body. Using any comparable yarn in a contrasting color, sew eyes with duplicate st. If desired, place small catnip sachet inside body. Weave in ends and sew up bottom seam.

IRIS SIDE-TO-SIDE SLEEVELESS TOP

-- *details* --

SIZES
To fit women's sizes Extra-Small (Small, Medium, Large, Extra-Large). Shown in Small.

FINISHED MEASUREMENTS
Bust: 30 (34, 38, 42, 46)" (76 [86.5, 96.5, 106.5, 117]cm)
Length: 22½ (23, 23¼, 23½, 23¾)" (57 [58.5, 59, 59.5, 60.5]cm)

YARN

3 LIGHT

Classic Elite Premiere (50% Pima cotton, 50% Tencel; 108 yds [99m]/50g) 2 (2, 3, 4, 5) skeins each of Bleached Orchid #5256 (A), Almost Green #5287 (B), and Natural #5216 (C). If substituting, use 620 (648, 810, 1,200, 1,410) yds (567 [592.5, 740.5, 1,097, 1,289]m) of 4-ply DK-weight yarn.

NEEDLES
One 24" (60cm) circular needle size 5 (3.75mm), or size to obtain gauge

NOTIONS
A smooth waste yarn, crochet hook size F/5 (3.75mm), tapestry needle

GAUGE
24 sts + 32 rows = 4" (10cm) in St st

-- *instructions* --

The smooth, lustrous Pima cotton and Tencel fibers in this yarn create a lovely drape—but these smooth fibers may stretch out over time, requiring frequent blocking. To combat the stretch, we've worked the garment from side to side so that when it's worn, the knitted fabric is pulled sideways rather than downward. You work from the center Back to the center Front, and then repeat around to the center Back again, following a deceptively simple color sequence.

Notes: Since this pattern is knit from side to side, exact row gauge is important so that the tank is the correct length. When changing colors at the beginning of your rows, carry the yarn along the edge by twisting all three strands around each other.

With waste yarn, CO 99 (102, 103, 105, 106) sts provisionally. If you aren't comfortable with the provisional cast-on (see page 238), you can always cast on as you would normally and then seam the edges together.

SECTION 1
Row 1 (WS): With A, purl across all sts.
Row 2: K1, M1, knit across.
Row 3: Purl across to last st, M1, p1.
Beginning with the 6-row section of color B, follow Color Sequence Chart section 1 throughout.

Rep increase Rows 2–3 until you have 122 (125, 126, 128, 129) sts, ending with a knit row.
Next row: Purl all sts, and at end of row CO sts for shoulder straps—135 (138, 139, 141, 142) sts.
Knit in St st for 20 (20, 20, 26, 34) rows, ending with purl row.
Next row: BO 29 (21, 13, 11, 11) sts, knit across—106 (117, 126, 130, 131) sts.
Purl one row.

BEGIN DECREASE
Row 1: K2tog, knit to end.
Row 2: Purl to last 2 sts, p2tog.
Rep Rows 1–2 until you have 93 (96, 97, 99, 100) sts, ending with a knit row.

-- *designed by Amie Gavin Glasgow* --

instructions continued

SECTION 2

Follow Color Sequence 2 throughout.

Row 1 (WS): Purl.

Row 2: K1, M1, knit across.

Row 3: Purl across to last st, M1, p1.

Rep increase rows 2–3 until you have 106 (117, 126, 130, 131) sts, ending with a knit row.

Next row (WS): Purl all sts. At end of row, CO 29 (21, 13, 11, 11) sts—135 (138, 139, 141, 142) sts.

Knit in St st for 20 (20, 20, 26, 34) rows.

Next row (RS): BO 13 sts, and knit across—122 (125, 126, 128, 129) sts.

BEGIN DECREASE

Row 1: K2tog, knit to end.

Row 2: Purl to last 2 sts, p2tog.

Rep Rows 1–2 until you have 99 (102, 103, 105, 106) sts, ending with a knit row.

Repeat Sections 1–2 once more.

FINISHING

Place sts from provisional cast-on onto another needle and graft together in the final row using kitchener stitch. If you opted not to use a provisional cast-on, bind off now and seam this edge to the cast-on edge. Sew shoulder seams.

EDGING

Around bottom hem, using A, pick up and knit 176 (202, 224, 247, 270) sts, being sure to pick up through any carried yarns from the color changes.

Starting with a purl rnd, work in garter stitch for 5 rows. BO all sts. Optional: Work single crochet around the neck and armholes. Weave in ends and block.

Color Sequence

SECTION 1

Color A	2 rows
Color B	4 rows
Color C	6 rows
Color A	4 rows
Color B	2 rows
Color C	4 rows
Color A	2 rows
Color B	6 rows
Color C	2 rows
Color A	6 rows

SECTION 2

Color A	6 rows
Color C	2 rows
Color B	6 rows
Color A	2 rows
Color C	4 rows
Color B	2 rows
Color A	4 rows
Color C	6 rows
Color B	4 rows
Color A	2 rows

-- details --

FINISHED MEASUREMENTS
(AFTER WASHING AND BLOCKING)
Ripple: 12" (30.5cm) square
Lace Leaf: 13" (33cm) square

YARN

Euroflax Originals from Louet (100% linen; 270 yds [247m]/100g) 1 skein Willow. (One skein will make both liners.) If substituting, use 135 yds (123.5m) of 4-ply sport-weight linen yarn for each basket liner.

NEEDLES
One set of size 3 (3.25 mm) dpns, or size needed to obtain gauge.

One 16" (40cm) size 3 (3.25mm) circular needle, or size needed to obtain gauge (optional)

NOTIONS
Stitch markers (5)

GAUGE
20 sts + 32 rows = 4" (10cm) in St st

STITCH GUIDE
KF&B
Knit through the front loop of a stitch and then, without taking it off the needle, knit through the back loop of the same stitch. You've created two stitches from one.

FIGURE-8 CAST-ON
Begin by lining up 2 dpns and wrapping your yarn around one, then the other, in the style of a figure-8. After you've made the required number of wraps, simply take your working yarn and begin knitting across the top row. Turn the needles and knit across the other row. One row will have stitches that sit backwards on the needles, so either knit through their back loops or correct their position before you knit them. After a few rows, tug on the CO tail to tighten up your center sts.

RIPPLE STITCH
Ssk, k2, YO, k2, YO, k2, k2tog, k1, ssk, k2, YO, k2, YO, k2, k2tog.

-- instructions --

What better way to present a gift of baked goods than wrapped in a handknit cozy? This durable linen yarn loves to be machine-washed and -dried, and it will grow softer and more lustrous with each wash. One hank makes two liners, and they knit up very quickly.

CENTER PATTERN FOR BOTH BASKET LINERS
Using a figure-8 cast-on, CO 4 sts (2 sts each on 2 needles). Kf&b of each stitch—8 sts.
Knit the next round.
Rnd 1: Mark the beginning of your round. Kf&b, place marker (pm), *kf&b twice, pm. Rep from * 2 more times, end with kf&b—16 sts. To avoid confusion, use a different color or shape stitch marker to indicate the beginning of your round.
Rnd 2: Knit all sts.
Rnd 3: *Knit to 1 st before marker, kf&b, slip marker (sm), kf&b. Rep from * around 3 more times, then knit to end.

Repeat Rounds 2–3 until you have 176 sts—44 sts between each marker. When you have enough sts, you can redistribute them evenly across 3 dpns and, when your piece is large enough, to circular needle.

RIPPLE BASKET LINER (LEFT)
Work the Center Pattern for basket liner, then:
Rnds 1, 5, and 9: Purl all sts.
Rnd 2: *Work the ripple stitch, kf&b, sm, kf&b, work the ripple stitch. Rep from * around 3 more times.
Rnds 3, 7, and 11: Knit all sts.

-- *designed by Amy King* --

--- *instructions continued* ---

Edge detail of Lace Leaf Basket Liner

Rnds 4, 8, and 12: *Knit to 1 st before marker, kf&b, sm, kf&b. Rep from * around 3 more times. Knit to the end of round.

Rnd 6: *Work the ripple stitch, k2, kf&b, sm, kf&b, k2, work the ripple stitch. Rep from * around 3 more times.

Rnd 10: *Work the ripple stitch, k4, kf&b, sm, kf&b, k4, work the ripple stitch. Rep from * around 3 more times. After Rnd 12, BO all sts loosely so the edges of your basket liner will lie flat.

LEAF LACE BASKET LINER (LEFT)

Work the Center Pattern for basket liner, then:

Row 1 and all odd-numbered rows: Knit.

Row 2: *Knit to stitch marker, sm, YO. Rep from * around 3 more times. Knit to the end of round.

Row 4: *Knit to 2 sts before the marker, YO, sl1 k1 psso, sm, YO, k1, YO, k2tog, YO. Rep from * around.

Row 6: *Knit to 2 sts before the marker, YO, sl1 k1 psso, sm, k1, YO, k1, YO, k1, k2tog, YO. Rep from * around.

Row 8: *Knit to 2 sts before the marker, YO, sl1 k1 psso, sm, k2, YO, k1, YO, k2, k2tog, YO. Rep from * around.

Row 10: *Knit to 1 st before the marker, YO, k1, sm, k2tog, k3, sl1 k1 psso, k1, YO. Rep from * around.

Row 12: *Knit to 1 st before the marker, YO, sl1, remove marker, k2tog, psso, replace marker, k1, sl1 k2tog psso, YO. Rep from * around.

Row 14: *Knit to 1 st before the marker, YO, sl1, remove marker, k2tog, psso, YO. Rep from * around.

Row 15: Knit all sts.

BO all sts loosely.

FINISHING

Weave in all ends, machine wash and dry to set and soften, place in basket, and fill with freshly baked muffins for a friend.

Edge detail of Ripple Basket Liner

PRINCESS MITTS

-- *details* --

SIZE

To fit a woman's hand, size Medium

FINISHED MEASUREMENTS

Circumference: 8" (20.5cm)

Length: 7½" (18.5cm)

YARN

Classic Elite Yarns Princess (40% Merino, 28% viscose, 15% nylon, 10% cashmere, 7% angora; 150 yds [137m]/50g) 1 skein Milord's Madder #3485. If substituting, use 150 yds (137m) of 4-ply DK-weight yarn.

NEEDLES

One set of size 6 (4mm) dpns, or size to obtain gauge

Two pairs of 16" (40cm) circular needles size 6 (4mm), or size to obtain gauge

NOTIONS

Cable needle, stitch markers, a darning needle

GAUGE

24 sts + 32 rows = 4" (10cm) in cable pattern

22 sts + 30 rows = 4" (10cm) in St st

STITCH GUIDE

M1R

Make a right-leaning increase by picking up the bar between sts from back to front and knitting into the front of the picked-up st.

M1L

Make a left-leaning increase by picking up the bar between sts from front to back and knitting into the back of the picked-up st.

--- *instructions* ---

When you find a luxurious four-ply yarn and want to take a small amount out for a test-knit, give these elegant fingerless mitts a try. They require only one skein of Classic Elite Princess, and the yarn's full-bodied, four-ply formation renders the cabled braid and ribbing beautifully.

Notes: In the first cable in the Four-Rib Braid Cable Pattern (Row 1), decrease by p2tog in the center of this stitch. In Row 33, M1 in the center purl stitch by purling into the front and back of the stitch. This will add the p2 for the rib.

CUFF

CO 48 sts and join in round, being careful not to twist. Work 14 rows in (k2, p2) ribbing for cuff. Place marker at beginning of round and after st 24 to help distinguish cable section from ribbing section.

FOUR-RIB BRAID CABLE

For the right-hand mitt, you'll work the ribbing/thumb gusset on the first 24 sts and the Four-Rib Braid cable

pattern on the second 24 sts. For the left-hand mitt, you'll work the Four-Rib Braid cable pattern on the first 24 sts and the ribbing/gusset on the second set of 24 sts. Finish thumb on 3 dpns.

Begin Four-Rib Braid cable chart.

Always k2 before the patt and (k2, p2) after the patt sts.

At the same time, on Row 3 of Four-Rib Braid Cable chart, begin to shape the thumb gusset in the ribbing sts. Follow the Thumb Gusset Charts to incorporate the increases into the (k2, p2) rib. The increase sts for the gusset will be worked before and after the third st for the right-hand mitt, and before and after the third to the last st for the left-hand mitt. To help you see where to make your increases, place a marker before

-- *designed by Jennifer Hagan* --

and after the M1 in the thumb gusset chart. As you increase, you will always slip the marker, M1, cont as established, and M1 before next marker.

Note: Work the first increase st by M1R and the second increase by M1L to create right- and left-slanting increases on either side of the gusset.

Once you have 13 sts between markers for gusset, work 3 more rows even and then place the gusset sts on a holder. Next row, CO 7 sts across the gap, and cont to end of round. Next round, begin decreases across top of thumb opening as follows.

FOR THE 7 CO STS:

Row 1: Ssk, k3, k2tog.

Row 2: Ssk, k1, k2tog.

Row 3: No decreases.

Row 4: S1 k2tog psso.

Cont the ribbing as established for rest of mitt.

On the cable section, cont Cable Pattern through Row 34. Then work (k2, p2) rib for 6 rows or until desired length. Try on the mitt periodically to ensure a good fit. BO all sts evenly.

THUMB

Place the first 6 sts from the holder on 1 dpn, the next 7 sts on a second dpn and pick up 7 sts from across the thumb opening on the third dpn. Work these 20 sts in (k2, p2) rib. Work thumb for 8 rows, or desired length. Again, try on the mitt to make sure of the fit. Bind off all sts evenly, leaving the thumb tip free. Weave in all ends, using the ends to close any remaining holes. Block to size.

Four-Rib Braid Cable Chart

 = K on RS

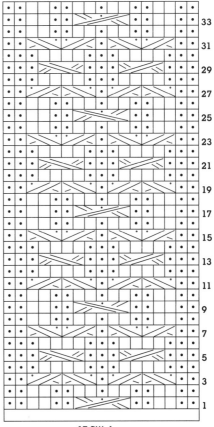

□ = K on RS

• = P on RS

= Slip next st onto cn and hold in back, k2, p1 from cn

= Slip next 2 sts onto cn and hold in front, p1, k2 from cn

= Slip 2 sts onto cn and hold in back, k2, k2 from cn

= Slip 2 sts onto cn and hold in front, k2, k2 from cn

= Slip 3 sts onto cn and hold in front, k2, slip purl stitch from cn back to left-hand needle and p, k2 from cn

= Slip 3 sts onto cn and hold in back, k2, slip purl stitch from cn back to left-hand needle and p, k2 from cn

FOUR-RIB BRAID CABLE

17 Stitches

Thumb Charts

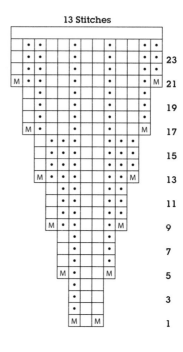

□ = K on RS

• = P on RS

M = Make 1 stitch

PRINCESS MITTS RIGHT THUMB GUSSET

PRINCESS MITTS LEFT THUMB GUSSET

Cabled Yarns

I'm veering away from convention here by using the term *cabled yarn* to define any yarn made up of multiple-plied yarns that are then plied together. Technically, this type of yarn has different names, depending on the direction in which the component strands were twisted and plied together in relation to the direction all *those* strands were plied into the final yarn.

When the finer individual strands are plied together in the S direction (counterclockwise) and then the resulting multiple-ply strands are plied together in the *opposite* direction (clockwise, or Z), you have a true *cable* yarn—sometimes also called grenadine, organzine, twisted rope, or cable cord. True cabled yarns really look like rope or a cable. They include Tahki Cotton Classic and Brown Sheep Cotton Fleece and Cotton Fine. The yarn is exceptionally balanced and strong.

When all the strands, at all stages of the game, are plied in the same direction (preferably S, or counterclockwise), you have a *multistrand* yarn, sometimes also called *S-on-S cabled*.

Currently the majority of commercial yarns fall into the multistrand yarn category—and of those, the majority come from Italian mills. Most are Merino, but some—such as the yarns from the Classic Elite Yarns Luxury Fibers Division—also include glorious amounts of cashmere and angora. Fewer true cabled yarns exist, and many of those are cotton or cotton blends. There is a difference in how these yarns knit up. True cabled yarns tend to produce even, open stitches and an overall rippled, almost pockmarked surface. This is because they have inner ply structures that move at an opposite angle to the outer yarn.

Multistrand yarns produce far more of a smooth, fluid surface that's aided by the fact that all the inner plies are moving at the same angle as the yarn. In simple stockinette, the left legs of the stitches tend to stack on top of one another, resulting in a faint vertical stripe up the fabric.

Karabella Aurora 8 multistrand yarn in stockinette stitch

The same yarn in a cable pattern (pattern on page 182)

But otherwise, the yarns' behaviors are similar enough that I've grouped them under the term cabled yarns. Purists, forgive me.

The presence of so many layers of twist gives cabled yarns an incredible stability and the strength to withstand far more abrasion than their once-plied counterparts. For this reason, although most sock yarns are traditional three- or four-ply yarn, you'll have great success using cabled yarns as well.

Cabled yarns produce a smooth fabric with beautiful stitch clarity that's enhanced by a visible ply structure. Although they can render a plush, fluid stockinette, they truly excel in rendering cables and more complicated stitchwork. The roundedness of cabled yarns gives those stitches a sculptural, three-dimensional quality.

While any fiber can be cable-spun, some fibers accept the spin better than others. My favorite would have to be the tightly plied, cable-spun Merino, such as Karabella Aurora 8, Filatura di Crosa Zara, Berroco Pure Merino, and Tahki Torino. You have crimpy, elastic Merino fibers spun and then plied at a near-perpendicular angle to create a plush, springy yarn with the feel of yeasted bread dough. Other cable-spun yarns, such as Alchemy Monarch, are loosely plied at an angle almost parallel to the yarn. The resulting yarn is still strong, but it has a far more fluid, relaxed feel that is better suited to more fluid, relaxed fibers. So if you're looking to substitute one cable-spun yarn for another, remember that the fiber content and the angle of the twist and ply will affect your results.

Both fiber contents and the angle of twists impact yarn. Berroco Pure Merino (top) is plush and elastic, with a crimpy Merino fiber plied at tight angles. Alchemy Monarch (bottom), on the other hand, is smooth and fluid with its loosely plied strands of cashmere and silk.

S
O
C
K

WAVY SOCKS

SIZE

To fit women's size Medium foot. (Knit the foot shorter or longer to fit your specific size.)

FINISHED MEASUREMENTS

Foot length: 9" (23cm)
Cuff length: 7" (18cm)

YARN

Karabella Aurora 4 (100% Merino; 197 yds [180m]/50g) 2 skeins #8170. If substituting, use 370 yds (338m) of multistrand DK-weight yarn.

NEEDLES

One set of size 2 (2.75 mm) dpns, or size to obtain gauge

NOTIONS

Tapestry needle

GAUGE

38 sts + 44 rows = 4" (10cm) in Wave Pattern

STITCH GUIDE

W&T
Wrap and turn. On the knit side, bring yarn to the front of your work as if to purl. Slip the next stitch, then bring yarn to the back of your work as if to knit, and slip the slipped stitch back onto the left-hand needle. Now turn your work. On wrong side rows, simply reverse the direction of the yarn.

C6F
Slip 3 sts onto cable needle and hold in front of work. K3 from the left-hand needle and then k3 from the cable needle.

C6B
Slip 3 sts onto cable needle and hold in back of work. K3 from the left-hand needle and then k3 from the cable needle.

WAVE PATTERN

Rnds 1–2: Knit.
Rnd 3: *C6F, k6; rep from * around.
Rnds 4–8: Knit.
Rnd 9: *K6, C6B; rep from * around.
Rnds 10–12: Knit.
These 12 rounds make up the Wave Pattern.

Cabled yarns are incredibly strong and stable, making them an ideal choice for socks. To keep the socks comfortable against your feet, we chose a smoother, low-relief, all-stockinette cable pattern that would show off the sculptural quality of the yarn while producing comfortable, entirely wearable socks.

LEG

CO 72 sts. Arrange your sts evenly over 4 needles (18 sts on each needle). Join in the round, marking the beginning of your round, and work (K2, p2) rib around. Work even in this ribbing pattern until your piece measures 2" (5cm) from the beginning.

Begin Wave Pattern and work until piece measures 8" (20.5cm) or until desired leg length, ending with Row 12 of the pattern.

HEEL

Put the instep sts on needles 2 and 3 on a stitch holder or scrap length of yarn. You will join them after you have turned the heel. Knit to the last st on needle 1, wrap and turn (w&t) the last st. Purl across needles 1 and 4 to the last st of your working sts, w&t.

Knit to 1 st before your last wrapped st, w&t. Purl to 1 st before your last wrapped st, w&t.

Repeat in this manner, working 1 fewer st each row

instructions continued

and always working a wrapped st before turning, until 12 sts remain without wraps and a RS row is facing. Knit over the 12 unwrapped sts to the first unworked, wrapped st. Work this st by picking up the wrap and knitting it together with your st. Wrap the next st so that it has 2 wraps and turn. Slip the first double-wrapped st and purl across to the first unworked, wrapped st. Pick up the wrap and purl it together with your st, w&t. Cont in this manner, working in the wraps and working 1 more st each row until you have worked all 36 sts again and your next row is a RS row. *You may need to pick up and work in an extra stitch on each end of the heel to prevent a hole when you start working in the round. Just knit them together in the next round.*

FOOT

Put instep sts back on needles 2 and 3 and begin working in the round again. Work needles 1 and 4 in St st, keep needles 2 and 3 in the Wave Pattern as established. Work until the foot measures 2" (5cm) less than the final desired foot length. Work one round with all sts in St st.

TOE

Rnd 1: Needle 1: Knit to the last 3 sts, k2tog, k1. Needle 2: K1, ssk, knit to end of the needle. Needle 3: Knit to the last 3 sts, k2tog, k1. Needle 4: K1, ssk, knit to end of the needle.
Rnd 2, all needles: Knit.
Work Rnds 1–2 until 36 sts rem (9 sts on each needle). Knit across needle 1. Break yarn, leaving a 12" (30.5cm) long tail.

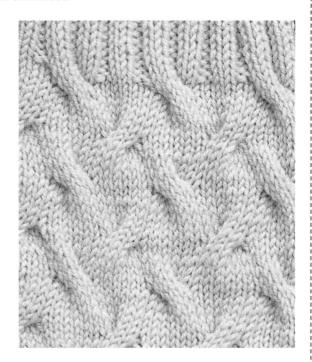

FINISHING

Graft the toe sts together using kitchener stitch. Weave in all ends.

XOX VEST

------ *details* ------

SIZES

Women's sizes Small (Medium, Large, Extra-Large). Shown in size Small.

FINISHED MEASUREMENTS

Bust: 34 (38, 42, 46)" (86.5 [96.5, 106.5, 117]cm)
Length: 19 (20, 21, 22)" (48 [51, 53.5, 56]cm)

YARN

Karabella Aurora 8 (100% extrafine Merino wool; 98 yds [89.5m]/50g) 6 (6, 7, 8) skeins #705. If substituting, use 550 (580, 680, 780) yds (503 [530, 622, 713]m) of multistrand, worsted-weight yarn.

NEEDLES

One pair of size 6 (4mm) straight needles and one set of size 6 (4mm) dpns, or sizes needed to obtain gauge

NOTIONS

Darning needle for seaming, stitch holders. If finishing neck with crochet, size G/6 (4mm) crochet hook

GAUGE

20 sts + 28 rows = 4" (10cm) over St st

STITCH GUIDE

C4B
Slip the next 2 sts onto cable needle and hold them to back of work, k2 from the left-hand needle, then k2 from the cable needle.

C4F
Slip the next 2 sts onto cable needle and hold them in front of work, k2 from left-hand needle then k2 from the cable needle.

CABLE PATTERN

Row 1: P2, k8, p2, k8, p2.
Row 2: K2, p8, k2, p8, k2.
Row 3: P2, C4B, C4F, p2, C4B, C4F, p2.
Row 4: K2, p8, k2, p8, k2.
Rows 5–8: Rep Rows 1–4.
Rows 9–10: Rep Rows 1–2.
Row 11: P2, C4F, C4B, p2, C4F, C4B, p2.
Row 12: K2, p8, k2, p8, k2.
Rows 13–14: Rep Rows 1–2.
Rows 15–16: Rep Rows 11–12.
These 16 rows are the Center Cable Pattern.

------ *instructions* ------

Cabled yarns always say "cables" to me, although I also love how they behave in simple stockinette. This vest is a compromise. The interlocking XOX cable pattern runs up the center and along each side of the neck, while a smooth stockinette hugs the body and keeps you toasty warm.

Note: This pattern is knit in two pieces. The Front piece has cabling along the neck that is continued after the shoulders are bound off. This cabling is grafted together and then seamed to the neck on the Back piece. So don't be put off when you see two tails hanging from the front of the vest!

BACK

CO 86 (94, 106, 114) sts.
Row 1: K2 *p2, k2; rep from * to end.
Row 2: P2 *k2, p2; rep from * to end.

Rep Rows 1–2 for 2½" (6.5cm), ending with Row 2. Work even in St st until your piece measures 12 (12½, 13, 13½)" (30.5 [32, 33, 34]cm) from the beginning. End with RS row facing.

SHAPE BACK ARMHOLES AND NECK
BO 4 sts at the beginning of the next 2 rows.
Next row: K1, k2tog, knit to the last 3 sts, ssk, k1. Purl the next row.
Rep these last 2 rows 3 more times—70 (78, 90, 98) sts remain.

------ *designed by Amy King* ------

Work even until the armhole measures 5 (5½, 5½, 6)" (12.5 [14, 14, 15]cm). End with RS row facing. K15 (15, 18, 19) sts and place on holder. You'll come back to them later. BO the next 40 (48, 54, 60) sts and knit to end of row.

Cont working the shoulder in St st, decreasing 1 st at the neck edge every RS row until you have 10 (10, 12, 12) sts remaining on the needles. Work even until the armhole measures 7 (7½, 8, 8½)" (18 [19, 20.5, 21.5]cm). BO all sts.

Attach yarn to the other shoulder and work the same way as the first shoulder.

FRONT

CO 94 (102, 114, 122) sts. *The difference in st count compensates for the 22 st cable section.*

Row 1: K2, *p2, k2; rep from * to end.
Row 2: P2, *k2, p2; rep from * to end.

Rep Rows 1–2 for 2½" (6.5cm), ending with RS row facing.

Next row: K36 (40, 46, 50) sts, work Cable Pattern over the next 22 sts, knit the last 36 (40, 46, 50) sts. Cont working the first and last 36 (40, 46, 50) sts in St st while working the middle 22 sts in the Cable Pattern as established until the entire piece measures 12 (12½, 13, 13½)" (30.5 [32, 33, 34]cm), ending with RS row facing.

SHAPE FRONT ARMHOLES AND NECK

BO 4 sts at the beginning of the next 2 rows. For the following rows, decrease 1 st at the armhole for every RS row 4 times. *At the same time,* start neck shaping as follows: Knit until there are 2 sts before the Cable Pattern begins, ssk, work across the first 11 sts of the Cable Pattern. Turn. Work the sts as they appear. Cont to work the neck decrease before the Cable Pattern every RS row until 22 (22, 24, 24) sts remain on the needle. Stop decreasing and work even until armhole measures 7 (7½, 8, 8½)" (18 [19, 20.5, 21.5]cm). End with RS facing. BO the next 10 (10, 12, 12) sts. Cont working the remaining 11 sts in the Cable Pattern, plus 1 knit st, until you have 6 (6½, 7½, 8)" (15 [16.5, 19, 20.5]cm) of cable. Put sts on a holder.

Attach yarn to the other side. You will decrease 1 st at the armhole every RS row 4 times. *At the same time,* start neck shaping as follows: Work across the 11 Cable Pattern sts, k2tog, work St st across the remaining sts. Work the WS sts as they appear. Cont to work the neck decrease after the Cable Pattern every RS row until 22 (22, 24, 24) sts remain on the needle. Stop decreasing and work even until the armhole measures 7 (7½, 8, 8½)" (18 [19, 20.5, 21.5]cm). End with WS facing. BO the next 10 (10, 12, 12) purl sts. Cont working the remaining 11 sts in the Cable Pattern, plus 1 knit st, until you have 6 (6½, 7½, 8)" (15 [16.5, 19, 20.5]cm) of cable. Graft this end with the other piece of cabling on the stitch holders.

FINISHING

Seam the Front and Back together at the sides. Join the shoulders together and seam the cable neck to the Back neck. If desired, work a single crochet stitch around the neck. Using your dpns, pick up and knit 76 (80, 84, 88) sts around the armholes. Join in the round and mark your beginning. Work (k2, p2) rib for four rounds, then loosely BO all sts in rib.

------ *details* ------

SIZE

To fit women's size Medium. To lengthen or shorten, simply increase or decrease the number of pattern repeats. (Each is approximately 1" [2.5cm].)

FINISHED MEASUREMENTS

18" (45.5cm) unstretched; will expand comfortably to a head circumference of 22" (56cm) or more

YARN

MEDIUM

Nashua Cilantro (70% cotton, 30% polyester; 136 yds [124.5m]/50g) 1 skein Ivory #003. If substituting, use 120 yds (109.5m) of multistrand worsted-weight yarn.

NEEDLES

One pair of size 7 (4.5mm) needles of your choice, or size to obtain gauge

NOTIONS

Cable needle, darning needle, stitch marker

GAUGE

22 sts + 32 rows = 4" (10cm) in St st

------ *instructions* ------

With headbands, we have far more room to play and create a high-relief, truly sculptural adornment. The sample shown was knit in a cotton blend, but you could just as easily make a decadent winter headband out of a multiple-ply Merino or one of the luscious cashmere blends from Classic Elite Yarns Luxury Fibers Division.

CO 28 sts using a provisional cast-on (see page 238). Begin Cable Chart and repeat 17 times. (For a shorter headband, work 16 chart repeats; a longer headband, work 18 repeats.) Leave sts on the needle.

FINISHING

Unravel the provisional cast-on and place those 28 sts on a second needle. With right sides facing you, join the seam with the kitchener stitch. Weave in ends and block to size. If you're not familiar with the provisional cast-on method, you can also use your preferred cast-on method, cast off all sts, seam the ends together, and hide the seam under your hair.

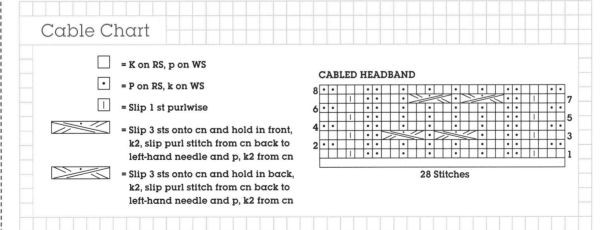

Cable Chart

☐ = K on RS, p on WS

• = P on RS, k on WS

⫿ = Slip 1 st purlwise

⟋⟍ = Slip 3 sts onto cn and hold in front, k2, slip purl stitch from cn back to left-hand needle and p, k2 from cn

⟋⟍ = Slip 3 sts onto cn and hold in back, k2, slip purl stitch from cn back to left-hand needle and p, k2 from cn

CABLED HEADBAND

28 Stitches

------ *designed by Jennifer Hagan* ------

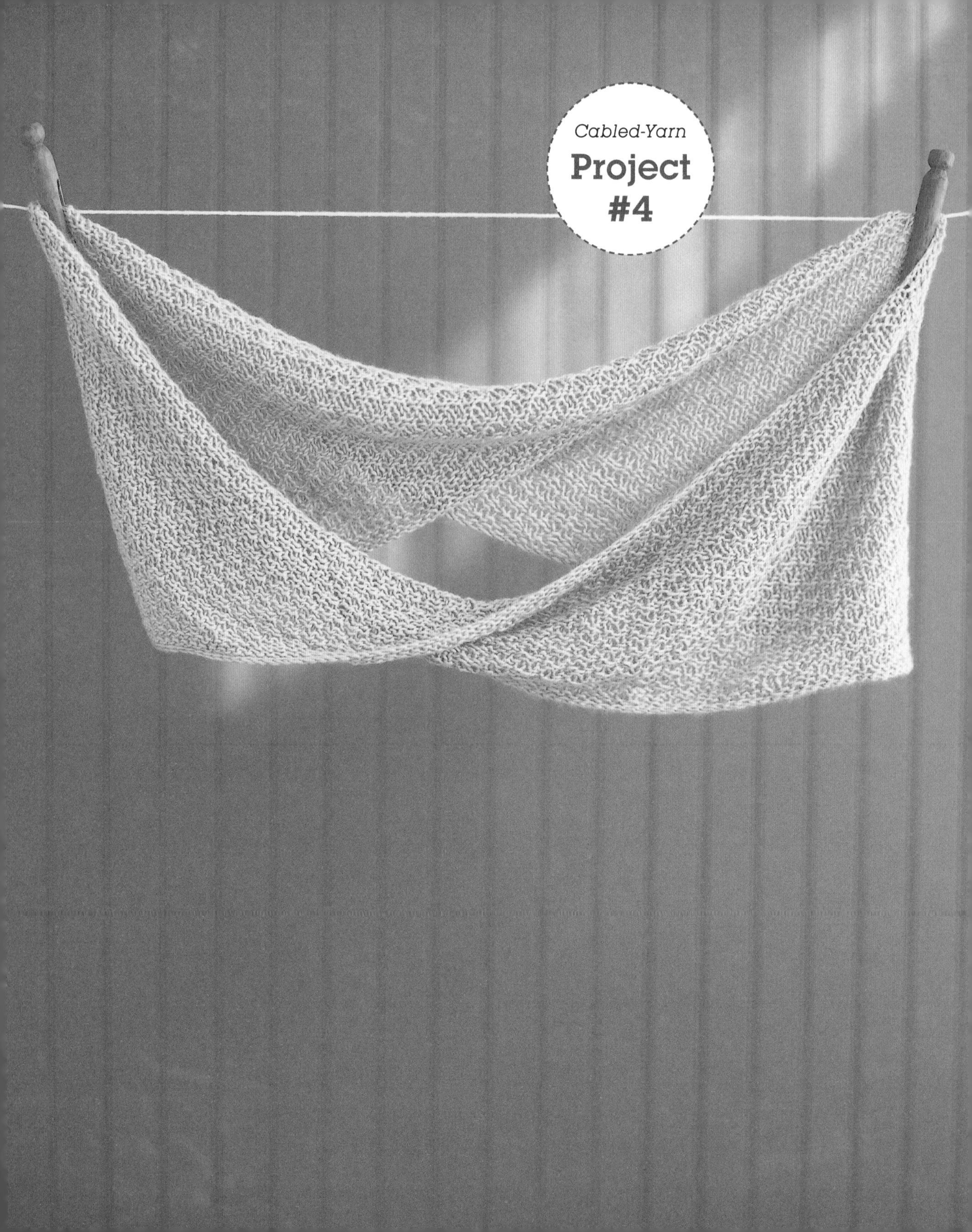
Cabled-Yarn
Project
#4

---

details

SIZE
To drape over an adult's shoulders

FINISHED MEASUREMENTS
Circumference: approx 24" (60cm)
Width: approx 10" (25.5cm)

YARN

SUPER FINE

Alchemy Yarns Monarch (70% cashmere, 30% silk; 156 yds [142.5m]/40g) 2 skeins Citrine. If substituting, 275 yds (251.5m) multistrand fingering-weight yarn.

NEEDLES
One 24" (60cm) circular needle size 7 (4.5mm)

NOTIONS
Stitch marker

GAUGE
24 sts + 32 rows = 4" (10cm) in Double Seed Stitch Pattern

DOUBLE SEED STITCH
Rnds 1–2: *K2, p2; rep from * to end.
Rnds 3–4: *P2, k2; rep from * to end.

---

instructions

Lest I mislead you into thinking that all cabled yarns are tightly plied, spongy Merinos, this yarn will set you straight. An astonishingly beautiful yarn, the multiple-ply Alchemy Monarch contains silk and cashmere fibers—an unexpected duo for this kind of yarn formation. On the skein it looks firm and flat, rather like embroidery thread. But it produces an extraordinarily soft, delicate, fluid knitted fabric with graceful drape, glorious sheen, and exceptional warmth.

I wanted to show off all these qualities, but I also knew that this yarn would be unforgiving of stitch irregularities because it's so smooth and fluid. A double seed stitch conceals any flubs and adds body and bounce to the fabric, while taking advantage of cashmere's softness and insulating qualities. Variations in tension would show up very clearly in plain stockinette, while a double seed stitch gives texture and relieves the pressure you might feel to make every stitch absolutely perfect.

This moebius would also be beautiful in similar multistrand yarns using pure silk or other fluid fibers such as bamboo or alpaca. The stitch pattern also helps break up pooling in hand-dyed colorways, so don't be afraid to experiment with those, too.

CO 168 sts. Marking the beginning of your sts, join to work in the round. Normally, when joining sts in the round you want to make sure you have no twists in your cast-on row. But in this case, you want to make sure there *is* one twist in your row—that is, somewhere in your cast-on row the base of the sts wraps over the needle once.
Work 4 rounds in garter stitch.

Next rnd: Begin double seed stitch and work until moebius is desired width. Finish with Rnd 4 of the double seed stitch.
Work 4 rounds in garter stitch. BO all sts loosely.

FINISHING
Wash in warm water with gentle soap and lay flat to dry, blocking to desired width and depth. Drape over shoulders and enjoy.

---

designed by Clara Parkes

Textured Yarns

Until now I've focused on the timeless classics, the essential yarn staples that are more influenced by Main Street than by Madison Avenue. They've always been in our local yarn stores and—we hope—always will. But the twist and ply of a whole other breed of yarns have been further manipulated to give the knitted fabric special texture and styling.

The benefit of these yarns is that they tend to do much of the heavy lifting for you—a welcome relief for relatively new knitters or anyone in need of a break and instant gratification. These yarns are specifically designed to make the simplest stockinette look like a work of art. Their drawback? As with the fashion world they attempt to follow, these yarns tend to come in and out of style far more quickly than their classic counterparts—sometimes seeing only one season in production.

Mills are constantly developing new methods to manipulate fibers into unusual yarns. Tapes, ribbons, tubes, furs and fluffs, ping-pongs, flags, knots, ladders, eyelashes, pigtails, and the list goes on and on with each season.

These unusual yarns work best in large, simple pieces of fabric where the yarn's innate texture can show through undiluted. This may be why novelty yarns have been so widely used for garter-stitch scarves and simple shawls. For more information on these yarns and for ideas on how to use them in designs, I recommend Laura Militzer Bryant's *The Yarn Stash Workbook*. As Creative Director of Prism Yarns, Laura has been deeply involved with novelty yarn innovation and has a great eye for its design potential.

Despite their ever-changing nature, novelty-style yarns can still be grouped into broader general categories that do stick around a while.

KNITTED TUBES

Sometimes yarn companies want visual depth without the body and weight of a standard multiple-ply structure. One way to do this is by taking a fine thread and knitting it into a soft tube that collapses onto itself, forming a narrow strand of flat yarn. It can look like a strand of homemade pasta, but if you hold it up to the light you'll see its honeycomblike, knitted loop formation.

Crystal Palace Cameo

Knitted tube yarns, also called tape yarns, are intriguing because the fibers move in a totally different direction than in standard spun yarns where the fibers flow more or less parallel to the strand. With a knitted tube yarn, you have fibers moving in a loopy formation that constantly shifts from parallel to perpendicular as each knitted stitch is formed.

This formation provides welcome stretch for inelastic fibers. If the fibers were stacked on top of one another and spun in the standard way, they might not yield at all under tension. But with the fibers forming perpetually enmeshed loops, your yarn tends to stretch more when you tug it. Keep this additional elasticity in mind if you're working with a yarn made from an innately elastic fiber, such as Merino.

Another quality of knitted tube yarns is that they can be deceptively bulky. I say *deceptively* because, while they may occupy the same amount of space as a standard plied yarn, they are essentially hollow at the core. In cellulose and cellulose-derived fibers, such as cotton, soy, bamboo, or corn, this abundance of air helps

the fabric breathe for perfect summertime wear. In warmer protein fibers, such as wool, the open fibers help trap still air and keep you warm.

The majority of knitted tube yarns available right now are made from cellulose and cellulose-derived fibers. We did have a brief glut of tube yarns made from marvelous blends of Merino, cashmere, angora, and other luxury fibers, but the mainstream market wasn't able to bear the high cost of these yarns and most of them have been discontinued, though I long for their return.

Meanwhile, the currently available knitted tube yarns are ideal for warm-weather clothing, like short-sleeved tops, tanks, lightweight sweaters, and shawls. You probably won't want to use these yarns for high-wear items, such as socks, which need a thicker, more robust yarn to withstand intense abrasion.

MIXING THICKNESSES
Thick/Thin Singles

Probably the simplest, most effective way to achieve texture in yarn is to vary its thickness at regular intervals. You'll most often find these thick/thin yarns in single-ply form, since adding more plies evens out a yarn's surface. Thick/thin yarns are available in solids and variegated colorways from many yarn manufacturers big and small, and in gauges that tend to err on the bulky side.

The thick/thin texture of Crystal Palace Yarns
Labrador single-ply yarn

If you're lucky, you can also find handspun thick/thin single-ply yarn at fiber festivals and select yarn shops. The irony here is that most handspinners produce a thick/thin yarn unintentionally when they first learn to spin. As their technique improves, it becomes harder to re-create that thick/thin texture, making a truly consistent thick/thin yarn the sign of an expert handspinner.

Thick/thin singles produce such a textured surface that you'll want to stick with simple stockinette, garter, and ribbing stitches. Much more elaborate stitchwork such as cables will easily get lost.

Multiple-Ply Textures

Another way to achieve easy surface texture in your knitting is to use a yarn that contains multiple plies of dissimilar thicknesses, textures, or fiber contents—or a bit of all three.

When you strand different components together, you get the smoother cohesion of a plied yarn but with the visual and tactile complexity of multiple materials. This generally allows you to do more than simple stockinette. Depending on the thickness of the yarn, you can also experiment with slip-stitch patterns, colorwork, and even lace.

The yarn choices within this category are so diverse that you'll really benefit from swatching samples before deciding on a final project. Try out stockinette, a few ribbing combinations, perhaps a cable or two. Switch needle sizes to see if it needs larger stitches or a tighter fabric. As you study the swatch with your eyes and hands, you'll find that the yarn tells you what to do.

Artyarns Silk Rhapsody consists of a superfine strand of brushed mohair and a luminous single ply of silk—the fiberly equivalent of mixing oil and water.

Alchemy Yarns Wabi-Sabi has two plies with different textures, thicknesses, *and* fiber compositions.

CHUNKY WINTER SET

SIZES

To fit a Child (Woman, Man). Shown in a Woman's size.

FINISHED MEASUREMENTS

Mitten circumference: 7½ (9½, 11)" (19 [24, 28]cm)
Hat circumference: 16 (18¼, 20½)" (40.5 [46.5, 52]cm)

YARN

Crystal Palace Yarns Labrador (100% wool; 90 yds [82m]/100g) 2 (3, 3) skeins Periwinkle #9628. If substituting, use 180 (270, 270) yds (164.5 [247, 247]m) chunky-weight yarn, preferably with a thick/thin texture.

NEEDLES

For mittens: One set of size 5 (3.75mm) dpns

For hat: One set of size 8 (5mm) dpns or 16" (40cm) circular needle

NOTIONS

Tapestry needle, stitch holder, stitch markers (3)

GAUGE

Mittens (on smaller needles): 16 sts + 24 rows = 4" (10cm) in St st
Hat (on larger needles): 14 sts + 20 rows = 4" (10cm) in St st

-- *instructions* --

Even the simplest stockinette stitching comes alive in a thick/thin single-ply yarn. As an added bonus, irregular stitches are all but concealed. A variegated colorway option in Labrador adds even more potential visual interest to this simple, classic set.

Notes: Both items in this set are knit at a decidedly finer gauge than specified on the yarn label. We did this to make sure no winter chill gets through when you wear the set outdoors.

MITTENS

CO 28 (36, 44) sts and join in the round, being careful not to twist sts. Place marker (pm) at the beginning of your round and work (k2, p2) rib for 2 (3, 3½)" (5, [7.5, 9]cm). Then work in St st for 2 (3, 4) rounds.

GUSSET THUMB INCREASE

Row 1: K1, pm, k1, M1, pm, knit to the end of round.
Row 2: Knit all sts, slipping the markers as you come to them.
Row 3: K1, sm, M1, knit to the next marker, M1, sm, knit to the end of round.
Rep Rows 2–3 until you have 9 (11, 13) sts between

markers—36 (46, 56) sts.
Knit 3 (4, 6) rounds even.
Next row: K1, remove markers as you go, place the next 9 (11, 13) sts on a holder, CO 3 sts for the thumb gap, knit to the end of round—30 (38, 46)sts.
Knit even for 2 (2½, 3)" (5 [6.5, 7.5]cm).

TOP DECREASE

(K4, k2tog) around, end with k0 (2, 4)—25 (32, 39) sts.
Knit even for the next 2 rows.
(K3, k2tog) around, end with k0 (2, 4)—20 (26, 32) sts.
Knit even for the next 2 rows.
(K2, k2tog) around, end with k0 (2, 0)—15 (20, 24) sts.
Knit even for the next 2 rows.
(K1, k2tog) around, end with k0 (2, 0)—10 (14, 16) sts.

-- *designed by Amy King* --

instructions continued

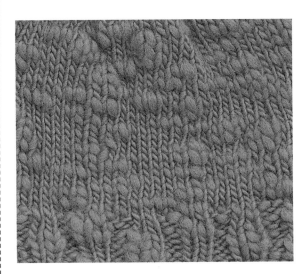

Knit even for the next 2 rows.

K2tog around—5 (7, 8) sts.

Knit even for the next 2 rows.

Cut yarn and a leave an 8–10" (20.5–25.5cm) tail. Using a tapestry needle, thread through the remaining sts and pull tight to close. Fasten off securely.

THUMB

Knit the 9 (11, 13) sts from the stitch holder. Pick up and knit 5 sts from the gap. Mark beginning of round and knit for 1" (2.5cm) even.

BEGIN DECREASE ROW

(K1, k2tog) around, end with k2 (1, 0)—12 (11, 12) sts.

Knit 2 rnds even.

Next decrease row: (K1, k2tog) around, end with k0 (2, 0)—8 (8, 8) sts.

Knit 1 rnd even.

Next decrease row: K2tog around—4 (4, 4) sts.

Cut yarn and leave a 6–8" (15–20.5cm) tail. Using a tapestry needle, thread through the remaining sts and pull tight to close. Fasten off securely, weave in all ends and block.

HAT

CO 56 (64, 72) sts. Join in the round, being careful not to twist stitches. Mark the beginning of your round and work (k2, p2) rib for 1½" (3.8cm). Work in St st until your hat measures 5 (6, 7)" (12.5 [15, 18]cm) from the brim.

BRIM DECREASE

Next rnd: (K2, k2tog) around—42 (48, 54) sts.

Knit 2 rounds even.

Next rnd: (K1, k2tog) around—28 (32, 36) sts.

Knit 2 rounds even.

Next rnd: K2tog around—14 (16, 18) sts.

Knit 2 rounds even.

Next rnd: K2tog around—7 (8, 9) sts.

Cut yarn and leave an 8–10" (20.5–25.5cm) tail. Using a tapestry needle, thread through the remaining sts and pull tight to close. Fasten off securely, weave in all ends and block.

ARCHITECT'S HAT

SIZE
To fit up to 22" (56cm) circumference

YARN

Alchemy Yarns Wabi Sabi (66% silk, 34% Merino; 86 yds [78.5m]/50g) 1 skein each of Persimmon #05F (A), Delphinium #25A (B), and Equinox #63C (C). If substituting, use 250 yds [229m] of 2-ply chunky-weight yarn, divided among three contrasting colors.

STITCH GUIDE
W&T
Wrap and turn. On the knit side, bring yarn to the front of your work as if to purl. Slip the next stitch, then bring yarn to the back of your work as if to knit, and slip the slipped stitch back onto the left-hand needle. Now turn your work. On wrong side rows, simply reverse the direction of the yarn.

NEEDLES
One 16" (40cm) circular needle size 10 (6mm), or size to obtain gauge

NOTIONS
Tapestry needle, stitch markers

GAUGE
14 sts + 20 rows = 4" (10cm) in St st

---- instructions ----

Multiple-ply yarns can play the mixed thickness game, too. In this case we chose a yarn that has two distinctly different plies made of two different fibers and two different textures. Brought together and knit up, they produce a finely rippled surface that makes even stockinette look interesting. The design draws from concepts of linear movement, 60-degree triangles, and the illusion of woven colors using slipped stitches and short rows.

Notes: The top of the hat is constructed in a series of six 60-degree triangles, which, when put together, form a circle (360 degrees). These triangles are formed through short-row knitting, employing a simple wrap & turn technique.

When picking up wrap & turn (w&t) stitches in short-row knitting, the wrap is knit together with the stitch it wraps. This step is unnecessary here, as the garter ridge and texture of the recommended fiber make the wrap hard to see.

TOP
With A, CO 12 sts.
*Row 1 (WS): K12.

Row 2: K10, w&t, k10.
Row 3: K9, w&t, k9.
Row 4: K8, w&t, k8.
Row 5: K7, w&t, k7.
Row 6: K6, w&t, k6.
Row 7: K5, w&t, k5.
Row 8: K4, w&t, k4.
Row 9: K3, w&t, k3.
Row 10: K2, w&t, k2.
Row 11: K1, w&t, k1
Next row (RS): Knit across 12 sts.

Rep from * 5 times more, for a total of 6 triangles. Sew edges of first and last triangle neatly together to form a circle.

instructions continued

BRIM

With B, pick up and knit 72 sts around outside of circle, placing marker (pm) at beginning of the round. Knit 1 round, purl 1 round to form a garter ridge.

With C, Knit 2 rounds.

With A, knit 1 round, purl 1 round.

BAND 1

Rnds 1–4: With B, *sl2 sts, k4; rep from * around.

Rnd 5: With A, knit.

Rnd 6: With A, purl.

BAND 2

Rnds 7–11: With C, *sl2 sts, k10; rep from * to marker.

Rnd 12: With A, knit.

Rnd 13: With A, purl.

Rep Band 2 (Rnds 7–13) once.

Rep Band 1 (Rnds 1–4) once.

With C, knit 2 rounds.

Change to B and knit 2 rounds.

With C, knit 1 round.

BO all sts as purlwise.

FINISHING

Weave in ends. Wash and block.

DIAMONDS AND PEARLS SHAWL

-- *details* --

FINISHED MEASUREMENTS
(AFTER WASHING AND BLOCKING)
Width: 56" (142cm)
Length: 19" (48cm)

YARN

Artyarns Silk Rhapsody (70% mohair, 30% silk; 260 yds [238m]/100g) 1 skein #RH123. If substituting, use 260 yds (238m) of 2-ply worsted-weight yarn, preferably a yarn with shimmer and drape.

NEEDLES
One 29" (73.5cm) circular needle size 9 (5.5mm), or size to obtain gauge

NOTIONS
Tapestry needle, stitch markers (4)

GAUGE
16 sts + 20 rows = 4" (10cm) in St st, blocked

-- *instructions* --

Plying dissimilar fibers together can produce even more visually dramatic results. For this shawl we picked Artyarns Silk Rhapsody, which mixes a smooth, shimmery, single-ply silk and a superfine strand of fluffy brushed mohair. The yarns are barely plied together, giving each component a distinct presence. But they complement one another perfectly in the finished fabric, the delicate halo of brushed mohair softening the brilliant sheen of the silk.

Notes: The stitch count jumps in Rows 31, 39, and 41 to create shoulder shaping. All those row-by-row instructions may seem daunting on paper, but after a short while you'll be able to read your stitches and understand your place in the pattern. The BO chosen for this pattern looks complicated when written out, but it's easy to complete and creates a wonderful airy edge that's very open to blocking.

CO 5 sts using the knitted cast-on or your preferred method.

Row 1: K1, place marker (pm), k1, pm, YO, k1, pm, YO, k1, pm, YO, k1—9 sts.

Row 2 and all even-numbered rows: Purl all sts.

In remaining rows, stitch markers should be slipped from left-hand to right-hand needle as the row is worked, remaining in the same position throughout. The markers will help you keep track of your place in the each row.

Row 3: K1, YO, k3, YO, k1, YO, k3, YO, k1—13 sts.

Row 5: K1, YO, k5, YO, k1, YO, k5, YO, k1—17 sts.

Row 7: K1, YO, k7, YO, k1, YO, k7, YO, k1—21 sts.

Row 9: K1, YO, k4, YO, k5, YO, k1, YO, k5, YO, k4, YO, k1—27 sts.

Row 11: K1, YO, k3, k2tog, YO, k1, YO, ssk, k4, YO, k1, YO, k4, k2tog, YO, k1, YO, ssk, k3, YO, k1—31 sts.

Row 13: K1, YO, k3, k2tog, YO, k3, YO, ssk, k4, YO, k1, YO, k4, k2tog, YO, k3, YO, ssk, k3, YO, k1—35 sts.

Row 15: K1, YO, k6, YO, sl1 k2tog psso, YO, k7, YO, k1, YO, k7, YO, sl1 k2tog psso, YO, k6, YO, k1—39 sts.

Row 17: K1, YO, k8, YO, ssk, k8, YO, k1, YO, k8, k2tog, YO, k8, YO, k1—43 sts.

Row 19: K1, YO, k20, YO, k1, YO, k20, YO, k1—47 sts.

Row 21: K1, YO, k22, YO, k1, YO, k22, YO, k1—51 sts.

Row 23: K1, YO, k1, *YO, k1, k2tog; rep from * 7 times, k2, yo, k1, YO, k2, *ssk, k1, YO, rep from * 7 times, k1, YO, k1—55 sts.

Row 25: K1, YO, k2, *YO, k1, k2tog, rep from * 8 times,

-- *designed by Shelia January* --

YO, k1, YO, *ssk, k1, YO; rep from * 8 times, k2, YO, k1—59 sts.

Row 27: K1, YO, k3, *YO, k1, k2tog; rep from * 8 times, k1, YO, k1, YO, k1, *ssk, k1, YO; rep from * 8 times, k3, YO, k1—63 sts.

Row 29: K1, YO, k30, YO, k1, YO, k30, YO, k1—67 sts.

Row 31: K1, YO, k32, YO, k1, YO, k32, YO, k1—71 sts.

Row 33: K1, YO, k8, YO, k9, YO, k9, YO, k8, YO, k1, YO, k8, YO, k9, YO, k9, YO, k8, YO, k1—81 sts.

Row 35: K1, YO, k7, k2tog, YO, k1, YO, ssk, k5, k2tog, YO, k1, YO, ssk, k5, k2tog, YO, k1, YO, ssk, k7, YO, k1, YO, k7, k2tog, YO, k1, YO, ssk, k5, k2tog, YO, k1, YO, ssk, k5, k2tog, YO, k1, YO, ssk, k7, YO, k1—85 sts.

Row 37: K1, YO, k7, k2tog, YO, k3, YO, ssk, k3, k2tog, YO, k3, YO, ssk, k3, k2tog, YO, k3, YO, ssk, k7, YO, k1, YO, k7, k2tog, YO, k3, YO, ssk, k3, k2tog, YO, k3, YO, ssk, k3, k2tog, YO, k3, YO, ssk, k7, YO, k1—89 sts.

Row 39: K1, YO, k10, YO, sl1 k2tog psso, YO, k7, sl1 k2tog psso, YO, k7, YO, sl1 k2tog psso, YO, k10, YO, k1, YO, k10, YO, sl1 k2tog psso, YO, k7, YO, sl1 k2tog psso, YO, k7, YO, sl1 k2tog psso, YO, k10, YO, k1—92 sts.

Row 41: K1, YO, k12, YO, k2tog, k8, YO, k2tog, k8, YO, k2tog, k11, YO, k1, YO, k12, YO, k2tog, k8, YO, k2tog, k8, YO, k2tog, k11, YO, k1—97 sts.

Row 43: K1, YO, k47, YO, k1, YO, k47, YO, k1—101 sts.

Row 45: K1, YO, k49, YO, k1, YO, k49, YO, k1—105 sts.

Row 47: K1, YO, k1, *YO, k1, k2tog; rep from * 16 times, k2, YO, k1, YO, k2, *ssk, k1, YO; rep from * 16 times, k1, YO, k1—109 sts.

Row 49: K1, YO, k2, *YO, k1, k2tog; rep from * 16 times, k3, YO, k1, YO, k3, *ssk, k1, YO; rep from * 16 times, k2, YO, k1—113 sts.

Row 51: K1, YO, k3, *YO, k1, k2tog; rep from * 17 times, k1, YO, k1, YO, k1, *ssk, k1, YO; rep from * 17 times, k3, YO, k1—117 sts.

Row 53: K1, YO, k1, *YO, k1, k2tog; rep from * 18 times, k2, YO, k1, YO, k2, *ssk, k1, YO; rep from * 18 times, k1, YO, k1—121 sts.

Row 55: K1, YO, k2, *YO, k1, k2tog; rep from * 18 times, k3, YO, k1, YO, k3, *ssk, k1, YO; rep from * 18 times, k2, YO, k1—125 sts.

Row 57: K1, YO, k3, *YO, k1, k2tog; rep from * 19 times, k1, YO, k1, YO, k1, *ssk, k1, YO; rep from * 19 times, k3, YO, k1—129 sts.

Row 59: K1, YO, k1, *YO, k1, k2tog; rep from * 20 times, k2, YO, k1, YO, k2, *ssk, k1, YO; rep from * 20 times, k1, YO, k1—133 sts.

Row 61: K1, YO, k2, *YO, k1, k2tog; rep from * 20 times, k3, YO, k1, YO, k3, *ssk, k1, YO; rep from * 20 times, k2, YO, k1—137 sts.

Row 63: K1, YO, k3, *YO, k1, k2tog; rep from * 21 times, k1, YO, k1, YO, k1, *ssk, k1, YO; rep from * 21 times, k3, YO, k1—141 sts.

Row 65: K1, YO, k1, *YO, k1, k2tog; rep from * 22 times, k2, YO, k1, YO, k2, *ssk, k1, YO; rep from * 22 times, k1, YO, k1—145 sts.

Row 67: K1, YO, k2, *YO, k1, k2tog; rep from * 22 times, k3, YO, k1, YO, k3, *ssk, k1, YO; rep from * 22 times, k2, YO, k1—149 sts.

Row 69: K1, YO, k3, *YO, k1, k2tog; rep from * 23 times, k1, YO, k1, YO, k1, *ssk, k1, YO; rep from * 23 times, k3, YO, k1—153 sts.

Row 71: K1, YO, k1, *YO, k1, k2tog; rep from * 24 times, k2, YO, k1, YO, k2, *ssk, k1, YO, rep from * 24 times, k1, YO, k1—157 sts.

Row 73: K1, YO, k2, *YO, k1, k2tog; rep from * 24 times, k3, YO, k1, YO, k3, *ssk, k1, YO; rep from * 24 times, k2, YO, k1—161 sts.

Row 75: K1, YO, k3, *YO, k1, k2tog; rep from * 25 times, k1, YO, k1, YO, k1, *ssk, k1, YO; rep from * 25 times, k3, YO, k1—165 sts.

Row 77: K1, YO, k1, *YO, k1, k2tog; rep from * 26 times, k2, YO, k1, YO, k2, *ssk, k1, YO; rep from * 26 times, k1, YO, k1—169 sts.

EDGING

Row 79: K1, *k1, (sl1 st back to left-hand needle, k1) 6 times, sl1 st back to left-hand needle, k3tog, BO first st on the right-hand needle by passing over the second st. Rep from * across row until the center st is the next st. Slip and knit the st before the center st 6 times, then sl1 back to left-hand needle and k2tog with the center st, BO first st on the right-hand needle afterwards. Cont from * until second half is completed, then cut end and pass through the last st, pulling tight.

FINISHING

Weave in all ends. Silk blocks well with heat blocking, as it retains the softness, drape, and shine. Since this shawl is a manageable size, you can pin it out on a heatproof blocking surface (especially pinning out all the edge loops) and then iron it flat with a dry iron on a silk setting.

Bouclé Yarns

Another way to create texture in yarn is to introduce intentional irregularities in the plying process. A classic example of this is bouclé yarn. Instead of feeding each ply together at an even pace to produce a smooth yarn, the mill intentionally feeds in one strand faster than the other so that it naturally loops back on itself before being secured by the other ply. This yarn is then re-plied in the reverse direction with a fine binder thread for stability, and the result is a "loopy" yarn called bouclé. Traditionally, bouclé yarns have been made from mohair with a wool or nylon binder, although you'll find a few more options today.

While bouclé yarns look gorgeous on the skein—especially when hand-dyed in variegated colors—they can be problematic to knit. Those open loops act as magnets for even the dullest-tipped needles, snagging again and again.

Most bouclés, whether simple or complex, want to be knit up in simple stockinette. Anything else will be totally lost beneath the wonderfully jumbled surface. Also know that the reverse side of your stockinette fabric tends to look more cohesive than the knit side. I've even turned garments inside out before seaming them to take advantage of this lovely texture.

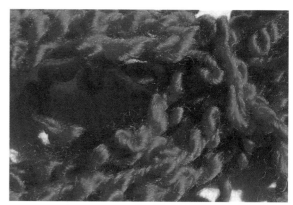

The textured bouclé in Debbie Bliss Astrakhan

HONEYCOMB BAG

-- details --

FINISHED MEASUREMENTS
Length: 11" (28cm), including handle
Width: 13" (33cm)

YARN

Debbie Bliss Cashmerino Astrakhan (60% Merino, 30% microfiber, 10% cashmere; 123 yds [112.5m]/50g) 2 skeins #15 (magenta) (A) and 1 skein #12 (periwinkle) (B). If substituting,

use 246 yds (225m) A and 120 yds (109.5m) B in worsted-weight bouclé or textured yarn.

NEEDLES
One pair of size 5 (3.75mm) needles

NOTIONS
Stitch holder, tapestry needle, ½ yd (.5m) cotton print fabric, sewing needle and thread, button, 1 yd (1m) suede cording

GAUGE
20 sts + 32 rows = 4" (10cm) in St st
24 sts + 40 rows = 4" (10cm) in pattern

STITCH GUIDE
KF&B
Knit through the front loop of a stitch and then, without taking it off the needle, knit through the back loop of the same stitch. You've created two stitches from one.

-- instructions --

More recently, general interest in the very basic bouclé yarns has faded in favor of more complicated, elaborate bouclé derivatives such as the soft, wonderfully textured Debbie Bliss Astrakhan that Teva Durham used for her charming Honeycomb Bag.

Stranding two colors of thick bouclé along the back of your work could be too dense and unruly with this yarn, so Teva chose a slipped-stitch colorwork pattern where only one color is worked each row.

Notes: This two-color pattern is easily worked in slip stitch. You only use one color of yarn in each row. Be sure to slip (or "sl" in the pattern) all sts purlwise so as not to change the orientation of the sts. Rather than cutting and rejoining colors, you can run them loosely up the edge of work, weaving them into the WS of the work. Or leave enough length to cut and weave in the ends later—although the texture in the yarn can make weaving in ends a challenge.

Front and Back are done in two identical pieces from bottom to handle top. All shaping is done within the pattern stitch: You begin with three repeats and then increase by one repeat (one-half repeat per side edge), which maintains staggered formation until seven repeats total. Then, to work even on same number of sts, you must

deliberately stagger the repeat in the stitch pattern, then the side edges are decreased within the pattern. The handle is worked from right edge and left edge up and grafted at the center top.

BACK/FRONT (MAKE 2 IDENTICAL)
With B, cast on 28 sts.

Row 1 (WS): Knit to end. Leave B there for Row 8 and carry up the edge.

Row 2 (RS): Join A and k1, sl3, k4, (sl4, k4) twice, sl3, k1.

Row 3: With A, p1, *sl2, p6; rep from * to last 3 sts, sl2, p1.

Row 4: With A, k1, *sl2, k6; rep from * to last 3 sts, sl2, k1.

-- designed by Teva Durham --

Row 5: Rep Row 3.

Row 6: Rep Row 4.

Row 7: Rep Row 3 and leave A for Row 10.

Row 8: With B, sl1, k3, (sl4, k4) twice, sl4, k3, sl1, CO 4 sts at end—32 sts.

Row 9: With B, knit across and CO 4 sts at end.

Row 10: With RS facing, join A, k1, sl3, k4, (sl4, k4) 3 times, sl3, k1.

Rows 11–15: Rep Rows 3–7.

Row 16: With B, sl1, k3, (sl4, k4) 3 times, sl4, k3, sl1, CO 4 sts at end—40 sts.

Row 17: With B, knit across and CO 4 sts at end—44 sts.

Row 18: With RS facing, join A and k1, sl3, k4, (sl4, k4) 4 times, sl3, k1.

Rows 19–23: Rep Rows 3–7.

Row 24: With B, sl1, k3, (sl4, k4) 4 times, sl4, k3, sl1, CO 4 sts at end—48 sts.

Row 25: With B, knit across and CO 4 sts at end—52 sts.

Row 26: Join A and k1, sl3, k4, (sl4, k4) 5 times, sl3, k1.

Rows 27–31: Rep Rows 3–7.

Row 32: With B, sl1, k3, (sl4, k4) 5 times, sl4, k3, sl1, CO 4 sts at end—56 sts.

Row 33: With B, knit across and CO 4 sts at end—60 sts.

MAIN BODY

Row 34: Join A and k1, sl3, k4, (sl4, k4) 6 times, sl3, k1.

Rows 35–39: Rep Rows 3–7.

Row 40: With RS facing, join B and sl1, k3, (sl4, k4) 6 times, sl4, k3, sl1.

Note: At this point, with 7 patt reps, you will not increase, but cont even in patt.

Row 41: With B, knit to end.

Row 42: Join A and k4, (sl4, k4) 7 times.

Row 43: With A, p5, *sl2, p6; rep from * to last 7 sts, s2, p5.

Row 44: With A, k5, *sl2, k6; rep from * to last 7 sts, sl2, k5.

Row 45: Rep Row 43.

Row 46: Rep Row 44.

Row 47: Rep Row 43.

Row 48 (RS): With B, k8, (sl4, k4) to last 8 sts, k8.

Row 49: With B, knit to end.

Rep Rows 34–49 once, then rep Rows 34–39 once.

SHAPE SIDE EDGE

Row 1: With B, BO 4 sts and cont across work as for Row 40—56 sts.

Next row: With B, BO 4 sts, k20 (begin count with last st from BO) and place them on a stitch holder for left edge handle, BO center 12 sts, k20.

RIGHT EDGE OF HANDLE

Preparation row: With RS facing, join A and k1, sl3, k4, sl4, k4, sl3, k1. Turn and work on these 20 sts for right edge of handle.

Row 1 (WS): With A, p1, (sl2, p6) twice, sl2, p1.

Row 2: With A, k1, (sl2, k6) twice, sl2, k1.

Row 3: Rep Row 1.

Row 4: Rep Row 2.

Row 5: Rep Row 1.

Row 6: Join B and BO 4 sts, k4 (begin count with last st from BO), sl4, k4, sl3, k1—16 sts.

Row 7. With B, BO 4 sts and knit to end—12 sts.

Row 8: Join A and k1, sl3, k4, sl3, k1.

Row 9: With A, p1, sl2, p6, sl2, p1.

Row 10: With A, k1, sl2, k6, sl2, k1.

Row 11: Rep Row 9.

Row 12: Rep Row 10.

Row 13: Rep Row 9.

Row 14: Join B and BO 4 sts, k4 (begin count with last st from BO), sl3, k1, CO 4 sts.

-------------------------------- *instructions continued* --------------------------------

Row 15: With B, knit to end—12 sts.

Rep Rows 8–15 three times, working final rep through Row 13 and then working final two rows without binding off or casting on as follows:

Final Row 14 with B: K1, sl3, k4, sl3, k1.

Final Row 15 with B: Knit to end.

LEFT EDGE OF HANDLE

Slip 20 sts from stitch holder onto needles and work to match other side, reversing shaping as follows: With RS facing, join A, work 3 reps, working Preparation Row through Row 13 as for Right Edge of Handle. Reverse shaping for Rows 14–15:

Rev Row 14: With B, CO 4 sts, sl4, k4, sl3, k1.

Rev Row 15: With B, BO 4 sts, knit to end—12 sts.

BOTTOM GUSSET

With A, CO 3 sts.

Row 1 and all WS rows: Purl all sts.

Row 2: Kf&b, k1, kf&b—5 sts.

Row 4: Kf&b, k3, kf&b—7 sts.

Row 6: Kf&b, k5, kf&b—9 sts.

Row 8: Kf&b, k7, kf&b—11 sts.

Cont even in St st until piece measures 11" (28cm). Decrease 1 st each edge every other row 4 times—3 sts.

Next RS row: K3tog, cut yarn, and pull through rem loop to secure.

FINISHING

Weave in ends and lightly block pieces. Since bouclé is a difficult yarn with which to sew, separate a strand of A and thread a tapestry needle. Graft right edge and left edge of handle at center top (side edge of rows), sewing 2 sts in from edge so honeycomb pattern appears to be continuous. Trace pieces for lining (see Lining instructions). Sew Gusset to Front and Back, and sew sides of purse, leaving top open.

LINING

Before sewing finished pieces together, arrange them flat on lining fabric and trace outline. Add ⅝" (16mm) selvedge all around. Sew lining front and back to lining gusset. Press seams outward and press handle seam edges inward (cut notches around curves to help edges to match knit pieces). Insert lining into purse and use small **whipstitches** to tack down edge around handle and top opening of purse. Sew the center of suede cording to lining at center back top opening of purse, trim and knot each end to desired length. Sew button to center front of purse 2" (5cm) down from edge.

Brushed Yarns

I magine loosely braiding your hair and then running a brush over the surface of the braid. This is pretty much how brushed yarns are created. Yarn manufacturers take a knitted tube or bouclé yarn and run it through a special machine with sharp teeth that rough up the fibers along the yarn's surface. The result is a marvelous, dimensionally stable yarn with an airy halo of fluff. Its common name is simply *brushed yarn*.

Traditionally, mohair has monopolized the brushed yarn market because its long, lustrous fibers lend themselves beautifully to the halo effect that comes from brushing. In recent years we've seen an influx of gorgeous, temptingly soft, brushed alpaca and alpaca blends. While they may look similar to mohair on the skein, their behavior is dramatically different. I'll explain why in a minute.

Brushed mohairs come in a variety of thickness and blends. First and most common is to mix the mohair with wool and a nylon **binder**—Classic Elite La Gran is a perennial favorite in this category. Next, the mohair can be blended only with wool—Anny Blatt's luminous Fine Kid is the best example here. And, finally, the mohair can be blended with wool and a small amount of silk, which gives an exquisite shimmer from beneath the halo of mohair fibers. This blend is often found in laceweight yarns where the silk can also lend marvelous drape. Here we have a tie between two classics, Rowan Kidsilk Haze and Knit One, Crochet Too Douceur et Soie.

Anny Blatt Fine Kid

But in all three cases, you have a dominant mohair presence that gives weight, body, and memory. Knit up, the mohair in these yarns produces a seemingly fluffy fabric that stays upright and perky in almost anything, from sweaters to blankets.

A much newer addition to the mainstream yarn world, brushed alpaca shares the length and luster of mohair. It's often marketed as a softer alternative to brushed mohair, which many people find too scratchy for next-to-the-skin wear. But mohair yarn that uses the highest-grade of kid and baby kid fibers will be just as soft as alpaca, if not softer.

Alpaca doesn't have quite the body or fiber memory of mohair, so it tends to have a heavier, flatter hand. The more undiluted alpaca you have in your brushed yarn, the more relaxed and fluid the fabric will be—perhaps to the point where all the brushed fluff lies flat like a furry tissue that's been through the wash.

This is why you'll generally find brushed alpaca yarns that also include some wool and nylon to keep the fabric firm and full-bodied. With 100 percent brushed alpaca yarns, such as Karabella's Brushed Alpaca, you may want to stick with high-drape, low-shape items, such as scarves, shawls, capelets, and ponchos. Don't bother with any stitchwork other than stockinette or garter, because the detail will be lost.

The brushed alpaca blends, such as Plymouth Baby Alpaca Brush or Blue Sky Alpacas Brushed Suri, will have a little more body for shapely garments—but drape and flatness will still be issues. One trick for adding body and firmness to brushed alpaca fabric is to use a smaller needle size than recommended on the label.

SCARUFFLE

-- *details* --

FINISHED MEASUREMENTS

Option A
Length: 46" (117cm)
Width: 5" (12.5cm)

Option B
Length: 50" (127cm)
Width: 7" (18cm)

YARN

Option A (near left): Rowan Kidsilk Haze (70% super kid mohair, 30% silk; 227

yds [207.5m]/25g) 1 skein Heavenly #592. If substituting, use 227 yds (207.5m) of fingering-weight brushed yarn of your choice.

Option B (far left): Hand Maiden Fine Yarn Rumple (100% silk; 328 yds [300m]/100g) 1 skein Sangria. If substituting, use 328 yds (300m) of fingering-weight bouclé or textured yarn of your choice.

NEEDLES

One 29" (80cm) circular needle size 4 (3.5mm), or size to obtain gauge

One 29" (80cm) circular needle size 11 (8mm), or size to obtain gauge

NOTIONS

Tapestry needle

GAUGE

12 sts + 16 rows = 4" (10cm) in garter st, lightly blocked. Because this is not a fitted garment, gauge is not too critical as long as the fabric remains open and airy. Option A uses a light, airy yarn while Option B uses a heavier yarn with more drape.

-- *instructions* --

Laceweight brushed mohair and silk are an ethereal combination. This simple pattern—part scarf, part ruffle—takes advantage of the relative drape of silk and mohair, while allowing the shimmer of the core silk to peek through the halo of mohair perfectly.

This pattern is equally well-suited to other silk-based yarns with a delicate slubby texture, where the drape and sheen will still come into play, so we created a second option using Hand Maiden Fine Yarn Rumple (far left). Have fun experimenting with other textured yarns, and don't be afraid to use this pattern for hand-painted or variegated yarns as well.

Notes: After the first 10 rows, the rest of the scarf is knit with short rows, which always leave some sts on the left-hand needle, no matter what needle is playing that role. If you must stop in the middle of a row to do something else (likely since there are upward of 300 sts in each row), you can pull all the stitches onto the cable part of the circular needle without folding your knitting or having long straight needles pointing in opposite directions like spears.

NECKBAND

CO 163 sts, using the knitted or cabled cast-on. Knit every row for 9 rows.

RUFFLE

Row 10: Knit into the front and back of each st to last st, k1—324 sts.

Row 11: Knit across row.

Row 12: Switch to larger needle and knit across row.

Row 13: K319 sts, leaving last 5 sts on the left-hand needle.

Row 14: Turn work and k314 sts, leaving last 5 sts on the left-hand needle.

Row 15: Turn work and k299 sts, leaving last 10 sts on left-hand needle.

Row 16: Turn work and k294 sts, leaving last 10 sts on left-hand needle.

-- *designed by Bess Haile* --

Row 17: Turn work and k290 sts, leaving last 14 sts on left-hand needle.

Row 18: Turn work and k286 sts, leaving last 14 sts on left-hand needle.

Cont in this manner, always increasing by 4 sts the number of sts left on left-hand needle every 2 rows, until piece measures 5" (12.5cm) long (7" [18cm] for Option B), or the desired length.

Last 2 rows: Turn and knit across all sts, including ones previously left on needle.

Final row: BO all sts very loosely.

FINISHING

Weave in all ends. Wash and block gently.

Chenille

Another yarn that produces a soft, furry surface is **chenille**, although it seems to be falling out of favor with knitters lately. Chenille yarn is created on a two-headed circular spinning machine. While the inner head rapidly plies fine binder threads together, the outer head runs "pile" threads back and forth in a zigzag formation. Each time they pass through the center, they are secured within those fine binder threads. Sharp blades then cut off the edges of the pile fibers, and you end up with the yarn we know as chenille.

The way chenille is manufactured involves quite a bit of twist that isn't always fully released at the mill. And this excess twist is perhaps the only serious drawback to chenille. As you unravel the yarn from the skein and start to work with it, you'll notice that it quickly gets twisted—not a big deal except that the yarn wants to be flat. Patient knitters will stop every few stitches or rows and untwist their work. Or you can place your skein on a vertical dowel (such as a paper towel holder), running the dowel through the very center of the skein. Using the outside end as your working yarn, you'll unwind the skein in such a way that less twist gets introduced.

Crystal Palace Yarns Cotton Chenille

After you've completed your garment, you'll likely encounter another problem. The yarn tends to work its way out of the fabric in little curled loops—this process is called **worming**. The best way to combat worming is by knitting as tight a fabric as you can, the idea being that the yarn will be better secured within that fabric.

The other thing you can do is stick with yarns that don't have a reputation for worming. Crystal Palace Yarns Cotton Chenille (made of, you guessed it, cotton) is my all-time favorite chenille because it does not worm and it wears like a dream.

Chenille yarns are also manufactured from synthetic fibers, and you'll even find exquisite silk chenilles from some of the boutique hand-dyers like Artyarns. The soft, fuzzy demeanor of chenille makes it perfect for pillows, afghans, baby blankets, shawls, stuffed animals, and even purses. Chenille yarns tend to have very little elasticity, and some of the synthetic chenille yarns tend to produce dense fabrics that don't breathe very well, making them rather unsuitable for women's clothing.

CLASSIC WASHCLOTH

------------------------------- details -------------------------------

FINISHED MEASUREMENTS

Before washing and drying: 12"
(30.5cm) square
After washing and drying: 10" (25.5cm)
square, or smaller, depending on how
hot your dryer gets

YARN

MEDIUM

Crystal Palace Yarns Cotton Chenille
(100% mercerized cotton; 98 yds

[89.5m]/50g) 1 skein Pistachio #1208
(A), 1 skein Powder Blue #5638 (B). If
substituting, use 90 yds (82m) A and
22 yds (20m) B, both in worsted-weight
cotton chenille. Because this is a
washcloth, it's important that the
chenille be cotton.

NEEDLES

One set of size 4 (3.5mm) needles, or
size to obtain gauge

NOTIONS

Tapestry needle

GAUGE

20 sts + 40 rows = 4" (10cm) in
garter stitch

STITCH GUIDE

GARTER STITCH
Knit all stitches on every row.

------------------------------- instructions -------------------------------

When I think of chenille, I think of cozy, old-fashioned bathrobes and plush towels and washcloths. This simple washcloth pattern was inspired by a set of colorful washcloths my grandmother had when I was growing up. I've never been able to find them since. The key is to use a smaller needle than the yarn requires, and then machine-wash and -dry the washcloth to tighten the fabric even more as part of the finishing process. These last forever and make wonderful gifts.

CO 56 sts with A and work 6 rows in garter stitch.
Stripe rows (RS): Attach B and work 6 rows in St st, twisting A up the edge as you go. When complete, cut B, leaving a generous tail for weaving.
Next row: With A, work the next 6" (15cm) in garter stitch, ending on WS row.
Next row (RS): Repeat Stripe Rows.
Rejoin A and work 6 rows in garter stitch, then BO all sts loosely.

FINISHING

Be sure to weave in all ends *before* washing. Then, place washcloth in warm soapy water, or run it through a wash cycle in your washing machine, and put it in the dryer. With wash, the cotton will shrink into a fuzzy, thick, wonderful fabric.

------------------------------- designed by Clara Parkes -------------------------------

The Felt Factor

When scale-laden protein fibers are submerged in hot soapy water (for example, when your much-labored-over handknit sweater is tossed in the washing machine by its clueless recipient), the fibers will swell, causing the ends of the scales to push out like an umbrella being opened. Agitate the fibers in the washing machine and all those scales begin to tangle with one another until they are inextricably enmeshed. The resulting matted shrunken material is commonly called **felt**. The felting of knitted items is actually called **fulling**, whereas felting is technically for raw fibers, but it's increasingly common to see the term *felt* used in all contexts, so I'm using it that way here.

Some protein fibers felt more readily than others, depending on the size and shape of the scales on their surface. Soft, short-staple wools, like Merino and Cormo, with their endless tiny scales, are eager, happy felters. The longer, smoother wools with larger scales, like Bluefaced Leicester and Wensleydale, are more work to felt. Alpaca and mohair, with their fewer, larger scales, felt more slowly but are worth the wait. The smooth, chevron-shaped scales in angora can add a beautiful halo to felted fabrics. Qiviut and camel have very few scales and will not felt readily.

Because the felting process depends on the presence of scales, fibers lacking scales won't felt—no matter how long you leave them in the washing machine. Synthetic fibers, cellulose and cellulosic fibers, and silk—they all have varyingly smooth surfaces that will not enmesh with one another in hot soapy water.

And even with fibers that *theoretically* have scales, some won't felt. The most notable is wool that's been specially treated to be machine-washable, since the superwash treatment involves removing or minimizing scales. The resulting smooth, scale-free surface won't felt in the washing machine and may actually stretch instead.

Also be aware that some white wools won't felt. Naturally bright white wools that haven't been bleached to oblivion will felt, such as the Fleece Artist Kid Aran used for the Calla Lily bag at right. But those that *were* extensively bleached and processed may be damaged to such a degree that the scales won't enmesh properly. If you aren't certain, try felting a test swatch first. It's the only way to know for sure if the skein you have will or will not felt.

And always remember to add soap or detergent to your water. This raises the pH of the water, which, in turn, encourages the felting process.

CALLA LILY BAG

FINISHED MEASUREMENTS (AFTER FELTING)

Base: 10" (25.5cm) long, 3½" (9cm) wide

Tall side: 12½" (32cm)

Short side: 6" (15cm)

Strap: 20" (51cm)

YARN

Fleece Artist Kid Aran (50% kid mohair, 50% wool; 438 yds [400.5m]/250g), 2 skeins Natural. If substituting, use 855 yds (782m) of 3-ply worsted-spun yarn containing protein fibers that will felt.

NEEDLES

Two pairs of 24" (60cm) circular needles size 11 (8mm), or size to obtain gauge

NOTIONS

Tapestry needle, stitch marker, safety pin

GAUGE

12 sts + 17 rows = 4" (10cm) in St st

-- instructions --

You'd think a white yarn from a company reknowned for its vibrant hand-dyed yarns wouldn't make sense. But this is no ordinary yarn, and Cat Bordhi is no ordinary designer. Below, she explains the genesis of this bag.

When Clara invited me to contribute a design inspired by a special yarn, I was in the mood to do a felted bag, and that meant the yarn simply had to be Fleece Artist Kid Aran. Fleece Artist is famous for hand-painted colorways that are so transporting that fans regularly find themselves hopelessly in love with colors they've always loved as well as others they've never even liked. But for this design I chose the simplicity of white. Kid Aran is a very special yarn, and I wanted to showcase its characteristics without the distraction of tempting colors.

Kid Aran is a three-ply yarn, worsted-spun of long fibers, half kid mohair and half wool, silken and sleek in the hand. It knits up into a supple and elegant fabric, wonderful for garments. But it is most delicious when felted, becoming lustrous and bumpy, with nubbles and knots of mohair tunneling in and out of the dense woolen surface. It is the most sensuous felt I know of. And this is an extraordinary "white"—like melting vanilla ice cream made with rich yellow egg yolks and pure vanilla.

The inspiration for the Calla Lily Bag arose from my love of flowing shapes and places to put things. I worked out the design by making paper models, and I have given you a paper model to cut out and put together, so you'll have a 3-D guide as you knit. Until the design was done, I'd planned to have a zipper close the central compartment (which is formed by the sandwiched inner walls of the outer compartments), but the finished bag had such beautiful calla lily–like lines that I could not bear to erase the flower's central curve by closing it. —CAT BORDHI

-- designed by Cat Bordhi --

-- *instructions continued* --

Note: Before you begin, you may find it helpful to make a photocopy enlargement of the bag model so you can understand how all the shapes and pieces come together.

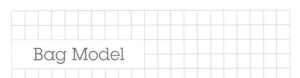

Bag Model

Making a model of the Calla Lily Bag

(Model represents unfelted proportions; bag will shrink more vertically than horizontally.)

Step 1: Trace or copy the pieces below, then cut around solid lines.

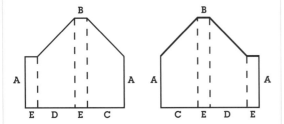

Step 2:
Fold one compartment along dotted lines and then attach side A to side A. Repeat with second compartment to make a mirror image of first compartment.

Step 3:
Attach each compartment to the rectangular base, matching edges with letters.

Step 4:
Attach strap to top of each compartment, making sure not to twist strap.

Step 5:
Join the edges of the compartments where they touch on each side of bag.

BASE

CO 84 sts and join in the round, being careful not to twist the sts. Place marker (pm). Knit for 6½" (16.5cm). Remove marker, and pin safety pin to this corner of the knitting.

FIRST COMPARTMENT

OUTER LONG SIDE

Find the midpoint of the 84 sts, fold your circular needle cable here, and pull out a few inches (about 8cm) of cable between the 2 sets of 42 sts. Hold the needle tips parallel. With second circular needle, k2tog (1 st from each tip), cont until the 2 lines of 42 sts are joined as a single line of 42 sts. Set aside empty needle.

FIRST SHORT SIDE

Place marker, and with the same needle, pick up 11 sts along one-half of the edge of this adjacent short side—53 sts on this needle.

INNER LONG SIDE

With the other circular needle, pick up 42 sts along the middle of the top layer of the Base, ending at the center of remaining short side.

SECOND SHORT SIDE

Cont with this needle, pick up 11 sts along one-half of the edge of this short side, ending at intersection with first needle. Each needle holds 53 sts.

Knit around on both circular needles *(one needle knits its own sts, then slides all its sts to rest in the middle of its cable, and gives the yarn to the other needle, which takes the yarn and does the same thing—one needle working while the other rests—round and round the knitting goes)* until the turns are wide enough to knit

instructions continued

all sts onto 1 needle. Set aside the empty needle. When the compartment measures 12" (30.5cm) from the base, begin shaping:

Row 1: BO first 11 sts after marker (bound-off sts are directly above the 11 sts picked up along first short edge). Knit until 1 st remains, pick up first bound-off st and knit it together with the final st, turn—95 sts.

Row 2: P2tog, purl until 2 sts remain, p2tog, turn—93 sts.

Row 3: K2tog, knit until 2 sts remain, k2tog, turn—91 sts.

Rep Rows 2–3 until 15 sts remain.

Work k1, p1 ribbing on these 15 sts until strap measures 25" (63.5cm). Cut tail and place sts on holder.

SECOND COMPARTMENT

Starting at the corner above the corner marked with a safety pin, pick up 84 sts from the cast-on edge. Once you finish joining the lines of 42 sts, you will be at the corner diagonally opposite the safety-pinned corner, ready to begin picking up 11 sts along the short edge, and so on. Follow the instructions for the first Compartment until 15 sts remain (do not knit another strap). Graft the 15 sts to the strap's 15 sts, checking to be certain the strap is not twisted.

FINISHING

Secure base layers: Spread compartments apart to reveal midline of base. Loosely sew through both layers along midline.

SIDES

Starting on one side of the bag, fold each compartment starting from where they meet at the base (a 12" [30.5cm] side grows beside a 22" [56cm] side), to iden-

tify a single vertical column of sts on each compartment. Sew these 2 columns of sts together (gently enough so the seam will not pucker when felting) from base up to top of 12" (30.5cm) side. Take a few extra sts here to secure the edge, then weave in ends. Repeat on the other side of bag.

FELTING

The bag will seem impossibly huge before felting, but the shrinkage will be dramatic. Place the bag in the washing machine with a pair of jeans or a half-dozen tennis balls. To protect your machine's filter, place the bag inside a large pillowcase secured with strong rubber bands or a zipper. Set machine for low, hot water, and add about an eighth of the usual amount of detergent. Set a timer and check progress after every minute or two, checking to be sure bag compartments are not turning themselves inside out—if so, turn them back before resuming felting. Reset the machine to continue agitating until the bag is the desired size. This yarn felts very quickly (my bag was done in 5–6 minutes) so keep a close eye on the progress. When the desired degree of felting has been achieved, remove it from the machine and submerge it in cold water to arrest the felting process. Block by patting and pulling into shape, then folding towels to fit inside each compartment. Wrap the entire bag in another towel, set it against the smooth area inside the washing machine, and spin dry in this position. Hang to finish air-drying.

RETRO CLOCHE

SIZE
One size fits most

FINISHED MEASUREMENTS
Felted brim circumference: 24" (60cm)
To adjust circumference, simply reduce or increase felting time until desired size is achieved.

YARN

Brown Sheep Yarns Lamb's Pride Worsted (85% wool, 15% mohair; 190 yds [174m]/113g) 1 skein each of Sapphire #M-65 (A) and Periwinkle #M-59 (B). If substituting, use 190 yds (174m) A and 80 yds (73m) B, both of single-ply worsted-weight wool.

NEEDLES
One 16" (40cm) circular needle size 10½ (6.5mm), or size to obtain gauge
Set of dpns size 10½ (6.5mm), or size to obtain gauge

NOTIONS
2 yds (2m) ¼-inch (6mm) ribbon in coordinating color, tapestry needle for weaving in ends, stitch marker

GAUGE
16 sts + 20 rows = 4" (10cm) in St st

At the *Knitter's Review* Retreat a few years ago, someone brought a lovely felted hat. I remember that, as people passed it around and tried it on, it looked good on every single person—something I'd never witnessed before or since. When I started writing this book, I knew I wanted to find that hat pattern. And I knew I wanted to show it in Brown Sheep Yarns Lamb's Pride, a classic yarn for felting.

With B, CO 110 sts. Join in the round, marking the beginning and being careful not to twist. Knit one round even.

Next rnd: K23, YO, k2tog, k2, (YO, k2tog, k3, YO, k2tog, k5) 6 times, YO, k2tog, k3, YO, k2tog, k2, YO, k2tog. Knit 8 rounds even.

Change to A and knit 16 rounds even.

(K9, k2tog) around—100 sts.

Knit 6 rounds even.

CROWN DECREASE
(K3, k2tog) around—80 sts. Knit 2 rounds even.

(K2, k2tog) around—60 sts. Knit 2 rounds even.

(K1, k2tog) around—40 sts. Knit 2 rounds even.

(K2, k2tog) around—30 sts. Knit 1 round even.

(K1, k2tog) around—20 sts. Knit 1 round even.

K2tog around—10 sts. Knit 1 round even.

K2tog around—5 sts.

Cut yarn leaving a 10" (25.5cm) tail. With a tapestry needle, thread tail through remaining sts and secure well.

FINISHING
Be sure to secure and weave in all ends before felting. Weave a piece of acrylic, superwash wool, or cotton string through the holes made in B for the brim at the beginning of the hat. (This will help you find them once the hat has been felted.) Place the hat in the washing machine with a towel, a pair of jeans, or several tennis balls to add friction. To protect your washing machine's filter, place the hat inside a pillowcase and zip it shut or secure it with a rubber band. Set the machine for a small load size, add a small amount of detergent, and use the hottest water your machine can provide. Begin to agitate, checking the hat's progress every minute or so. You do not want it to rinse and spin. Continue felting until the hat has reached the desired size. Immediately pull it out of the washing machine and submerge it in cold water to arrest the felting process. To block, place the hat on your head, fold up the cuff, and tug it to the desired shape. Tighten and retie the piece of string so that it's the right size. Remove the hat from your head and let it dry, standing in shape. Once dry, replace the string with a satin ribbon and tie securely into a knotted bow.

W E'VE BEEN ON A JOURNEY LEARNING ABOUT THE ESSENTIAL BREAD-AND-BUTTER STAPLES OF OUR YARN STASHES. YARN COMPANIES COME AND GO, BUT THESE FIBERS, PREPARATIONS, AND FUNDAMENTAL *TYPES* OF YARNS ENDURE. THIS INFORMATION IS JUST THE TIP OF THE ICEBERG. WHAT LIES AHEAD IS THE FUN PART: EXPERIENCING IT FOR YOURSELF.

Go to your stash, close your eyes, and pick a skein of yarn. Without looking at it, touch the yarn, smell it, rub it against your cheek, and try to guess what fiber it is. Open your eyes and read the label. Were you right? Close? Terribly wrong? Don't worry—sometimes you'll hit the nail right on the head, and sometimes the right clues will lead you in a different direction. Keep going.

Look at the yarn. Is it a single, a plied yarn, or a more complex textured yarn? How is it made up? If it's a plied yarn, how many plies are there, what direction are they twisted, and at what kind of angle? Think back to what you've read. Based on this fiber and this type of spin, how *should* the yarn behave? Consider the fiber content. Does it make sense to you that the fiber has been spun this way?

Grab some needles, cast on a few stitches, and start swatching. See what happens when you switch from bamboo to birch to aluminum to casein to ebony needle, or when you change from a size 8 to 9 to even 10 needle, or when you squeeze those same stitches on a size 4.

Open up your mind and tune in all your senses. Are your needles growing listless? Add some purl stitches. Does the yarn need discipline? Switch to a pair of sharper-tipped needles. Try stacking your purl stitches on top of one another to see how the ribs look. Awkward and forced? Switch needles. Switch stitches. While we tend to approach yarns with a general idea of what we want to do with them, sometimes we have to set all preconceived notions aside and do what the yarn tells us. And every yarn will reveal its potential to you if you listen to it long enough. Keep trying new things and keep experimenting.

I realize that some yarns will always pose a challenge. Perhaps the fiber is of a poor quality, or the mill forced the fiber into shapes it didn't want to take, or the dye house used one too many chemicals. Some yarns are just damaged goods that have lost their ability to whisper to you. In those cases, honor the yarn as best you can but know when to give up and move on.

When yarn, needles, and stitch come together in perfect harmony, when your yarn speaks and it's what you, too, have been dreaming—it's a match no other yarn can set asunder. The work flows, it pleases your hands, it excites your mind, and it calms your soul. Time stops. You feel as if you could knit forever.

Let the journey begin.

Care & Feeding

WASHING HANDKNITS

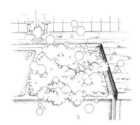

I love dropping my handknits into a sink of warm, soapy water. It's a sensual experience, feeling the garment soften and relax in the water, watching the bubbles swish to and fro as I gently squeeze the fabric, and, of course, smelling that heavenly blend of wet fibers and gentle soap. I've even been known to wash my superwash-wool socks by hand just for the sheer pleasure of it.

But many still warn us that the only way to safeguard our precious handknits is to have them dry-cleaned. For most fibers, just the opposite is true. Dry cleaning involves applying chemical solvents to fabric. These chemicals can inadvertently strip the fibers of their natural moisture and luster. Careful handwashing with a gentle, biodegradable soap, on the other hand, will leave your garments supple and lustrous for years and years.

Other people refuse to wash garments by hand—especially socks—because they just don't believe they'll get as clean as they would in the washing machine. My answer: If you trust your hands to wash your hair properly, then you can trust them to keep your clothes clean as well.

Dropping a much-labored-over handknit into a sink of water the first time can be a bit nerve-wracking, so let me walk you through the steps. This is the standard procedure for all handknits. Please make note of the fibers you're washing and check the Special Fiber Notes at the end of this section before proceeding.

FILL THE SINK. After you've taken a few deep breaths to control any racing pulse or trembling hands, get started by filling a sink with lukewarm water and adding a mild soap. When washing protein fibers, I prefer soaps specifically formulated for woolens, such as Eucalan or Kookaburra woolwashes—but you can also use a gentle shampoo (after all, protein fibers are hair, too, right?). When in doubt, and for all other fiber types, I'll often use Ivory Dishwashing Liquid. When washing protein fibers, you want to steer clear of any harsh detergents that could strip the fibers of their luster.

SUBMERGE. Drop your handknit into the water and gently tap it down until the whole garment is saturated. Squeeze the handknit gently a few times to make sure all the soap has reached the nooks and crannies of the fabric, and then let the handknit rest for about five minutes. With protein fibers you generally want to keep agitation to a bare minimum.

RINSE. Squeeze the handknit together so that the soapy water runs through one final time and drains out as you lift the handknit out of the water. Now drain the sink and refill it with water, being extra careful to keep the rinse water the same temperature as the wash. Rapid temperature changes can cause protein fibers to felt together.

Drop the handknit back in the sink, tap it down, squeeze gently, pull it together, lift out, drain the sink, refill, and repeat as many times as necessary until the rinse water runs clear.

BLOT. Pull the handknit together in your hands and give it a good squeeze, being careful not to wring or twist it. You want to remove the bulk of excess water. Next, lay the handknit out on a towel. For extra absorption, I like to cover the handknit with a second towel, too. Now roll it up and gently press to remove more water. You can also put the handknit in the washing machine and set it to spin for about ten seconds—but don't let it spin more than that or you'll risk stretching or creasing the fabric.

DRY. Now simply reshape the handknit (some will need it more than others) and let it dry, flat, away from heat. You can either dry it flat on a towel or use a mesh-covered sweater rack, which keeps the handknit elevated so that air can circulate underneath.

STORE. In the case of handknits, I'd say no coat hangers, period. Hanging handknits—wools, cottons, or most other fibers—invites stretching, and you may also end up with large, hanger-shaped nubs protruding from where each shoulder should be. Fold your clean handknit and store it flat. Some even fold up their woolens in tissue paper.

That's it! Now reward your bravery with a cup of tea or a piece of chocolate—or better yet, both.

SPECIAL FIBER NOTES

Protein Fibers

All protein fibers are susceptible to moths. The best way to prevent moth damage is to keep your woolens clean, especially before storing them for any period of time. Perspiration and food stains or crumbs are especially attractive to moths. If you suspect an infestation, immediately take all your woolens out of the house and vacuum the storage area thoroughly.

To kill the eggs and larvae, you can either wash the garment and let it dry outside in the sunshine (something eggs and larvae dislike immensely) or place the garment in your freezer for about a week. I still recommend washing the garment and setting it outside to dry, preferably in a bright area. If you're worried about direct sunlight damaging the fibers simply place the garment in an area that's indirectly well-lit.

I do not recommend storing your woolens with traditional mothballs containing naphthalene or paradichlorobenzene. While naphthalene vapors are highly toxic to moth eggs and larvae, they have also been found to be potentially carcinogenic to both humans and pets. More recently, naphthalene has been replaced by paradichlorobenzene, which is also used in toilet deodorizer products. An EPA-registered pesticide, paradichlorobenzene may reasonably be anticipated to be a carcinogen at high exposures, according to the Department of Health and Human Services. While both products have proven effective against moths, be mindful of the risks before using them.

A more indirect route is to store your woolens with sachets of herbs considered to have moth-deterrent qualities—including wormwood, rue, rosemary, mint, thyme, cloves, lavender, and pennyroyal. The theory behind herb sachets is that their strong fragrance may cloak the fiber's attractive scents, leading moths elsewhere. But unlike the chemical pesticides in mothballs, herb sachets do not actively stifle eggs or larvae.

Specific protein fibers may have additional needs beyond what I've described already. Here's a list of the most common care issues.

ALPACA AND LLAMA: Support your wet garment carefully, as the fibers may stretch under the wet weight. Both fibers are a little slower to felt, but they will felt.

ANGORA: Fibers are far less elastic, so handle your wet garment with care. You don't want the weight of the wet fibers to stretch your fabric out of shape. When storing your angora garment, remember that the fibers don't like to be flattened. Try to reserve an open spot at the top of a shelf for any angora handknits. To bring back the fluff in a compressed item, put it in a dryer and let it tumble on air dry—without heat—for five minutes or so.

CAMEL: If you're using a predominantly camel blend with no superwash fibers, you're in for a treat. After you've washed the garment and let it dry almost completely, toss it in a cool dryer with a towel or another fabric to introduce friction and let it tumble on air dry for about ten minutes. I know this goes against much of what I've told you about protein fibers, but trust me. When you pull your garment out of the dryer, you'll be amazed at the transformation. Those previously polite, obedient little fibers will have suddenly risen, freeing themselves from the tyranny of stitches to produce a glorious halo of fibers—you'll swear there was angora in the mix. (The best yarn I've ever seen for this is Caravan, a camel/wool blend from Just Our Yarn.) Because yarns differ, I strongly advise you to try this on a swatch first.

CASHMERE: Avoid undue agitation and keep the water temperatures constant, as cashmere felts easily.

MOHAIR: Fibers are less elastic than others, so be extra careful to support the whole garment when lifting it out of the wash to avoid undue stretching. When using brushed mohair yarns with nylon binders, avoid *any* heat-based blocking or else you'll have a melted mess on your hands.

QIVIUT: These fibers bloom beautifully with the wash, and they don't felt as easily, so you can relax a little.

SILK: Bombyx silk is highly susceptible to acid and alkali, and it can be damaged by heat and sunlight. Never use a chlorine bleach on silk, and if you must block the garment with an iron, use the lowest heat possible. If you happen to perspire (or leave deodorant residue) on a silk garment, be sure to wash it quickly. You don't want to let any stain sit on silk for long. Thanks to its slightly different chemical composition, Tussah silk is more rugged than Bombyx. It's more resistant to acid, alkali, and sunlight, although you should still practice a regular care regimen. Also, lacking the sulfur that moths generally seek, silk is less prone to moth damage than wool and other protein fibers.

Cellulose Fibers

While clothes moths primarily go for protein fibers, they've occasionally been known to munch on cotton fibers as well. But the biggest foes of cellulose fibers are mold and mildew. Keep garments clean and store them in a cool, dry place whenever possible.

Here are some specific requirements for different cellulose fibers.

COTTON: Cotton can be washed and dried at high temperatures using any decent laundry detergent without damage. Likewise, the fiber can withstand periodic bleaching and ironing, although you should always use a color-safe bleach and test a small area first. Because cotton fibers lack elasticity, be sure to lay your garment flat to dry rather than hanging it—unless you *want* the garment to stretch.

LINEN: Linen is an easy-care fiber. Unless you're working with a very special yarn that blends linen with other, more delicate fibers, most linen yarns actually don't mind being tossed in the washing machine and the dryer, as long as you pull the item out of the dryer before it is completely dry. Linen grows softer and more lustrous the more you wash it. (But always check the yarn label, just in case. If it says *handwash only* but you want to machine-wash it, just knit a test swatch, toss it in the washer, and see what happens.) You can use most detergents and even diluted bleach, if necessary, but stay away from acids, such as vinegar. That's the one thing linen doesn't like.

HEMP: As with linen, hemp grows softer and more comfortable to wear with each wash. It can also be machine-washed and -dried, but be sure to pull it out of the dryer before it is completely dry.

Regenerated Cellulose and Cellulosic Fibers

ACETATE: Because acetate is easily damaged by acetone, the main ingredient in nail polish remover, I advise you not to wear an acetate sweater when giving yourself a manicure. In fact, some would advise against wearing *any* handknits while giving yourself a manicure, but I'll leave that choice up to you.

RAYON: Respect the label with rayon—if it says *dry clean only*, do it. Some rayons don't like to be handwashed.

Synthetic Fibers

These are all intentionally easy-care, wash-and-wear fibers. Unless the yarn label indicates otherwise, most synthetics can be machine-washed and -dried. To reduce the risk of static electricity, add a dab of fabric softener to the rinse cycle (or, if washing by hand, add a little bit of hair conditioner to the rinse). The only thing to be watchful of with synthetics is heat—especially with microfiber. If you're machine-drying a garment, keep the setting on low and remove the item as soon as it's dry or even a little beforehand. Likewise, if blocking is necessary, make sure you only use a warm iron, not a hot one.

REMOVING ODORS FROM YARN

Yarn has a tendency to absorb the smells of its surroundings. This is especially true in environments in which cigarette smoke, mildew, strong perfume, or mothballs are present. Here are some tips for removing strong scents from your yarn.

First, if the scent isn't too overpowering, it may be removed simply by airing the yarn (or knitted garment) outdoors on a sunny, breezy day. At a minimum, the exposure to sunlight will kill any potential moth larvae in the yarn.

However, if that doesn't work and you're ready to bring on the heavy artillery, pick up a bottle of Febreze the next time you go to the grocery store. Febreze is a fabric freshener and odor remover made by Procter & Gamble. Simply spray your yarn or garment evenly until the surface is slightly moist, and then let it dry. If Febreze is not available in your area, you may also try putting the yarn in a bag with a scented dryer sheet.

Many people may be hesitant to spray their yarn with chemicals, or they may be highly sensitive to the synthetic fragrance in Febreze and scented dryer sheets. In this case, you may also want to try the following:

- *Put approximately ¼ cup (60 ml) coffee beans, baking soda, or kitty litter in a breathable fabric or mesh bag. Place this bag, along with your yarn or garment, in a self-sealing plastic bag and let it sit for a few days.*

- *Fill a spray bottle with a solution of one part water, one part vodka. Spray the yarn or garment lightly and allow to dry. Optional step: Pour a small amount of vodka in a separate glass. Add some tonic and enjoy!*

Note: I've heard some people recommend spraying with a similar solution of water and vinegar, but be careful what you're spraying. Some fibers, such as linen, are easily damaged by acids.

Knowing What You Have: WPI

What happens when you come across a gorgeous skein of yarn that you want to use—only it has no label? How do you figure out what needle size to use, what its ideal gauge is, and how many yards of yarn it might contain?

For the answer, look no farther than your standard household ruler. At some point over the centuries some wise person figured out that if you wrap yarn around a ruler and measure how many wraps are in 1 inch (2.5cm) (or **WPI**), no matter what kind of ruler you use, it'll always tell you that yarn's gauge.

Simply wrap your yarn around the ruler, being careful not to pull the yarn too tight, overlap the strands, or leave gaps between them. Once you've wrapped your yarn around an inch (2.5cm) of the ruler, count the number of wraps you have made. If you're measuring a particularly bulky yarn, you can also wrap it around several inches of the ruler and then divide by the number of inches wrapped to get a good average.

Now for the fun part, translating that WPI into more meaningful numbers. The chart here comes from one of my absolute favorite knitting references, Priscilla A. Gibson-Roberts and Deborah Robson's *Knitting in the Old Way*. The authors kindly permitted me to excerpt it here for your benefit. Simply match your WPI number to the closest corresponding gauge, yarn category, and needle size that will work for your yarn.

WRAPS PER INCH AND APPROXIMATE YARDAGE REQUIREMENTS

Estimating gauge, needle size, and amount of yarn for a plain sweater, adult medium, 36–38-inch chest with 4–6 inches of ease.

YARN		WRAPS PER INCH	TYPICAL GAUGE IN STOCKINETTE STITCH		APPROXIMATE NEEDLE SIZE		APPROX. YARDAGE
			stitches per inch	stitches per 10 cm	US sizing	metric sizing	
Ultra-fine *	baby to lace weight	18	8+	32+	00, 0, 1, 2	2–3mm	1,800–2,200
Fine *	fingering weight	16	6–8	24–32	2, 3, 4	3–3.75mm	1,600–1,800
Medium **	sport weight	14	5–6	20–24	4, 5, 6	3.75–4.5mm	1,400–1,600
Heavy **	worsted weight	12	4½–5	18–20	7, 8, 9	5–6mm	1,200–1,400
Bulky ***		10	3½–4	14–16	10, 10½, 11	6.75–7.5mm	1,000–1,200
Very bulky ***		8 or less	2–3	8–12	13, 15	9–10mm	800–1,000

* Measure over 1 inch to determine wraps per inch.
** Measure over 2 inches and divide by 2 to determine wraps per inch.
*** Measure over 3 inches and divide by 3 to determine wraps per inch.

"Wraps per inch and approximate yardage requirements" developed by Priscilla Gibson-Roberts. Reprinted by permission from *Knitting in the Old Way* by Priscilla A. Gibson-Roberts and Deborah Robson (Fort Collins, Colorado: Nomad Press, 2004).

CYCA Numbers Explained

In an attempt to standardize common yarn weight terms, which can still vary from place to place, the Craft Yarn Council of America released its own Standard Yarn Weight System. Each pattern in this book includes information on suitable substitute yarns, and it includes the equivalent CYCA category number. You can use the chart below to match number to yarn, but be aware that each category can span a range of gauges.

Abbreviations and Techniques

ALT: Alternate.

BO: Bind off.

CABLED CAST-ON: This is almost identical to the knitted cast-on except that instead of knitting into the front of each stitch on the left-hand needle, you will place the tip of your right needle *between* the two stitches closest to the edge of your left needle. Wrap the yarn around as if to knit, pull the loop through, and place it back on the left needle so that the left side of the new loop sits on the back of the needle. Continue to knit between the two stitches closest to the edge of the left needle, placing the new stitch back on the needle, until you've cast on the desired number of stitches.

CxB Replace x with the number specified in the pattern and proceed as follows: Divide x by 2 to get y. Slip the next y stitches onto cable needle and hold them to the back of the work; knit y stitches from the left-hand needle then knit y stitches from the cable needle.

CxF Replace x with the number specified in the pattern and proceed as follows: Divide x by 2 to get y. Then, slip the next y stitches onto cable needle and hold them in front of the work; knit y stitches from left-hand needle, then knit y stitches from the cable needle.

STANDARD YARN WEIGHT SYSTEM
Categories of yarn, gauge ranges, and recommended needle sizes.

YARN WEIGHT SYMBOL & CATEGORY NAMES	1 SUPER FINE	2 FINE	3 LIGHT	4 MEDIUM	5 BULKY	6 SUPER BULKY
TYPES OF YARNS IN CATEGORY	Sock, Fingering, Baby	Sport, Baby	DK, Light Worsted	Worsted, Afghan, Aran	Chunky, Craft, Rug	Bulky, Roving
KNIT GAUGE RANGE* IN STOCKINETTE STITCH TO 4 INCHES	27–32 sts	23–26 sts	21–24 sts	16–20 sts	12–15 sts	6–11 sts
RECOMMENDED NEEDLE IN METRIC SIZE RANGE	2.25–3.25 mm	3.25–3.75 mm	3.75–4.5 mm	4.5–5.5 mm	5.5–8 mm	8mm and larger
RECOMMENDED NEEDLE IN U.S. SIZE RANGE	1 to 3	3 to 5	5 to 7	7 to 9	9 to 11	11 and larger

CDD (CENTER DOUBLE DECREASE): You'll work a center double decrease when you need to decrease two stitches evenly, so that the stitches lean against one another like a rooftop. There are a few ways to complete a CDD, so be sure to read the pattern to see which technique the designer specifies. The most common decrease, also called a double vertical decrease because it creates a vertical stitch up the center line of the decrease, is achieved as follows: slip 1 stitch knitwise, then knit the next 2 stitches together, then pass the slipped stitch over the decreased stitch and off the needle. Another variation, also called a double left-slanting decrease, results in a center stitch that tilts to the left. This is done as follows: Slip 2 stitches together knitwise, knit 1 stitch, and then pass both slipped stitches together over the knit stitch and off the needle.

CN: Cable needle.

CO: Cast on.

CONT: Continu(e)(ing).

DEC: Decreas(e)(ing).

DOUBLE YARN-OVER: Work as a regular yarn over except wrap the yarn *twice* around your needle.

DPN(S): double-pointed needle(s).

FLEXIBLE CAST-ON: Any cast-on technique that produces a more flexible edge. Here I'd recommend the cabled cast-on or the long-tail cast-on.

FOLL: Follow(s)(ing).

I-CORD: Using double-pointed needles, cast on the number of stitches specified in the pattern (usually 1–3). Knit one row, then slide the stitches to the other side of the double-pointed needle, pull the working yarn tight across the back, and knit them again. You're effectively creating a knitted tube. Repeat for the desired length.

INC: Increas(e)(ing).

K: Knit.

KF&B: Knit through the front loop of a stitch and then, without taking it off the needle, knit through the back loop of the same stitch. You've created two stitches from one.

KNITTED CAST-ON: Create a slipknot and place it on the left needle. Insert your right needle into that stitch as if to knit, wrap the yarn around your needle, pull the loop through the stitch and toward you, and then place it back on the left needle, twisting your stitch slightly so that the left side of that new loop sits on the back side of the left needle. Repeat for the desired number of stitches.

KTBL: Knit through the back loop.

KTBL-YO-K: Knit 1 stitch through the back loop, then wrap the yarn over your RH needle, and then knit into the front loop of the same stitch. You've created three stitches from one.

K2TOG: Knit 2 stitches together.

K2TOGTBL: Knit two stitches together through the back loops of both stitches.

K2TOG-K3TOG-PSO: Knit two stitches together, knit the next three stitches together, and then pass the first decrease over the second decrease and off your needle.

K3TOGTBL: Knit three stitches together through the back loops of all three stitches.

LONG-TAIL CAST-ON: The success of the long-tail cast-on depends on the tail being truly long enough to accommodate all the stitches you need to cast on. To get a general idea of how much yarn you need per stitch, wrap the yarn around your needle once and measure it. Multiply this times the total number of stitches you're casting on, add a few inches for good measure, and you'll be set.

Create a slipknot with the abovementioned long tail. Place this slipknot on a needle and hold it in your right hand so that the tail hangs closest to you. With your left hand, poke your thumb and index finger toward you between the two hanging strands of yarn, grab them with your other fingers so that they are secured on the palm of your left hand, and then twist your hand backward while opening up your thumb and index finger so that they make a V. The yarn is wrapped around each finger in the right position for your next step.

Insert the tip of your needle through the bottom of the loop on your thumb and upward. With that yarn still on the needle, hook the needle over the top and around the back of the loop on your index finger, and bring the needle back through the loop on your thumb. While keeping the strands secured in the palm of your hand, let your thumb slip out of the loop and pull the tail gently to tighten the newly formed stitch on your needle. Then move your fingers back into the original V position and continue casting on this way until you've reached the desired number of stitches.

M1: Make 1 stitch by picking up the strand between your needles and placing it on the left-hand needle, and knitting it through the back loop.

M1R: Make a right-leaning increase by picking up the strand between your needles from back to front, and knitting into the front of the picked-up stitch.

M1L: Make a left-leaning increase by picking up the strand between your needles from front to back and knitting into the back of the picked-up stitch.

P: Purl.

PATT(S): Pattern(s).

PM: Place marker.

PROVISIONAL CAST-ON: A provisional cast-on is used when you want to access your cast-on stitches later—for example if you want to create a hemmed cuff on a pair of socks. My favorite provisional cast-on is actually a *crochet* provisional cast-on, and it comes to us from Lucy Neatby. She walks you through it in her *Knitting Essentials 2* DVD.

You'll need a knitting needle that's the size required for your project, plus a crochet hook and a length of scrap yarn that's the same thickness as your project yarn but, ideally, in a different color so you can see it clearly. Be sure you have enough yarn to cast on all the stitches required.

Create a slipknot on your crochet hook, which you'll hold in your right hand. Place the knitting needle to the left of the crochet hook so that they are parallel to one another, with the working yarn running from the crochet hook and *behind* the knitting needle and held in your left hand. With the crochet hook, reach over the top of your knitting needle and wrap the yarn around the hook, then pull it through the slipknot. You have now created one stitch on the knitting needle.

Before you can repeat this step, you'll need to move your working yarn around your knitting needle and to the back again. Now you're ready to reach the crochet hook over the top of the knitting needle, wrap the yarn around the hook again, and pull it through the loop on your hook.

When your total number of desired stitches is on the knitting needle, make an emergency crochet chain with a few more stitches just using the crochet hook and not catching the stitches in the needle. Your provisional cast-on is complete. When you're ready to unravel your provisional cast-on, simply find that emergency crochet chain and tug the end to unravel the whole chain and release those cast-on stitches.

P2TOG: Purl 2 stitches together.

P2TOG-TBL: Purl 2 stitches together through the loops at the back of the needles. This creates a twisted decrease.

PSSO: Pass slipped stitch over worked stitch and off right-hand needle.

REM: Remain(s)(ing).

REP: Repeat.

REV ST ST: Reverse stockinette stitch. Instead of knitting on the right side and purling on the wrong side, you purl on the right side and knit on the wrong side.

RND(S): Round(s). When working in the round, this constitutes one "row" of knitting.

RS: Right side, generally the side of the garment that will face out once it's done.

SL: Slip a stitch without working it. Usually followed by the number of stitches to slip.

SL1 K1 PSSO: Slip 1 stitch as if to knit, knit 1 stitch, pass slipped stitch over knit stitch and off right-hand needle.

SL2 K1 PSSO: Same as above but slip 2 stitches instead of 1.

SL1 K2TOG PSSO: May also be written as CDD, or center double decrease. Slip 2 stitches as if to knit, knit 1, pass slipped stitches over that stitch and off right-hand needle.

SEED ST: Seed stitch. First row, (knit 1, purl 1) to end. Next row, purl the knit stitches and knit the purl stitches.

SSK: Slip 1 stitch as if to knit, then slip the next stitch as if to knit. Then insert left-hand needle into the front of these stitches from left to right, and knit both stitches together onto your right-hand needle.

SM: Slip marker.

ST(S): Stitch(es).

ST ST: Stockinette stitch.

TBL: Through back loop(s).

W&T: Wrap and turn. On the knit side, bring yarn to the front of your work as if to purl. Slip the next stitch, then bring yarn to the back of your work as if to knit, and slip the slipped stitch back onto the left-hand needle. Now turn your work. On wrong side rows, simply reverse the directions of the yarn.

WET-BLOCKING: Wet the pieces of your project (or the entire project if you've already assembled it or if it's one piece) and lay them out on a large flat surface. Stretch them to desired size and shape, pin if necessary, and let dry. If you don't want to completely submerge the pieces in water before blocking, you can always moisten them with a spray bottle filled with water.

WOOL ROUND HOOK: A crochet term for wrapping the yarn around your crochet hook to form a stitch.

WS: Wrong side, generally the side of the garment that will *not* face out when done.

WYIB: With yarn in back of work.

WYIF: With yarn in front of work.

YD(S): Yard(s).

YO: Yarn over. Literally, wrap your working yarn over the right-hand needle from front to back to create a new stitch.

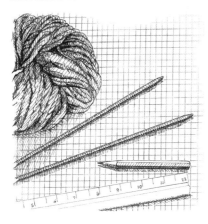

Resources

I've listed many yarns, farms, mills, companies, spinneries, and fiber-related organizations throughout this book. What follows is a comprehensive list of each, followed by a link to their most direct online presence.

In terms of yarn companies, some provide online ordering, others will direct you to retailers that carry their yarns, while smaller companies will encourage you to contact them directly—with instructions on how to do so. In terms of mills and spinneries, you'll find out more about their services and get contact information. LYS owners, consider using this list as a springboard for finding new yarns or even connecting with a spinnery to create your own custom yarn.

In all cases, these links will set you on the right path to discovery.

And when in doubt, don't forget Google. This is my favorite way to quickly find an LYS that carries a specific yarn. A recent search on the term *Koigu* brought 239,000 results including yarn stores and tales from other knitters. Never underestimate the power of a simple search.

Alchemy Yarns
www.alchemyyarns.com
Alice Starmore
www.virtualyarns.com
Anny Blatt
www.annyblatt.com
Artyarns
www.artyarns.com
Bartlett Yarns
www.bartlettyarns.com
Beaverslide Dry Goods
www.beaverslide.com
Belfast Mini Mills
www.minimills.net
Berroco
www.berroco.com
Blackberry Ridge Woolen Mill
www.blackberry-ridge.com
Blue Moon Fiber Arts
www.bluemoonfiberarts.com
Blue Sky Alpacas
www.blueskyalpacas.com
Bouton d' Or
www.boutondor.com

Brooks Farm Fiber
www.brooksfarmyarn.com
Brown Sheep Company Inc.
www.brownsheep.com
Buckwheat Bridge Angoras
www.bwbagoats.com
Cascade Yarns
www.cascadeyarns.com
Classic Elite Yarns
www.classiceliteyarns.com
Crystal Palace Yarns
www.straw.com
Dale of Norway
www.daleofnorway.com
Debbie Bliss
www.debbieblissonline.com
Dzined
www.dzined.com
Elsa Sheep and Wool Company
www.wool-clothing.com
Eucalan
www.eucalan.com
Fibre Co.
www.thefibreco.com
Filatura di Crosa
www.tahkistacycharles.com
Fleece Artist
www.fleeceartist.com
Green Mountain Spinnery
www.spinnery.com
Habu Textiles
www.habutextiles.com
Hand Jive Knits
www.handjiveknits.com
Hand Maiden Fine Yarn
www.handmaiden.ca
Harrisville Designs
www.harrisville.com
Hemp for Knitting
www.hempforknitting.com
Henry's Attic
845-783-3381 (wholesale only)
Hope Spinnery
www.hopespinnery.com
Just Our Yarn
www.justouryarn.com
Karabella
www.karabellayarns.com
Knitpicks
www.knitpicks.com

Koigu
www.koigu.com
The Kookaburra Company
www.kookaburra.com
La Lana Wools
www.lalanawools.com
Lily Sugar 'n' Cream
www.sugarncream.com
Lorna's Laces
www.lornaslaces.net
Louet Sales
www.louet.com
Malabrigo
www.malabrigoyarn.com
Marr Haven Farm
www.marrhaven.com
Mission Falls
www.missionfalls.com
Morehouse Merino
www.morehousefarm.com
Mostly Merino
www.mostlymerino.com
Mountain Colors
www.mountaincolors.com
Nashua Handknits
www.westminsterfibers.com
Noro
www.eisakunoro.com
Ohio Valley Natural Fibers
www.ovnf.com
Oomingmak Musk Ox Producers'
Cooperative
www.qiviut.com
Pakucho
www.perunaturtex.com
Peace Fleece
www.peacefleece.com
Pine Tree Yarns
www.pinetreeyarns.com
Rovings
www.rovings.com
Rowan
www.knitrowan.com
Satakieli
Sold in the U.S. by:
www.schoolhousepress.com
www.woolywest.com
South West Trading Company
www.soysilk.com

Spirit Trail Fiberworks
www.spirit-trail.net
Spunky Eclectic
www.spunkyhats.com
Tahki Stacy Charles
www.tahkistacycharles.com
Taos Valley Wool Mill
www.taosfiber.com/woolmill
Tierra Wools
www.handweavers.com
Tongue River Farm
www.icelandicsheep.com
Valley Yarns
www.yarn.com
Vermont Organic Fiber Co.
www.vtorganicfiber.com
Wool in the Woods
www.woolinthewoods.com
Yarns International
www.yarnsinternational.com
Zeilinger Wool Co.
www.zwool.com

RESOURCES FOR NOTIONS

HONEYCOMB BAG (page 208)
Cotton print fabric lining from Purl
Patchwork, www.purlsoho.com

Raffia flower button from Greenberg &
Hammer, www.greenberg-hammer.com

VINES CARDIGAN (page 102)
Rhinestone clasp from Windsor Button,
www.windsorbutton.com

SEASCAPE BOLERO (page 78)
Handblown-glass buttons from Moving
Mud, www.movingmud.com

Recommended Reading

The highly skilled yarn whisperer needs just a few core books to guide her on her path. Not all are in print now, but you can still find copies in used bookstores or online at sites like Powells.com or Alibris.com.

You have the yarn, you know what it wants to be, but you need some technical help in getting there. This is where Ann Budd's *The Knitter's Handy Book of Patterns* and *The Knitter's Handy Book of Sweater Patterns* come in. These amazingly helpful resources provide foundation patterns for just about everything. Plug in the gauge and measurements, and off you go.

If you want to do a little more off-road knitting, say, to figure out how to make a sweater that fits the difficult-to-fit perfectly, switch over to *Knitting in the Old Way* by Priscilla A. Gibson-Roberts and Deborah Robson. Borrowing from traditional knitting techniques around the world, they show you how to conceive, design, and knit gorgeous sweaters without a pattern.

But what about when you want to adorn this project with unusual stitches? That's where Barbara Walker's *Treasury of Knitting Patterns* series comes into play. Let them serve as the master stitch atlas for your knitting road trip.

A few of the patterns in this book call for techniques that may not yet be easy for the novice knitter—kitchener stitch, figure-8 cast-on, applied I-cord, provisional cast-on, and so on. Here you'll want a solid how-to reference book, something every knitter should have in his or her library. Vicki Square's *The Knitter's Companion* is one of the handiest out there, partly for its portable size and partly for its vast coverage of techniques. For those times when you need to bring out the big guns, I urge you to invest in a copy of Montse Stanley's *Knitter's Handbook*. And to see many of these techniques in action, treat yourself to a set of Lucy Neatby's *Knitting Essentials* DVDs. They're among the finest how-to DVDs I've seen yet.

If you want to learn more about fibers, keep an eye out for a little booklet called *Fibre Facts*, written by Bette Hochberg. It's an invaluable gem. She covers everything, including the notorious "burn" test you can perform to figure out what fibers are in your yarn. Susan Drummond's *Raising Angora Goats* has valuable fiber information about both angora and cashmere goats. Angora buffs will want to track down a copy of Erica Lynne's *Angora: A Handbook for Spinners*. For a great exploration of natural fibers, check out Barbara Albright's *The Natural Knitter*.

Whenever I'm not quite sure of something, or I just feel like escaping into the land of facts-I-didn't-know-I-didn't-know, I open June Hemmons Hiatt's *The Principles of Knitting*. This near-encyclopedic tome ventures into every nook and cranny of knitting with great detail and precision. Now out of print, it's worth whatever price you pay for a used copy.

Among the knitting-related periodicals currently in print, I treat two with special reverence: *Interweave Knits* and *Wildfibers*. Their integrity, intelligence, and exceptional beauty are unparalleled. *Interweave Knits* focuses on the knitter's journey, with patterns and technical how-tos and thoughtful feature stories, while *Wildfibers* focuses on the fibers themselves, with stories of the animals whose fiber we love, the places they live, and the people who raise them. (You can find both magazines at your LYS.)

If you want to take a little journey back in time and learn more about the traditions from which we've all emerged, make yourself a cup of tea and curl up with Anne Macdonald's *No Idle Hands: The Social History of American Knitting*, or, if you want to look back further to the fiber arts in colonial American days, dip into Laurel Thatcher Ulrich's *The Age of Homespun*. Both provide a deep connection with knitters past.

And to connect with knitters present, I hope you'll venture over to knittersreview.com/forum. The community arm of *Knitter's Review*, the forums are a warm, supportive place where tens of thousands of people just like you come together to share ideas, tips, resources, and stories. I'll be there!

About the Designers

ADRIAN BIZILIA (pp. 121, 148)

Adrian Bizilia lives and works in Boston, with her husband and faithful dog Shambles, in a house full of wool and yarn. She's made things all her life, studying everything from metalsmithing to glass-blowing in college, but didn't discover her true passion, knitting, until about five years ago. She added dyeing and spinning to the mix not long after and now spends her days happily immersed in all things woolly. You can visit her on the Web at helloyarn.com.

CAT BORDHI (p. 224)

Cat Bordhi is the innovative author of *Socks Soar on Two Circular Needles*, *A Treasury of Magical Knitting*, *A Second Treasury of Magical Knitting*, and *New Pathways for Sock Knitters, Book One*. Her Nautilus Award–winning novel *Treasure Forest* is woven together with golden threads of knitting and spinning, including a treehouse knit directly into a tree. She teaches knitting and publishing workshops in Canada and the United States, and loves to unearth new possibilities in knitting.

TEVA DURHAM (p. 208)

Designer Teva Durham launched one of the first Internet knitting pattern sites, loop-d-loop.com, in 2000. She is the author of *Loop-d-Loop Crochet: More Than 25 Novel Designs For Crocheters (and Knitters Taking up the Hook)* and *Loop-d-Loop: More Than 40 Novel Designs For Knitters*. Fall 2007 brings an exciting new venture for Teva—a collection of yarns and patterns through Tahki Stacy Charles. Teva lives in New York City with daughter Olivia who, at 4½, already exhibits signs of craft obsession with her own stash of fabric and yarn (mostly pink).

JACKIE ERICKSON-SCHWEITZER (p. 98)

Jackie Erickson-Schweitzer is a longtime knitting enthusiast who enjoys capturing the melody of color/texture and harmonizing it with style and function. Her motto is, "There is no bad yarn; only a yarn looking for a purpose." She is the owner of HeartStrings FiberArts, a showcase for her original knitting pattern designs and publications. Her interest in the myriad fiber arts extends beyond knitting to include dyeing, spinning, and weaving.

NORAH GAUGHAN (p. 134)

A professional knitting designer for more than twenty years, Norah Gaughan has freelanced for major yarn companies and knitting magazines, designed pattern stitches for ready to wear, and been the design director for two major yarn companies. During a "hiatus" between design-director gigs, Norah wrote *Knitting Nature, 39 Designs Inspired by Patterns in Nature*. Currently the design director at Berroco, Norah and Margery Winter have teamed up to provide knitters with hundreds of new knitting patterns each year.

AMIE GAVIN GLASGOW (pp. 160, 164)

Knitter, spinner, designer, and yarn shop habitué, Amie Gavin Glasgow teaches knitting and spinning in the Baltimore-Washington metropolitan area. She documents her frequent fiber exploits in her blog at http://rosebyany.blogspot.com.

JENNIFER HAGAN (pp. 72, 90, 172, 186)

Jennifer Hagan has been an avid needleworker for most of her life, learning crochet at her grandmother's knee as a preteen. Later, as a young mother of three daughters, she set about learning smocking, French hand-sewing, crewel work, and needlepoint before finally catching the knitting bug. Ever since, all the other crafts have taken a distant backseat to knitting. In 2004, she was inspired to create her own designs, which you can view at the Figheadh Yarnworks website, figheadh.com. Read about her knitting exploits and discoveries on her blog at http://figknits.blogspot.com, where you'll also learn that Jennifer loves hiking and camping in the Pacific Northwest with her husband, Fred. You'll probably also see considerable bragging about her three now-grown daughters and her two grandsons.

BESS HAILE (p. 214)

Bess Haile is a Virginia girl whose romance with fiber began at age seven with a fully working, hand-cranked toy Singer sewing machine. Though sewing was her first love, she flirted with knitting at various times over the years, and in 1998 her knitting fire was reignited by the timely receipt of a Patternworks catalog. Amazed at how yarn had developed and blossomed since her last foray into a yarn shop, she succumbed to temptation and was soon hooked again. Many sweaters, socks, hats, and mittens later, she found a less expensive way to acquire lavish novelty yarns: handspinning. Now she teaches knitting and spinning to innocent bystanders in fiber shops and at regularly scheduled workshops. A library director in real life, Bess lives with her husband and three dogs near Tappahannock, in what she likes to refer to as Upper Tidewater Virginia. You can visit her blog at http://likethequeen.blogspot.com.

LANA HAMES (p. 156)

Already an avid knitter for many years, Lana Hames attended her first Stitches show in 1997 and was overwhelmingly inspired. At the same time she was taking fiber classes at the local art school and was introduced to hemp, the world's oldest and strongest fiber. Thinking hemp might make an exceptional yarn, she began working and playing with this idea. It wasn't long before her first hemp sweater was designed and knit—and she still wears it to this day. At the encouragement of friends and family, Lana opened Lanaknits Designs in 2000. Since then she has worked endlessly to develop a hemp yarn line that is a true yarn, not a coarse string. Her designs and yarns have been well received, with features in knitting publications including *Interweave Knits*, *Knitter's Magazine*, and *Vogue Knitting*. Lanaknits Designs and her hempforknitting yarn line have grown since their humble beginnings, and Lana now has several employees working in the studio in downtown Nelson, British Columbia, where Lana and her family have lived for nearly thirty years.

SHELIA JANUARY (pp. 94, 110, 129, 202)

Shelia January has been a knitter since she was eight years old, following on the heels of learning embroidery and crochet a couple of years before then. Growing up on a farm in Oregon, she continued knitting and doing other handwork, earning spending money in the '60s by crocheting "hip" vests for her mother's and grandmother's friends. Knitting saved her sanity while attending college, while working for twenty-eight years in the financial services industry, and finally, while preparing to retire to a farm in Oregon, where she now lives. She became a spinner 5½ years ago and now collects spinning wheels as well as yarn. She knits and designs with her homespun yarn as well as with commercial yarn, and has taught spinning and knitting at retreats and shops in New York, Massachusetts, and Virginia. You can visit her blog at www.letstalkstash.blogspot.com.

AMY KING (pp. 102, 106, 140, 168, 179, 182, 194, 228)

Amy King has been knitting and working on creating a SABLE stash since she was a little girl. She now obsessively knits and designs while running a business and chasing her two little girls. For more information, visit her website, www.spunkyeclectic.com.

ELANOR LYNN (p. 114)

Elanor Lynn is as passionate about teaching knitting as she is about knitting itself. "It's not about what I can do, it's about what *you* can do" she is fond of saying to her students. Her first book of baby knits, *Country Living Cozy Knits for Cuddly Babies* contains many of her adult patterns scaled down for smaller sizes, including suggestions on how to improvise on her designs. She also published an essay, "Paris Charm Blanket," in Lela Nargi's anthology *Knitting Memories*, recounting the story of how she came to knit a blanket based on the arrondissements of Paris before and after (but not during) her first trip to Paris last year. She is currently plotting an economic revolution founded on community activism through the needle arts. You can contact her at elanorknits@yahoo.com.

TARA JON MANNING (p. 152)

Knitting author and designer Tara Jon Manning finds inspiration for her work in nature, the Eastern arts, and the exploration of the connection between craft and spirituality. Tara pioneered the "mindful knitting" movement, and she continues to gain popularity through her lectures, workshops, and knitting retreats. She is the author of *Nature Babies: Natural Knits and Organic Crafts for Moms and Babies*, *Mindful Knitting*, *Compassionate Knitting*, *The Gift Knitter*, and *Men in Knits*. Tara lives with her family in Boulder, Colorado. For more information, visit her website, www.tarahandknitting.com.

GINA WILDE (pp. 78, 198)

Gina Wilde lives in the country about an hour north of San Francisco, where she enjoys knitting, playing guitar, and hanging out with her multispecies family, including her partner, two teenage daughters, an array of amazing nonfiber-gifting animals, and beautiful flower gardens. Gina is the president, cofounder, and artistic director of Alchemy Yarns.

MARGARET KLEIN WILSON (p. 86)

Margaret Klein Wilson moved to a hillside farm in southern Vermont in 1988 and acquired a few Merino sheep to keep the farm fields open. A year and three bags of wool later, Mostly Merino was born. This fiber studio specializes in hand-dyed luxury Merino and mohair knitting yarns, patterns, and knitting kits. A self-taught shepherd, dyer, and designer, Margaret finds her inspiration as much in the process and collaborative nature of bringing wool to market as she does in the satisfaction of keeping sheep. Each stage of having her yarns produced is one of affection, attention, nuance, and craftsmanship. Margaret is the author and editor of *The Green Mountain Spinnery Knitting Book*. Her writing has appeared in *Interweave Knits*, *Handwoven*, and *Knit Lit: I*, *II*, and *III*. Mostly Merino yarn was also featured in Teva Durham's book *Loop-d-Loop*.

Acknowledgments

First and foremost, I must thank the designers who graciously lent their creative spirits to this endeavor—Adrian Bizilia, Cat Bordhi, Teva Durham, Jackie Erickson-Schweitzer, Norah Gaughan, Amie Gavin Glasgow, Jennifer Hagan, Bess Haile, Lana Hames, Shelia January, Amy King, Elanor Lynn, Tara Jon Manning, Gina Wilde, and Margaret Klein Wilson. I thank you from the bottom of my heart. You heard my ideas, trusted the vision, and responded with items of great beauty.

There were several occasions when something needed to be knit and there were no more hands to knit it. Knitters Catherine Shumadine, Lindsey-Brooke Hessa, Cindy Grosch, and Lauren Lax responded quickly and ably, and this book is all the more lovely because of it. My thanks to Anjeanette Milner for her pursuit of technical accuracy, Peggy Greig for her beautiful charts, and Alexandra Grablewski for her inspiring photography. And thank you to my friends and colleagues Pam Allen and Linda Cortright for standing by with insight and understanding.

A deep tip of the hat goes to Rosy Ngo at Potter Craft for immediately getting why this book needed to be written and letting me be the one to write it—and to Mona Michael and Erin Slonaker for so wisely shepherding it through production. To my agent, Linda Roghaar, thank you for so ably shepherding *me* through the process.

To my dear *Knitter's Review* family, thank you for proving that people really *do* want to know more about yarn. And thank you for letting me do what I love every week. You are my inspiration.

I must also express special gratitude to my close friends and family members who have willingly allowed every visit and vacation to be hijacked by wool festivals and yarn shops. Special love to my nieces Hannah and Emma and my baby nephew William, who all patiently endured months of being told no, their auntie couldn't come out to play. To Don and Robert, for knowing just when I *did* need to be taken out into the wide blue ocean to play. Above all, to Clare for believing, encouraging, listening, and providing endless cups of tea when I needed them most.

My parents taught me from a very early age that you can succeed at living a creative and fulfilling life, and I thank them both for that priceless lesson. I will be forever grateful to my grandma for first putting yarn and needles in my hands, inspiring the medium through which my own creative life would take shape.

Glossary

ACRYLIC: A synthetic fiber containing a chemical base of 85 percent to 90 percent vinyl cyanide or acrylonitrile.

ANGORA: The hair of an angora rabbit. (Not to be confused with the angora *goat*, which produces mohair.)

ARTIFICIAL SILK: An early term for the manufactured fiber now known as rayon.

AWN: The slightly finer protector hair on the angora rabbit. Awn is one of three types of fiber that the rabbit grows.

BAMBOO: A relatively recent addition to the fiber family and primarily coming from China, bamboo fiber is derived from the cellulose in the bamboo stalk. Bamboo fiber is unique in that it contains an antibacteria and bacteriostasis bio-agent.

BATT: The thick, lofty, blended continuous mass of fibers produced by a carding machine. This tends to be the first in a series of steps that align the fibers and remove any irregularities in preparation for spinning.

BIAS: A naturally occurring tilt in fabric that was knit using an unbalanced yarn (i.e., one with excess twist in one direction). The fabric leans in the direction of that excess twist in an attempt to release it.

BINDER: A fine thread normally used in novelty-style spinning to help reinforce the positioning of other fibers.

BLEED: The release of excess dye during the washing process. Normally this is a result of the yarn not being sufficiently rinsed after it was dyed.

BOLL: The seed pod of the cotton plant. The cotton fibers grow around the seeds inside the boll until the outer shell cracks open to reveal mature fiber-covered seeds.

BOMBYX SILK: A fine white lustrous silk produced by the *Bombyx mori*, the most common type of silkworm.

CAMELID: A member of the Camelidae family. Consists of the bactrian and dromedary camel as well as the alpaca, llama, guanaco, and vicuña.

CARDING MACHINE: The machine that loosens up fibers, opens up natural lock formations, and removes dirt and unsuitable neps of fiber in preparation for spinning. It usually consists of several series of large, opposing cylinders lined with tiny teeth. As the cylinders rotate, the fibers move through the carder and the teeth catch the fibers, stripping them from one cylinder and pulling them onto the next. Also called a carder.

CASHGORA: A relatively new breed resulting from efforts to cross-breed angora and cashmere goats. Technically, the cashgora breed is $3/4$ cashmere and $1/4$ angora goat.

CASHMERE: The downy undercoat of the cashmere goat. Fibers are harvested in the spring when the animal sheds its coat.

CHENILLE: A fuzzy yarn composed of short pieces of fiber that lie perpendicular to the yarn's core. Chenille is created on a two-headed circular spinning machine. While the inner head rapidly plies fine binder threads together, the outer head runs "pile" threads back and forth in a zigzag formation. Each time they pass through the center, they are secured within those fine binder threads. Sharp blades then cut off the edges of the pile fibers, and you end up with the yarn we know as chenille.

COLOR POOLING: A phenomenon that can occur with yarns that have been dyed multiple colors at regular intervals, most often those that were dyed by hand. When knit up at just the right gauge and circumference—usually in narrower items such as socks—the multiple colors can stack on top of one another from row to row, forming strong "pools" of color.

COMMUNITY SPINNERY: A term I use to describe a spinnery (i.e., a company that processes fiber into yarn) that has committed to business practices that help serve and sustain its local community. This may include buying fibers from nearby sheep farms, bartering its services with other fiber-related organizations in the area, using environmentally friendly processing and/or dyeing techniques, providing ownership and continuing education opportunities for employees, etc.

CORN: A relatively new biotech development, corn fiber is made from the naturally occurring starch in corn. These starches are broken down into sugars, fermented, and separated into polymers. The resulting paste-like substance is extruded into fine, delicate strands that are processed and spun into yarn. When knit, it produces a soft, comfortable fabric similar to cotton. When shucked, steamed, and dotted with butter, it is also delicious.

COTTON: The soft fibers that grow around the seeds inside the *Gossypium* seed pod. At maturity the pod pops open, like popcorn, to reveal the mass of fibers and seeds inside.

CRIMP: The natural wave that runs along a shaft of fiber. Most often this term is used in relation to protein fibers, especially wool. Different sheep breeds grow hair with different crimp patterns ranging from extremely fine (12 crimps or more per inch) to rough (3 crimps or fewer per inch). The ideal fiber has a finer, uniform crimp along its entire length.

DEGUMMING: The process of soaking a silk cocoon in hot soapy water to soften its gummy outer coating (called sericin) and separate the silk fibers from the dead chrysalis at the core. Once the cocoon has been degummed, the individual silk filaments are ready to be unraveled (or reeled) and made into yarn.

DEHAIRING: While sheep tend to grow a uniform coat of fiber, some other animals—especially ones living in extremely cold climates—grow what is called a "dual coat." An outer layer of long, thick, and strong guard hairs protect the delicate and extremely warm "down" hairs closest to the skin. Knitters want the down hairs, but they don't want the guard hairs—so it is necessary to "dehair" the fleece to separate the guard hairs from the down. Fibers requiring dehairing include cashmere, yak, camel, and qiviut.

DENIER: A unit of measurement used in the textile industry to indicate a fiber's linear mass density. Canada and Europe tend to use another measurement called the "Tex." The knitting world focuses more on a fiber's micron count than its denier. Just remember that the lower the denier, the finer the fiber.

DOWN: The fine insulating fibers that grow closest to the skin on dual-coated animals. Perhaps the best-known down fiber is cashmere, but others include qiviut, yak, and camel.

DYE LOTS: A batch of yarn that's dyed at the same time is considered one "dye lot" because all the yarn experiences the same precise dye blend. Sometimes even the smallest environmental variable can cause a subtle difference in hue from batch to batch, so manufacturers almost always provide a dye lot number on the yarn label. (Always check this number when buying yarn to make sure all the skeins come from the same lot.) Some hand-dyers follow such intimate and quixotic processes that they don't assign dye lots at all, because each skein may be slightly different.

DYED IN THE WOOL: Fibers that have been dyed prior to being spun into yarn. This process has the added benefit of allowing yarn companies to blend small amounts of different shades to build heathered and visually complex colors of yarn.

DYESTUFFS: A common term for the materials that give color to fiber (i.e., dye).

FELT: The dense fabric produced by submerging protein fibers in hot soapy water and subjecting them to sustained agitation. Also what happens when you machine-wash a handknit wool sweater by mistake. (The felting of knitted items is actually called "fulling," whereas felting is technically for raw fibers, but it's increasingly common to see the term "felt" used in all contexts.)

FIBROIN: The fine liquid thread that the silkworm secretes through two salivary glands on its head. As it is secreted, this thread is coated with a second material called sericin, which hardens upon contact with the air and helps protect the cocoon (and the fine fibers).

FINENESS: A key criteria that yarn companies use when selecting wool. Most often this fineness is measured in terms of the fiber's average micron, or diameter.

FLAX PLANT: The plant whose stalk is transformed into linen fiber.

FLEECE: The mass of fiber shorn from a sheep. A fleece will contain everything that was on the sheep at the moment it was shorn—including vegetable matter (often simply referred to as "VM"), dirt, and lanolin.

FULLING: The felting of knitted items. Increasingly people are using the terms "felting" and "fulling" interchangeably.

GIN: A machine that quickly separates cotton fibers from their seed pods. Also a popular beverage at knitting parties and the source of woe the following day.

GUANACO: A wild South American descendant of the Camelidae family. The soft fibers of its undercoat can range from 14 to 18 microns. This, combined with the guanaco's protected species status, make guanaco an extremely rare and coveted fiber.

GUARD HAIRS: The longer, coarse hairs that many animals grow along their outer coat. They're sometimes also called "protector" hairs because they protect the animal's softer insulating undercoat of down fibers.

GUERNSEY: A warm, tight-knit, distinctively patterned, hard-wearing sweater from the British Channel Island of Guernsey.

HALO: A term of endearment for the fuzzy blur of loose fiber ends that can develop on knitted fabric, especially after it's been washed and worn a few times. Angora and qiviut have especially magical haloes.

HAND: The way a fiber, yarn, or fabric responds to human touch. Also sometimes referred to as "handle."

HAND-DYED: Fiber or yarn whose dye was applied by hand rather than by machine. Techniques run the gamut from dipping different sections of a hank into different dyes, or dropping the whole hank in a vat of dye, but the ultimate point is that the dye was introduced to the yarn by hand.

HAND-PAINTED: Fiber or yarn whose dye was applied by hand in a painterly fashion. True hand-painted yarns also convey a sense of personal color artistry that goes beyond simply dunking skeins in a big vat and letting them simmer.

HUACAYA: The most common of the two alpaca breeds, the huacaya grows a dense fleece with moderate crimp.

HYGROSCOPIC: A material that readily absorbs and retains moisture. Wool and other protein fibers (including silk) are all extremely hygroscopic, able to absorb several times their weight in moisture while remaining warm and dry against the skin.

IMMERSION DYE: The most common large-scale commercial dye method, in which entire hanks of spun yarn are immersed in large vats of dye.

KETTLE-DYED: Generally considered a smaller-scale dye process in which hanks of yarn are suspended over, or lowered into, large kettles of dye. Sometimes the dye is intentionally only partially stirred so that the resulting yarns will have subtle variations in saturation.

LANOLIN: The greasy substance that is secreted from the sheep's sebaceous glands. Lanolin helps repel water from the sheep's coat, keep the sheep warm, and protect the sheep's skin from infection. Some wool yarns are processed so rigorously that no lanolin remains in the fibers, while others retain varying amounts of the substance. Some knitters insist on knitting with lanolin-rich yarns because they like how the lanolin acts as a natural moisturizer for their own skin. Others consider lanolin-rich yarns too raw and avoid them.

LLAMA: A South American descendant of the Camelidae family that is often used as a guard animal for sheep and alpaca farms. The llama grows a true dual coat, with an undercoat that can range from supersoft to coarse.

LOFT: The open and elastic quality that a fine, well-developed crimp can add to yarn, especially wool. Because this same crimp contributes to a yarn's elasticity, loft and elasticity are often considered together.

LONGWOOLS: A category of sheep breeds that grow longer hair averaging anywhere from 5 to even 12 inches in length. These fibers tend to be thicker, stronger, and rougher, with an open wavy crimp and lustrous appearance.

LYCRA: The trademark name for the synthetic fiber spandex.

LYOCELL: A member of the rayon family that's marketed in the United States under the trademark Tencel. Made from wood pulp.

MERCERIZED: Cotton that has been specially treated in a caustic soda solution to permanently swell and straighten the fibers. Mercerized cottons tend to be stronger, denser, and more lustrous than their untreated counterparts. Named after John Mercer, who discovered the process by accident in 1844.

MERINO: The oldest sheep breed—and certainly one of the most prevalent and prized—the Merino produces a fine fleece of soft and springy fibers. Many other sheep breeds were developed from Merino strains, including Rambouillet, Corriedale, and Polwarth.

MICROFIBER: A synthetic fiber that is one denier or less.

MICRON: A common unit of fiber diameter, one micron equals one thousandth of a millimeter, or .00004 inch. Because a fiber's diameter directly influences its softness and value, the micron count is frequently used in discussions of fiber quality. The lower the micron count, the softer and more desirable the fiber.

MICROSPINNERIES: An unofficial term I use to describe small commercial spinneries. It usually implies a certain degree of artistry that may be missing in the larger, industrial spinneries.

MILL ENDS: Leftovers from spinning mills, sometimes in odd dye lots or strange yardages and often sold on large cones at discount.

MODAL: A subset of rayon and the registered trademark of Lenzig AG, Modal is a soft, smooth fiber made from the reconstituted cellulose in beech trees.

MOHAIR: The curly and lustrous fiber from the angora goat. The softness varies dramatically with age, running from delicate silkiness to a harsh ruggedness suitable only for rugs and upholstery.

MOLTING: The shedding of old hairs, usually in spring. Many of the most prized fibers—such as cashmere, camel, yak, and qiviut—are harvested during the molting season.

MORDANTS: Those substances that bind dye to fiber. Some dyes—especially natural dyes, i.e., dyes obtained from plants, animals, and minerals—require mordants to set the color. The specific mordant you use will further impact the color you get.

MULESPUN: While I love the image of mules sitting at spinning wheels, this term actually refers to yarns that were spun on a machine called a "spinning mule." This machine—of which only a few remain in operation today—closely replicates the draft-twist-release movements of the hanspinner to produce a true woolen yarn. The movement is slow and plodding, rather like the steady walk of a mule, which is perhaps where the machine got its name.

NEPS: Small tangled or matted clumps of fibers that are removed during the carding process.

NOIL: The short fibers that are removed during the combing and carding process. These fiber are often collected and blended for use in other yarns, especially those where an irregular texture is desired. Silk noil produces an especially lovely yarn with an earthy and organic feel.

NOVELTY YARNS: By their simplest definition, novelty yarns are yarns whose construction differs from the standard single- and multiple-ply form and that, when knit up, produce an unusual textured effect. While novelty yarns have existed for more than half a century, modern computerized equipment has elevated them into the realm of complex and sophisticated architectural masterpieces with elaborate pom-poms, fringes, railroads, you name it. These yarns derive their maximum benefit from simple stitchwork and open shapes, or when used sparingly as embellishment.

NYLON: A synthetic fiber developed by DuPont in 1935, nylon is a generic name for synthetic linear polymers. The nylon used for knitting yarn is formed from polymer chips that are melted, extruded through the tiny holes of a spinneret, cooled and conditioned, and then cut into regular lengths that are processed and spun into yarn.

PASHMINA: While reference books from the mid-1900s define pashmina as the fine downy undercoat of goats raised in Kashmir and other northern Indian provinces, the term has evolved over time to describe almost anything soft—silks, wools, and even synthetics. As a result, the word "pashmina" is no longer a legally recognized labeling term in the United States.

PILLS: Small clumplike tufts of fibers that can gather on a fabric's surface after a sustained period of friction. The tiny ends of fiber catch on one another and slowly work their way out of the fabric. Thus, the more fiber ends you have per inch of yarn, the more likely it will pill. But the fiber quality, processing, preparation, tightness of twist, and ply structure can also impact a yarn's pilling potential.

PLIES: Individual strands of twisted fiber that, when further spun together, form a complete yarn. While a single ply isn't always considered a complete yarn, it is a yarn nonetheless.

POLYESTER: Nearly indistinguishable from nylon, polyester is a synthetic fiber that was first developed in 1953 and is made from polymers of polypropylene and polyethylene. In the U.K. it is known as Terylene.

PYGORA: A relatively new breed created by ongoing efforts to cross-breed the pygmy and angora goat.

QIVIUT: The downy (and heavenly) undercoat of the musk ox. Qiviut is sometimes also spelled qiviuq, qiviuk, qiveut, or qiviut. In Alaska, this term is trademarked for products made from qiviut fiber and designed, knitted, and sold by the Oomingmak Musk Ox Producers' Cooperative.

RAYON: The oldest of all manufactured fibers, rayon is made from the cellulose in wood pulp.

REELED SILK: The finest and most expensive grade of silk, reeled silk isn't seen much in the handknitting market because it's normally reserved for industrial weaving and fabric yarns. Reeled silk is made from the perfectly continuous silk filaments that are unwound directly from the cocoons, and then twisted together.

ROVING: A continuous strand of (relatively) parallel fibers that have been carded or combed and to which a slight twist has been applied. Consider it a well-yeasted bread dough that's risen several times and is finally ready to be formed into its final loaf shape and put in the oven.

S TWIST: Yarn that is twisted counterclockwise, or to the left, when spun. If you examine a strand of yarn, you'll see that the plies (or the fibers, if it's a single) move in a diagonal direction. If that diagonal moves from top left to lower bottom right (as with the letter S), it's an S-twist yarn.

SCALES: A microscopic layer of cells that coat the outside of any animal-grown protein fiber, including human hair. Their size and the degree to which they overlap influence how a fiber looks, behaves, and feels against the skin—and all three factors can vary widely depending on the animal.

SEACELL: Manufactured by Zimmer AG under the trademark SeaCell, this fiber is made from 95 percent lyocell and 5 percent seaweed. In yarn form, it has the soft, breathable, comfortable elements of lyocell infused with trace elements and seaweed extracts.

SERICIN: A liquid secreted by the silkworm that covers and protects the fine strands of fiber that make up its cocoon. This material hardens upon contact with the air.

SERICULTURE: The cultivation of silkworms for the production of silk.

SOY: A lustrous fiber manufactured from the soy pulp that remains after soybeans have been pressed and their oil removed. The soy proteins are then isolated and rendered into a liquid state and wet-spun with polyvinyl alcohol.

SPINNERET: Comparable to a small shower head with microscopic holes (sometimes as fine as five-thousandths of an inch in size), the spinneret is what gives form to individual strands of manufactured fiber. The material—whether it's soy, corn, viscose rayon, polyester, nylon, you name it—is forced through the spinneret, and the resulting streams of liquid undergo various treatments to become spinnable fiber.

SPUN SILK: Yarn made from silk fibers that have been cut into standard lengths, carded together, possibly also combed, and then spun. Generally made from the waste silk produced by the reeling process, spun silk can also be made from the broken cocoons in which the moth was allowed to pierce a hole and escape into the bright blue yonder.

STAPLE LENGTH: The average length of a fiber in its most natural form, and usually in a group. This term is used for everything from wool to cotton to yak. Manufactured and regenerated fibers have no "natural" staple length because they rely on machines to chop the fibers into predetermined staple lengths that vary depending on the yarn being produced.

STIFLING: The process of killing the silkworm's chrysalis in order to obtain premium unbroken silk filament from the cocoon. This is normally done by prolonged exposure to heat.

SUPERWASH WOOL: Wool that has been specially treated so that it can be washed in a machine without risk of felting. This treatment usually involves the elimination or minimization of the scales that line the surface of wool fiber. Although knitters commonly use the term "superwash" to define any machine-washable wool, superwash is actually a trademark of the International Wool Secretariat in London and can only be used if the yarn has passed their inspection. If not, yarn companies will simply list "machine-washable" on the label.

SURI: The less common of the two alpaca breeds, the suri grows a long fleece with a silken luster.

TENCEL: The exclusive trademark name under which lyocell fiber—made from wood pulp—is sold and marketed in the United States.

TUSSAH SILK: Produced by the wild or semicultivated silkworm, Tussah silk is stronger than Bombyx but with a slightly coarser feel and a duller, more matte appearance.

TWIST: The gravity of our yarn world, twist is the essential energy that holds fibers together.

VAT-DYED: As with kettle-dyed, this is generally considered a smaller-scale dye process in which hanks of yarn are suspended over, or lowered into, large vats of dye. Sometimes the dye is intentionally only partially stirred so that the resulting yarns will have subtle variations in saturation.

VICUÑA: The most graceful of the South American descendants of the Camelidae family, the vicuña grows one of the softest fibers on earth, averaging 10–15 microns. Vicuña fiber has only recently been reintroduced into the world market and is available in extremely small quantities at a high price.

VISCOSE PROCESS: The most common process for creating rayon fiber from wood pulp. After being chopped up and soaked in a caustic soda solution, the pulp is squeezed, shredded, and fermented. It's then treated with carbon bisulphide, which forms a cellulose xanthate compound. This compound is then mixed with a weak solution of caustic soda and aged again before being filtered and finally forced through a spinneret into a coagulating bath of sulfuric acid, where those streams of liquid harden into strands of fiber. Essentially, the materials are broken down into raw cellulose that's regenerated into spinnable fiber.

WOOL: In the very broadest possible terms, wool is simply the hair grown on a sheep. The variety of length, crimp, softness, and luster among different sheep breeds—and sheep themselves—is almost infinite.

WOOLEN-SPUN: Yarn in which the fibers receive only minimal order and alignment prior to spinning, resulting in a lofty jumble of different-length fibers going every which way. Woolen-spun yarns tend to be loftier and warmer, but often at the expense of durability.

WORMING: A common phenomenon in which chenille yarns wriggle (or "worm") their way out of a knitted fabric and form loops on the surface. The larger your needles and looser the work, the greater the chenille's potential to worm.

WORSTED-SPUN: Yarn in which the carded fibers have been further combed so that the fibers are of uniform length and lie parallel to one another. What you lose in loft and warmth, you make up for with a smooth, lustrous, and hard-wearing yarn. Those extra processing steps create more waste, which is why worsted-spun yarns tend to cost more than their woolen counterparts.

WPI: Wraps per inch. A common way to determine a yarn's ideal gauge and needle size is to wrap it around a ruler and count the number of wraps that occur in one inch. (See the chart on page 236.) The WPI measure is especially helpful for handspun yarn or yarn whose label was lost long ago.

YAK: A member of the bovine family, the yak is native to the rugged, high-altitude regions of Tibet, Mongolia, and south central Asia. To keep itself warm in winter, the yak grows a marvelous insulating layer of down fibers. Come spring, those fibers are harvested as the animal sheds its coat. The rough guard hairs are separated and used for other purposes, while the soft down is set aside for the yarn market.

Z TWIST: Yarn that is twisted clockwise, or to the right, when spun. If you examine a strand of yarn, you'll see that the plies (or the fibers, if it's a single) move in a diagonal direction. If that diagonal moves from top right to lower bottom left (as with the letter Z), it's a z-twist yarn.

About the Author

CLARA PARKES

Every knitter dreams of ditching it all and staying home to play with their yarn. My moment came after college, after living in France, and after almost a decade working in high-tech publishing in San Francisco. I was writing about the technology that was transforming every aspect of society, and yet I felt that none of it stacked up against a single pair of handknit socks.

While some would have looked at their surroundings and slapped themselves back to reality with a "what, are you crazy?!" I actually answered the call. I quit my job, let go of my apartment, packed my trusty Toyota, and headed east to the tiny coastal Maine town where six generations of my family have spent their summers. I renovated an old farmhouse that had belonged to my great aunt. I took freelance jobs to cover the bills. But more to the point, I stayed at home and played with my yarn.

My grandma formally introduced me to yarn when I was twelve. She—always clad in a handknit Icelandic cardigan—caught me eyeing her yarn basket covetously during a winter visit, and the connection was immediate. While I lived mostly in an Arizona house devoid of wool, every June my mother would load us into the car and drive east to Maine. Our destination was a town

halfway up the coast with a population of 900. It had one market, one church, one garage, one marina, and one singularly marvelous little yarn store.

The shop was like your old-fashioned candy store. But instead of sugary confections, the shelves were packed with skeins of pure, lanolin-rich wool in every imaginable color, imported directly from Norway.

For many years, that was my only experience of yarn. As life took me away from Maine for longer and longer periods, I had only to pick up a skein and smell it to evoke foggy mornings by the wood stove, evenings by kerosene lamp, and the faraway gentle ring of the bell buoy in the harbor.

Then a curious thing happened. I started venturing into other yarn stores and buying other yarns. My experience of knitting began to change. Sometimes it was good, but often . . . not so. My hands were often restless, projects piled up, I grew demoralized. Had I lost the love? Was this the end for me and knitting?

A chance reunion with that original Norwegian wool made it blatantly clear that it was the yarn that was impacting my experience. I craved to know more. How could yarn have this kind of effect? What makes one yarn more memorable than the next? Why do some yarns last, and others show wear immediately? Is there such a thing as "good" and "bad" yarn?

Out of this quest was born KnittersReview.com, which I launched in September 2000. The goal was simple: Fueled by my renewed passion for knitting, and drawing upon my high-tech years as a writer, editor, reviewer, and website producer, I would publish honest and in-depth reviews of yarns, books, tools, and other items that shape our knitting experience. I would find those yarns that made my hands sing, and I'd let you know when a yarn snagged, bled, or pilled. And I'd do it every week, through wind and sleet and snow and hail. It is a labor of love that I now share with more than 30,000 knitters each week. This book is a distillation of everything I've learned on my yarn journey so far, and I hope you enjoy it.

Index

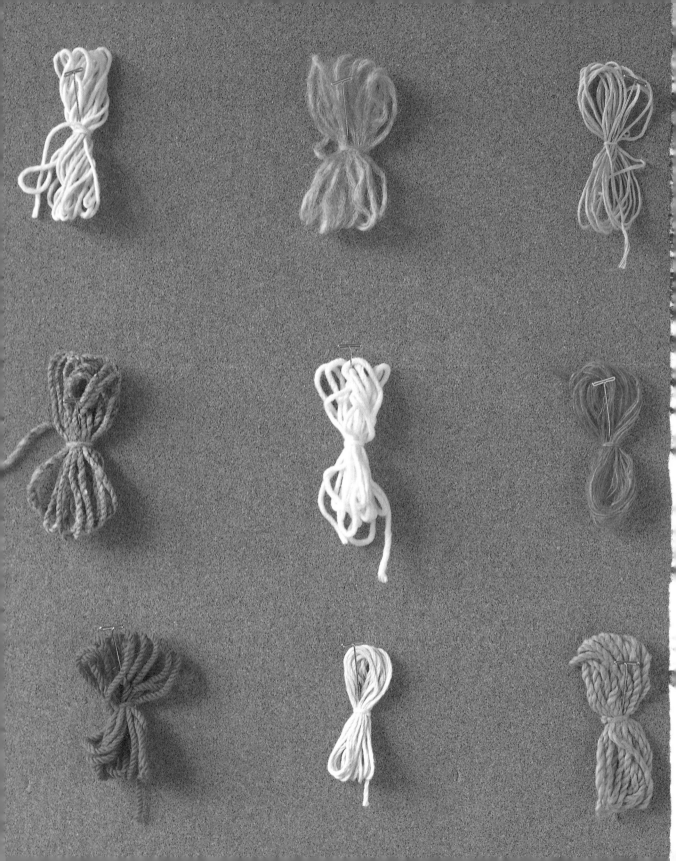

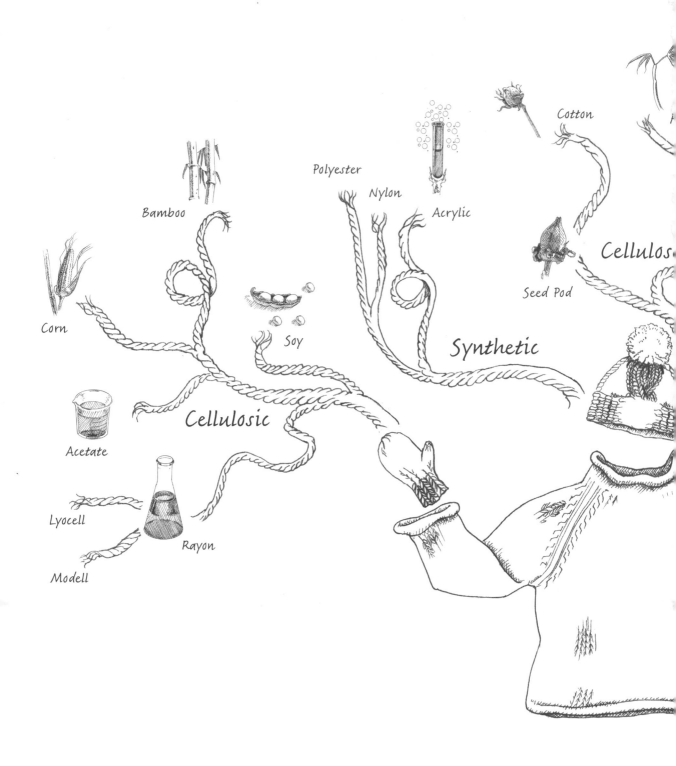

Bamboo

Polyester

Nylon

Acrylic

Cotton

Cellulos

Corn

Soy

Seed Pod

Synthetic

Cellulosic

Acetate

Lyocell

Rayon

Modell